RED ACROPOLIS,
BLACK TERROR

ALSO BY ANDRE GEROLYMATOS

The Balkan Wars

RED ACROPOLIS, BLACK TERROR

THE GREEK CIVIL WAR AND THE
ORIGINS OF SOVIET-AMERICAN
RIVALRY, 1943–1949

ANDRÉ GEROLYMATOS

BASIC

BOOKS

A Member of the Perseus Books Group
New York

Published by Basic Books
A Member of the Perseus Books Group

Books published by Basic Books are available at special discounts for bulk purchases in the United States by corporations, institutions, and other organizations. For more information, please contact the Special Markets Department at the Perseus Books Group, 11 Cambridge Center, Cambridge MA 02142, or call (617) 252-5298, (800) 255-1514 or e-mail special.markets@ perseusbooks.com.

Gerolymatos, André.
    Red Acropolis, Black Terror: The Greek Civil War and the origins of Soviet-American rivalry, 1943–1949 / Andre Gerolymatos.
        p. cm.
    Includes bibliographical references and index.
    ISBN 0-465-02743-1
    1. Greece—History—Civial War, 1944–1949.   I. Title: Greek Civil War and the origins of Soviet-American rivalry, 1943–1949.   II. Title.
DF849.52.G47 2004
949.507'4—dc22

                                                        2004007702

Designed by Lisa Kreinbrink
Set in 12-point AGaramond by the Perseus Books Group

04 05 06 / 10 9 8 7 6 5 4 3 2 1

To Beverley
For many long days and nights
and beautiful sunsets to come.

TABLE
OF CONTENTS

ACKNOWLEDGMENTS

THE IDEA FOR A BOOK ON THE GREEK CIVIL WAR EMERGED FROM several pleasant meetings with John Donatich in New York. A number of books have appeared in Greek, especially after the fall of the junta in 1974, such as George Margaritis's monumental study of the 1946–1949 military operations, and the declassification of the Greek general staff history of the conflict is providing intriguing possibilities for future research. However, with the exception of Polymeris Voglis's *Becoming a Subject: Political Prisoners during the Greek Civil War* (Berghahmn Books, 2002) and Charles R. Shrader's *The Withered Wine: Logistics and the Communist Insurgency in Greece, 1945–1949* (London: Praeger, 1999), histories of the Greek civil war available in English are essentially confined to Edgar O'Balance's *The Greek Civil War, 1944–1949* (New York: Frederick A. Praeger, 1966) and C. M. Woodhouse's *The Struggle for Greece, 1941–1949* (Chicago: Ivan R. Dee Publisher, 1976).

These studies focus primarily on the impersonal military and political events of the war. They continue to provide excellent service to students of history, yet the Greek civil war has been etched on an entire generation of Greeks, whose voices, with some notable exceptions, have remained mute in English. I have tried to tell their story by combing individual accounts of the pivotal events—in effect giving the conflict a face. Insofar as I have succeeded, it is only through capable and encouraging support from friends, students, and colleagues.

I am grateful to Chip Rossetti, history editor for Basic Books, for his excellent editorial skills, insightful suggestions, and commitment. Vanessa Rockel, who has worked with me on previous projects, has once again proven to be a capable and thorough researcher with an aptitude for tackling complex historical problems. I am indebted to Ron McAdam, who generously shared his memories of the December Uprising, and to Leo and Kostas Katsuris for kindly allowing me to record what are still very painful memories. Dione Dodis not only gave me considerable insight into her experiences during the December Uprising but also put me in touch with Roxanne Fessas, who shared with me her mother's unfinished memoir of the terrible ordeal she suffered as a captive of the KKE. Also, thanks to Dora Antonakopoulou for her help.

Rigas Rigopoulos, who lived through the occupation, is a fine writer, whose account, *The Secret War: Greece–Middle East, 1940–1945* (Paducah, Kentucky: Turner Publishing Company, 2003), offers a rare glimpse into the murky world of espionage in occupied Greece. I am also grateful to Gerasimos Apostolatos for advice and suggestions about events on the December Uprising, as well as for his encyclopedic memory of sources. Konstantinos Yannakogeorgos is a mine of information on Greek history and, on more than one occasion, has been kind enough to find for me rare Greek accounts of the civil war as well as providing timely and useful advice. Dinos Siotis has been a friend for more than two decades, and I have relied on him for help on numerous occasions. He is generous with his time, and as a poet and publisher, he is an outstanding representative of Greece in North America.

I would also like to thank Kostas Dedegikas, a former student, now an inspired graphic artist, for the maps; Panos Pappas, a friend and colleague, for timely assistance; and Maria Hamilton, without whose support this and a number of other projects would not have seen the light of day. John Taylor guided me through the maze of documents at the National Archives, Washington, D.C., and I, as well as a multitude of scholars, owe him a debt of gratitude. Simon Fraser University's small Social Sciences and Humanities Research Council (SSHRC) grant contributed to completing the research on this project, along with the support of John Pierce, dean of arts.

I will always pay homage to my parents, Sotos and Maria, for helping me understand this difficult period of Greek history without prejudice or malice. Finally, my wife, Beverley, is the reason for all that is good in my life, and her understanding, patience, and love have enabled me to overcome many a hurdle. She shared with me the ordeal of completing this project and spent long hours rendering rough drafts into a comprehensible manuscript. If this book falls short of achieving its objectives, the fault is mine.

ANDRÉ GEROLYMATOS
MARCH 2004
NORTH VANCOUVER

LIST OF TERMS

AAA	Struggle, Restoration, Independence
Africa Corps	German army in North Africa
AKE	Agrarian Party of Greece
AMFOGE	Allied Mission for Observing the Greek Elections
AMM	Allied Military Mission
Andartes	Greek resistance fighters
Arvanitis	Greek-speaking Orthodox Albanians
ASO	Antifascist Military Organization
BDDFA	British Documents on Foreign Affairs
BEF	British Expeditionary Force
BMM	British Military Mission
C	head of British Secret Intelligence Service
CAB	cabinet papers
capetanios	guerrilla leader
CID	Committee of Imperial Defense
Cominform	Information Bureau of the Communist Parties
Comintern	Communist International (Third)
Committee of Six Colonels	minor resistance group in Athens
COS	chiefs of staff
CPSU	Communist Party of the Soviet Union
DGFP	Documents on German Foreign Policy
EAM	National Liberation Front
EDES	National Democratic Greek League
EEAM	National Workers' Liberation Front
EKKA	National and Social Liberation

ELAS	National Popular Liberation Army
ELD	Union of Popular Democracy
EON	Greek Youth Organization
EP	National Civil Guard
ethnikophron	nationalist-minded
Evzone	traditional guard of the Tomb of the Unknown Soldier
FO	Foreign Office (British)
FRUS	Foreign Relations of the United States
GAK	General Archives of State (Greece)
GDA	Greek Democratic Army
gendarmerie	national provincial police
GHQ	general headquarters
GNA	Greek National Army
Goudi	Greek army barracks outside Athens
Harling Mission	SOE operation to destroy the Gorgopotamos viaduct
Helldiver	U.S. dive-bomber
IAEA	Historical Archive of the National Resistance (Greek)
IDEA	Sacred Association of Nationalist Officers
JUSMAPG	Joint U.S. Military Advisory and Planning Group–Greece
KKE	Communist Party of Greece
Lebanon Charter	agreement of 20 May 1944 establishing the Government of National Unity
Marita	codename of German invasion of Greece and Yugoslavia
ME	Middle East
MI	military intelligence
MI5	British security and counterintelligence service
MI6	British Secret Intelligence Service
MI9 (N Section)	British service responsible for assisting the escape of prisoners of war
MID	Military Intelligence Directorate (British)
Midas 614	SOE Greek espionage and sabotage group
Military Hierarchy	monarchist faction of Greek generals in 1943
MIR	Military Intelligence Research
NARA	National Archives and Records Administration
NARS	National Archives of the United States
NATO	North Atlantic Treaty Organization

November 17	Greek Marxist-Leninist terrorist group
Operation Noah's Ark	British plan designed to harass the German retreat from Greece
OPLA	Organization for the Protection of the People's Struggle
OSS	Office of Strategic Services
PASOK	Pan-Hellenic Socialist Movement
PEAN	Pan-Hellenic Union of Fighting Youth
PEEA	Political Committee of National Liberation
PESE	Friendly Society of the Army of Liberation
PRO	Public Records Office
Prometheus II	SOE espionage network in Athens
PWE	Political Warfare Executive (British)
RG	Record Group
Rizospastis	KKE daily newspaper ("The Radical")
RN	Royal Navy
SAS	Special Air Service
Section D	forerunner of SOE
Security Battalions	collaborationist units during the Axis occupation
SIS	Secret Intelligence Service (British)
SKE	Socialist Party of Greece
SOE	Special Operations Executive (British)
UNRRA	United Nations Relief and Rehabilitation
UNSCOB	United Nations Special Committee on the Balkans
USAGG	U.S. Army Group–Greece
USSR	Union of Soviet Socialist Republics
Wehrmacht	The army of the Third Reich
White Terror	postwar period of ultra-right-wing violence
WO	War Office
X	ultra-right-wing organization
YVE	Defenders of Northern Greece

CHRONOLOGY

1821	The Greek War of Independence against the Ottoman Empire.
1830	Great Britain, France, and Russia recognize Greece as a sovereign state.
1833	Otto of Bavaria is crowned as Othon I of Greece.
1844	The new constitution establishes Greece as a constitutional monarchy.
1897	The Greek-Ottoman War. Greece is defeated in just three weeks of fighting.
1910	In the wake of a coup by military officers, Eleutherios Venizelos wins a landslide victory in the elections and institutes major reforms.
1912	The First Balkan War. Greece, Serbia, Montenegro, and Bulgaria defeat the Ottoman Empire.
1913	The Second Balkan War. Greece, Serbia, and Montenegro defeat Bulgaria.
1914	Outbreak of the First World War.
1916	Venizelos forms a revolutionary government in northern Greece. The beginning of the Great Schism.
1917	Great Britain and France force King Constantine to abdicate in favor of his son Alexander.
1922	The Greek-Turkish War. The Greek army is defeated in Asia Minor; Constantine is forced to abdicate for a second time.
1923	Treaty of Lausanne (24 July) establishes the borders of Greece and Turkey. Both countries also agree to a population exchange in which more than 1.5 million Greek Orthodox are forced to relocate to Greece.
1924	Greece becomes a republic.
1924–1926	A succession of military coups undermines the new republic.
1935	The Venizelist faction in the armed forces attempts a coup and fails. The officer corps is purged of antimonarchists.

1935   The monarchy is restored after a fraudulent plebiscite; George II returns
        to Greece.

1936   (4 August) Ioannis Metaxas, with the support of King George, estab-
        lishes a dictatorship.

1940   Italy attacks Greece. The Greek army scores a number of impressive vic-
        tories and pushes the Italians back to Albania.

1941   (6 April) The German army, with support from Bulgaria, invades Greece.

1941   King George leaves Greece, and a Greek government-in-exile is set up in
        London and Cairo.

1941–1944 Greece is occupied by the Axis (Germans, Bulgarians, and Italians). A re-
        sistance evolves but is divided between left- and right-wing organizations.

1942–1943 The SOE establishes the British Military Mission in Greece to coordi-
        nate the Greek guerrilla forces.

1942   The British SOE, along with ELAS and EDES, destroys the Gorgopota-
        mos viaduct.

1943   (April) Ioannis Rallis, with permission from the Germans, creates the
        Security Battalions.

1943   (August) A delegation representing the Greek resistance travels to Cairo,
        but all efforts at a political compromise with the Greek government-in-
        exile and the British fail.

1943   (8 September) Italy surrenders.

1943   (12 October) The first round of the Greek Civil War begins.

1944   (29 February) The Plaka Agreement ends the first round of civil war.

1944   (March) The PEEA is established.

1944   (17–20 May) The Lebanon conference and the creation of a Govern-
        ment of National Unity.

1944   (July) The British Military Mission is joined by the American Office of
        Strategic Services (OSS) and is renamed the Allied Military Mission.

1944   (28 July) A Soviet Military Mission arrives in ELAS territory.

1944   (August) EAM agrees to join the Government of National Unity.

1944   (26 September) The Caserta Agreement is concluded.

1944   (9 October) The Churchill-Stalin Percentage Agreement divides the
        Balkans into spheres of influence.

1944   (17 October) The Greek government returns to liberated Athens.

1944	(Sunday, 3 December) Demonstrators are fired upon by police in Constitution Square.
1944	(4 December–January 1945) The December Uprising.
1945	(4–11 February) The Yalta Conference.
1945	(12 February) The Varkiza Agreement ends the December Uprising.
1945–1946	Period of White Terror as ultra right-wing gangs persecute former members of ELAS as well as those in EAM and the KKE.
1946	(30–31 March) Communists attack Litochoron, launching the third round of civil war.
1946	(31 March) First postwar Greek general election.
1946	(July) Markos Vaphiadis organizes communist forces into military units.
1946	(Summer) Fighting escalates in the countryside.
1946	(1 September) Plebiscite restores monarchy.
1946	(28 October) KKE proclaims establishment of the Greek Democratic Army.
1947	(12 March) Proclamation of the Truman Doctrine.
1948	(May) Murder of CBS correspondent George Polk.
1948	(15 November) Markos Vaphiadis is removed and Zachariadis completes the organization of the Greek Democratic Army into a conventional force.
1949	(10 July) Tito closes Yugoslavia's border to the Greek insurgents.
1949	(5–16 August) Offensive of the Greek National Army in Grammos and Vitsi.
1949	(24–31 August) Final offensive in Grammos.
1949	(26 August) Albanian communist government disarms and detains Greek insurgents.
1949	(16 October) Radio Free Greece (the KKE radio) announces the end of the insurgency.
1952	Greece becomes a member of NATO.
1967–1974	A junta of colonels establishes a military dictatorship.
1974	Turkish invasion of Cyprus.
1981	Greece joins the European Community.
1981	(October) PASOK (the Hellenic Socialist Movement), led by Andreas Papandreou, brings to power the first Greek socialist government since the end of the civil war.
1991	The breakup of Yugoslavia and the reemergence of the Macedonian issue.
2003	Trial of members of November 17.

INTRODUCTION

IN THE LATE FALL, ATHENS CAN BE UNCHARACTERISTICALLY
cold and grim and is occasionally punctuated with bone-chilling rain.
Brisk winds sweep the narrow streets and a lemon yellow sun deceives
the expectation of warmth during the short days of late autumn. The
day 29 November 1922 dawned reluctantly, revealing a city shrouded in
a gray pall, a fitting setting for a day weighted down by so much drama
and history.

Despite the cold rain that drizzled from early morning, approximately 150 men clustered in a field adjacent to the Goudi military barracks just a few kilometers north of Athens. They stood silently,
consumed by the restless energy of anticipation. They had come here
to witness the execution of six men. For two years, Dimitris Gounaris,
Prime Minister; Georgios Hatzianestis, Commander-in-Chief of the
Greek Army; Georgios Baltazzis, Foreign Minister; Nikolaos Stratos,
Minister of the Interior; Nikolaos Theotokis, Minister of War; and Petros Protopapadakis, Finance Minister, individually and collectively,
had directed the Greek state. Now they were the most despised men in
Greece.

The Six, as they came to be known, had been tried by military court
martial and condemned to death for high treason.[1] Under their stewardship the Greek army had been defeated in Turkey, which terminated any
hope of redeeming the ancient territories of Greece in Asia Minor. The
Great Idea, the short phrase that encompassed all the hopes and aspira-
tions of generations of dreamers, ambitious politicians, and kings, had
now turned into a frenzy of blame.

In this lonely field close to 11:30 A.M., these once powerful men stood at the edge of their lives. For most of them, the journey to the firing squad had originated in the highly charged politics of Athens and led to the city's Averoff prison, where they had spent the night waiting anxiously for a decision on life or death by a military court that was less interested in justice than in the politics of retribution.

Colonel Katsigiannakis, the deputy commander of the gendarmerie, had the onerous task of informing the Six that the decision of the court martial was death, but the officer could not bring himself to face the condemned. He tried to pass on the responsibility to a subordinate, and when that failed, he even pleaded with an inmate of Averoff prison, but he, too, declined. Finally, Colonel Katsigiannakis worked up sufficient courage to inform the Six that at 11:00 A.M. they were to be transferred. Although this meant execution, the authorities in Averoff prison were simply unable to put into words the fact that these men were going to die.

A little past 10:30 A.M. the families of the prisoners were permitted a last farewell. The condemned men were granted the last rites. A monk was brought into the prison and reluctantly performed the ceremony, protesting that he could not minister to men responsible for the deaths of priests and the destruction of churches.

Twenty-five minutes later the six prisoners and their guards were herded into two trucks, accompanied by about a dozen officers and gendarmes in automobiles. The procession, led by an ambulance that would later serve as a hearse, then headed to the place of execution. The small convoy sped along one of the main boulevards in Athens toward the military barracks of Goudi. The street was lined with soldiers, who stood in the rain hoping to get a glimpse of the men who had cheated them of victory, but the trucks were covered. If most Athenians nursed a secret desire for the Six to be spared, the army needed and demanded a human sacrifice.

At 11:05 A.M., the trucks slowly disgorged their reluctant passengers. Almost immediately, the clusters of soldiers and nervous spectators milling about in the chilly November morning assumed the shape of three sides of a rectangle. An army captain collected the prisoners and with his sword pointed each one to his last patch of earth. The first four moved quickly to the designated firing zones, but the last one, Dimitris Gounaris (the former prime minister), still suffering from typhoid fever, had to be assisted by Protopapadakis, who helped the sick man to his designated spot and then swiftly took his own place. Behind each man, a shallow grave had been prepared to accommodate his body prior to final burial in a proper cemetery.

At that moment, six firing squads of five men (one for each prisoner) presented arms, but the officer in charge noticed that one squad numbered six instead of the assigned five. He ordered one of the soldiers to retire, but the man demanded to keep his place. The spectators quietly whispered that the soldier had to be from Asia Minor and wanted to collect his pound of flesh. A few minutes later, another commotion broke out as a young officer scuffled with a civilian. He proved to be a journalist who had pulled out a black package of cigarettes, which the officer had taken to be a camera (photos of the execution were forbidden). The ensuing struggle brought nervous laughter from the spectators, and for a few moments almost all forgot the grizzly ordeal that was to take place.

Five minutes later, the officer in charge, Colonel Neokosmos Grigoriadis, proceeded to read the charges and specifications; however, soon his voice failed, as did his courage. After a few vain attempts at preserving his dignity, he collapsed to the dank ground, and Colonel Peponis, the secretary of the court martial, snatched the paper from his unconscious colleague's hand to finish reading out the document. The officer in charge of the firing squads offered each of the condemned men the traditional option of saying a few last words, followed by the ritual presentation of the blindfold, but the Six refused both. Once again the command was given to the firing squads to present arms.

The privilege of completing the execution was awarded to a veteran and amputee of the lost war in Turkey. The man, struggling with his crutches, slowly approached the line of soldiers and took his place. At this point, the only sounds came from the priest reading a final prayer, and then the veteran straightened up and, in a clear voice, gave the commands to "aim" and "fire." Thirty-one rifles concentrated on the Six, and in a split second, the air exploded. Five of the six collapsed almost immediately; the sixth, Hatzianestis, former field marshal of the Greek army, hesitated and, clutching his throat, spun downward onto the wet earth, gasping for life.[2] Before the officer in charge could administer the coup de grâce, the soldier from Asia Minor (who had held his fire) took matters into his own hands. He dropped to one knee, took aim, and shot the field marshal in the head, exploding the cranium and staining the ground with a puddle of blood. Five more shots penetrated the sudden silence as the officer in charge mercifully terminated the agony of the rest.[3] A light rain peppered the spectators, who stiffly abandoned the field, some only partly conscious that this particular execution had now solidified the political schism that had dogged Greek society from the beginning of the nineteenth century.

MANY OF THE KEY INDIVIDUALS WHO LATER CONTRIBUTED TO the sequence of events that led to the civil wars of the 1940s directly or indirectly had a role in the trial and execution of the Six. Colonel Nikolaos Plastiras, "The Man on the Black Horse," as his friends and followers liked to call him, was typical of the professional Greek officer of that time—a man of humble origins who had found success and social mobility through a military career. As one of the primary leaders of the Revolutionary Committee, Plastiras, more than anyone else, was responsible for the execution of the Six. Later he argued that he had condoned the death of the Six in order to prevent a larger massacre of Royalist officers, politicians, civil servants, and even ordinary civilians, and in a last interview just before his death in 1952, he claimed responsibility for the inevitability of the execution. After 1922, he led two abortive coups in the 1930s to prevent the restoration of the monarchy, which in fact paved the way for the restoration of King George II in 1935 and the establishment of a dictatorship a year later. In 1945, Plastiras became prime minister, and under his stewardship Greece entered the final round of the civil wars in 1946.

General Ioannis Metaxas, a fanatical monarchist and friend of King Constantine, as well as of the Six, headed a dictatorship from 1936 to 1941. Once in power, Metaxas persecuted and imprisoned many of the officers involved in the execution and in the abolition of the monarchy.

During the Metaxas rule, the Communist Party of Greece (KKE) was elevated to the status of a national threat, and its members were declared traitors and anti-Christian. The security services arrested hundreds of communists and thousands of Greeks suspected of being left-wing sympathizers. Many of them underwent torture and were condemned to long prison sentences.

According to some accounts, communists were made to sit on blocks of ice while force-fed castor oil. The victims suffered horribly from uncontrollable diarrhea, but the objective of the torture was to strip them of any semblance of dignity. Another, less invasive but equally devastating, technique was to arrest suspected communists or leftist sympathizers and offer them the option of going to prison (which also implied torture) or signing a declaration of repentance renouncing "Godless communism." Although at the time, the KKE's membership did not exceed 2,500 members, the overzealous police and gendarmes by 1940 had collected over 50 thousand such declarations.

Lists of these declarations were published in the *Government Gazette* as well as in right-wing newspapers, with predictable results. Thousands of innocent people were compromised as subversives. Many of them lost their jobs and friends and ultimately found refuge by joining the Communist Party. In a bizarre twist of fate, the Metaxas dictatorship came close to destroying the KKE but in the long run secured for the communists a pool of future recruits. Certainly, many of those who signed the declaration of repentance harbored an almost visceral hatred for the Metaxas regime, which also extended to the monarchy that had kept the dictator in power.

Post–civil war Greek governments adopted many of the techniques of the dictatorship, including the use of internal exile, as well as torture, as a means of rehabilitation. After the Second World War, the Greek army, with the connivance of the government, established a number of detention centers including the prison island of Makronisos, which surpassed the medieval horrors of Devil's Island and resembled the gulags of Siberia. Inmates were used as forced labor in near primitive living conditions, given little food, often deprived of water, and periodically beaten. Those marked for special treatment, particularly well-known

communist cadres or former resistance leaders, were tortured exten-
sively, and if that did not break their spirit, the authorities had more in-
genious and sadistic means at their disposal. Recalcitrant prisoners, or
those who did not cooperate, had their feet and hands bound and were
placed in a sack along with four or five cats, then immersed in a few feet
of water. After a few minutes, the victims became so badly mauled that
some died later from hemorrhage.

Another character in the drama of 1922 was General Theodore Pangalos, the erratic and rabid antimonarchist member of the Revolutionary Committee. Pangalos organized one coup in 1925 and ruled Greece
as a petty dictator for six months. The Pangalos interregnum was brief
and ridiculous. The more outrageous examples of his legislation included the devaluation of the currency by simply having all the paper
notes cut in half, the imposing of a dress code for women by decreeing
that women's skirts fall to the ankle, and the hanging of two civil servants for corruption. With the exception of the last, which for a brief
moment in time shook up the civil service, the rest of his legislation was
consigned to comic obscurity. Inflation continued to soar regardless of
Pangalos' intervention, and the result of his foray into fashion was that
for at least six months, Greek policemen could legitimately stare at
women's mid-calves.

During the occupation (1941–1944), however, Pangalos and his associates played a much darker role. Many of his supporters joined the infamous Nazi-controlled Security Battalions who fought the left-wing
resistance. In 1944, under British command, the officers of these quisling units participated in the December Uprising and afterward contributed to the White Terror that forced many on the left to take up
arms and organize guerrilla bands. In 1946, these units formed the nucleus of the Communist Democratic Army and managed to exact their
pound of flesh from the government forces in retaliation.

In 1922, George Papandreou was a rising star in the Venizelist camp,
closely linked, though not a participant, with the leaders of the military
coup that toppled King Constantine. In the fall of 1944, he was brought
out of occupied Greece by the British Special Operations Executive to
head a government of national unity that included representatives of

communists and socialists. Less than two months after liberation, the Government of National Unity collapsed, but Papandreou remained prime minister, and under his tenure the British and Greek government forces fought the left-wing resistance during the December Uprising, which paved the way to the final round of civil war in 1946.

Some of the lesser figures in the events of 1922, such as Colonel Stefanos Sarafis (although a junior member of the Revolutionary Committee), played a greater role after 1941. During the occupation, Saraphis was appointed commander-in-chief of the National Peoples' Liberation Army (ELAS), the left-wing resistance army, controlled by the KKE, which came close to enabling the Greek communists to take over Greece after liberation. Sarafis was not a communist but had remained a committed Venizelist with social democratic views. Like many officers of his generation he opted to join ELAS in order to fight the Axis as well as to prevent the return of a British-imposed monarchy.

There were many others present on that cold November morning who—in one fashion or another—had had a hand in turning the pages of history, initiating a cycle of division, revenge, retribution, and finally civil war. Yet, individually none of these men possessed the charisma to attract a mass following and impose their will on events. Many were middle-rank officers who later achieved higher office because circumstances created opportunities for advancement, not as a reward for participating in a particular movement or party. Allegiance to the monarchy or the Venizelist-Republican cause was motivated by loyalty to a specific faction, more to secure promotion than owing to political dogma. Collectively the officer corps lacked a common ideology and vision for the Greek state; that was left to the Communist Party of Greece (KKE).

Certainly on that fateful day, it was unlikely that anyone from the KKE would have been welcome at any official event, let alone permitted to witness the execution. In 1922, prior to the Asia Minor disaster, the communists could boast fewer than 1,500 members. As a political party, the KKE remained on the periphery of the political scene and had been further marginalized by opposing Greek irredentist policies. For the most part, KKE members were in the throes of ideological bloodletting, consumed by the ebb and flow of events in the Soviet Union and the Communist International.

The communists were concentrated in the poorer districts of Athens and Piraeus and had failed to make an impact on mainstream voters. Their focus was on the small working class in Athens, Piraeus, Thessaloniki, and some of the larger towns. Most KKE activity was confined to penetrating labor organizations and distributing leaflets and the party newspaper, *Rizospastis* (the *Radical*), or huddling in small coffee shops to debate endlessly the finer points of Marxism.

All that changed in 1922. The tidal wave of refugees from Asia Minor provided the KKE with its only consistent supporters. A large number of the members of the central committee and politburo, including Nikos Zachariadis, the secretary General of the KKE from 1924 to 1952, and Markos Vaphiadis, the commander of the Greek communist forces in 1946, came from the working-class neighborhoods of Constantinople, Smyrna, and other large cities of the Ottoman Empire.

Later, Greeks from Asia Minor filled the higher ranks of the left-wing resistance and the Democratic Army, but in the 1920s and 1930s the refugees provided the KKE with votes, which elected the first communist deputies in the Greek parliament in the interwar period. During the civil war in 1946–1949, the refugee-dominated region of Western and Central Macedonia and Thrace became one of the principal bases of operations for the Democratic Army, which brought about yet one more onslaught of misery for the victims of the Great Idea—a notion of a greater Greece.

The harsh life of the refugees in the sprawling shantytowns of Athens and Piraeus became a breeding ground of discontent and political dissent and a source of the malaise that permeated Greek society in the 1920s and 1930s. In 1922 hundreds of thousands left the shores of Turkey on anything that floated and were dumped on the quays of Greek harbors, while others made the long trek from Eastern Thrace. All arrived half starved, stripped of possessions and dignity, and consigned to makeshift camps stalked by disease and famine. Thousands packed into overcrowded churches, and still more overflowed into the streets, finding shelter in doorways and filthy alleys.

The helplessness and hopelessness of the refugees was compounded by the Great Depression, which further degenerated their harsh environment into an appalling poverty. Thousands perished, and for the survivors even hope was an extravagance few could manage. The Greek authorities had been overwhelmed in 1922 when the refugees first arrived, but in 1929 they simply gave up. The limited and modest welfare services of the Greek state simply could not deal with the over 1.5 million unexpected new residents in addition to the swelling ranks of the poor and unemployed caused by the collapse of the Greek economy in 1929.

Throughout this period, the political establishment remained impotent and, instead of confronting these upheavals, simply turned inward. Since the establishment of the Greek state, irredentist policies had offered a convenient distraction for politicians and the general public from the complex social and economic issues that confronted the new country. The end of the Great Idea exposed the stark realities of a divided society and a fragile financial infrastructure. The military coup of 1922, coming in the wake of defeat and after such a dramatic sociological upheaval, not only imposed political change but undermined the notion of constitutional legitimacy.

Fundamentally, the Revolutionary Committee demonstrated that power could be achieved through the bayonet—a lesson that the military would not forget and would repeat throughout the next two decades. As a result, the economic crisis of 1929 was exacerbated by political uncertainty, as a succession of governments followed each other with dizzying regularity. A series of coups and countercoups occasionally punctuated the bleak Greek political landscape, but the objectives of the conspirators were self-serving and had little to do with achieving economic stability for the country.

Consequently, the inability of the Greek state to cope with these upheavals diminished the legitimacy and moral authority of the Greek political establishment. Greece in the 1920s and 1930s went adrift; hence, when a fraudulent plebiscite brought back the monarchy in 1936, the Greek nation simply acquiesced. A year later, when Ioannis Metaxas imposed a dictatorship, it simply underscored the political bankruptcy of the Greek state.

The Fourth of August Regime, as the dictatorship was called, established order and made the trains run on time, but generated neither popular support nor mass opposition—only begrudging tolerance. Metaxas ruled for four years over a country scarred by social divisions and an economic system in tatters, and badly served by its traditional political leaders. For a brief period, when the Greek army defeated the Italian invasion of Greece in 1940, there was national consensus on defending the country and unity of purpose, but these ideals disintegrated after the German occupation in April 1941.

From 1941 to 1944, Greece was dominated by the Axis forces, the vicissitudes of famine, and the politics of the resistance, whereupon the KKE emerged to challenge the traditional political leadership of the state. The story of the Greek civil war is inextricably tied to the efforts of the communists, who wanted to impose a political solution on the postwar Greek constitution by the force of arms. After decades of oppression and fear it was difficult for the KKE and its supporters to place their faith and their security in the "bourgeois" political process. The KKE leadership for most of the 1920s and 1930s functioned underground and practiced politics through conspiracy. Despite the rhetoric of popular democracy and representation of the masses, few KKE members ever succeeded in getting elected, let alone having any experience in government.

The KKE rose to prominence as a result of the occupation and came to dominate the left-wing resistance movement because of better discipline and an ability to function in a clandestine environment. However, even though the KKE emerged as a major force in postwar Greece, it was outmaneuvered by the provisional government and militarily defeated by the British army in the 1944 December Uprising.

Despite the outbreak of hostilities in 1946, some of the communist leaders still believed that after 1944 they could achieve power through revolutionary means. The drift to the final round of the Greek civil war was, in part, precipitated by the inability of the communist leadership to control events and secure a place for the KKE as a legitimate party in the Greek political spectrum. Another factor for the final round of the civil war was the failure of the provisional government and its British sponsors to come to terms with the resistance and the end of the politics of the prewar era.

Yet, what pushed Greek society over the chasm into civil war was the enduring national schism that had permeated Greece from independence, emerged into a political movement in 1916, received greater impetus with the execution of the Six, and solidified with the Metaxas dictatorship. After 1941, the chronic division between the Venizelist-Republicans and the royalists underwent a metamorphosis, forcing the old combatants to choose between the left-wing resistance dominated by the KKE and the right-wing factions supported by the monarchy and the British. However, the issue of the monarchy remained as the common denominator and icon of division.

The traumatic experience of occupation and resistance exposed the bankruptcy of the old political system, but not the ingrained divisions of Greek society. These found expression and power in the resistance movement, which offered a means of fighting the hated occupation forces and at the same time created an opportunity to set new political parameters for the period after liberation. This desire for a change from the prewar political and social status quo was exploited by the KKE to create a mass resistance movement which was ultimately betrayed when the communists attempted to seize power by force of arms. The hundreds of thousands who had flocked to the left-wing resistance during the occupation but would not join the KKE's insurrection in 1943 and 1944 were marginalized.

Postwar Greek governments suspected anyone who had taken part in the resistance in general, and particularly those in the organizations led by the KKE. The result was that most of the veterans of the resistance were disenfranchised and terrorized by right-wing gangs. Many, once again, turned to the KKE as the only alternative to persecution, prison, or death and sought refuge in the mountains. By 1946, the few dispersed bands in northern Greece and the Peloponnese became the nucleus of the communist Democratic Army that condemned Greece to the most destructive last act of the civil war.

The causes of the three Greek civil wars from 1943 to 1949 are manifold and complex. The period between 1922 and 1941, however, set into motion the process of political fragmentation that was triggered on the morning of 29 November 1922. Both periods were dominated by the issue of the monarchy, which forced Greek society to align itself for or against the crown. In this contest, the moderates were squeezed out and compelled to join the left, which placed them on the side of the KKE, or the right, which forced them to accept the monarchy and by extension an authoritarian political system. The radicalization of Greek society created a harsh and unforgiving environment in the postwar period that made compromise next to impossible.

To some extent, the story of the Greek civil wars revolves around these political realities and the personalities who attempted to impose their will on events but in the process succeeded in unleashing a cycle of violence that pitted Greeks against other Greeks, killing thousands and condemning the country to poverty for a generation.

1

HISTORICAL BACKGROUND

ON 9 SEPTEMBER 1935, GENERAL GEORGE KONDYLIS, GREEK minister of war and "king maker," decided to terminate the troubled Greek Republic. At midnight, he summoned Major-General Christos Panagiotakos to a hurried cabinet meeting. A few hours earlier Kondylis, a crusty old republican officer, had demanded that Premier Panagiotis Tsaldaris abdicate in favor of the monarchy. In a show of force, Kondylis deployed dozens of army units, accompanied by armored cars, in and around Athens. Much to the surprise of Kondylis, Major-General Panagiotakos had mobilized the Goudi garrison, just outside Athens, in support of the premier. For a few hours, soldiers loyal to one or the other general squared off along the streets in the center of the capital.

Kondylis was furious, and when General Panagiotakos arrived, the two men got into a heated argument. Finally, Kondylis ordered Panagiotakos to withdraw his forces. Panagiotakos refused to obey, whereupon Kondylis directed the nearest guard to arrest the general. The guard tried to apprehend Panagiotakos on the threshold of the chamber, but the general managed to break free. First Kondylis, then his aide, Lieutenant Loukidis, joined the struggle to arrest Panagiotakos, who was by this time assisted by his brother, a republican deputy. For several minutes, two generals, one junior officer, one parliamentarian, and one soldier slugged it out just outside the cabinet room. In this fracas, Loukidis pulled out his revolver and shot at Panagiotakos, who had also received a bayonet thrust in his jaw. This pathetic tragicomedy was a fitting spectacle in the theater of the absurd that passed for government. Neither Kondylis' coup to end the republic nor Panagiotakos' attempted countercoup to support the government had any constitutional basis. These dramatic events were manifestations of the military supremacy in Greek politics.

For most of the twentieth century, the Goudi barracks became synonymous with Greek national restlessness and the staging ground for coups, countercoups, and executions. In 1909, the army, in a fit of righteous indignation, temporarily seized the state. The move was a delayed reaction to Greece's 1897 defeat by the Ottoman Empire as well as a heightened sense of resentment against the ingrained corruption of the ruling establishment. The minuet of party factions, combined with greed and acrimonious partisan politics, led the country to disaster in 1922. That year, the army took direct control of the state to exact retribution for the political incompetence and criminal negligence that had damaged national interests.

By the late summer of 1922, after its defeat in Turkey, the army was streaming back to Greece in disgrace. As the soldiers returned home, stalked by the odium of failure, a tide of refugees flooded the sun-drenched harbors of Athens and Thessaloniki. This sea of human misery was the price Greece had to pay for a military adventure that had begun in 1919, but whose origins had been intertwined with the inception of the modern Greek state.

The Great Idea, the notion that the new Greece could incorporate all Greeks living within the Ottoman Empire as well as the territories that fell within the boundaries of the Byzantine Empire, was born from the idealism of nineteenth-century Greek nationalism. This vision of a greater Greece represented a link with the glories of classical Greece and the grandeur of Byzantium. The Great Idea had also served as a common bond and a source of identity for Greeks in and outside Greece. Although the appetite for territorial aggrandizement may have perished on the battlefields in Turkey in 1922, the aftershock of that costly delusion generated a continuum of upheaval that had only partially abated by 1949.

In 1922, assigning blame had become the order of the day. Someone had to pay for the Asia Minor catastrophe and atone for the sin of defeat, and it was left to the military to choose the sacrificial victims. By the second week of September 1922, elements of the Greek army that had retreated to the islands of Lesbos and Chios rebelled, and a group of angry Greek officers once again took control of the Greek state.[1] Ordinary soldiers, bone weary and hungry, followed their officers because circumstances left them little choice. The government in Athens appeared helpless, overwhelmed by the magnitude of the defeat and the daunting refugee problem.

In late September, a few army units reached Athens and with little resistance took over the state and proclaimed a new order.[2] The principal leaders of the coup and members of the subsequent Revolutionary Committee included Colonel Stylianos Gonatas, Colonel Nikolaos Plastiras, and Captain Nikolaos Phokas. For the sake of appearances and under pressure from the British and French, the colonels set up a puppet government led by S. Krokidas. A short while later that government was replaced by one headed by Colonel Gonatas, dropping any pretense of civilian rule. On 26 September the military issued an ultimatum to the government, demanding, among other things, the removal of King Constantine, who agreed to leave Greece, which he did on 30 September (he died in Palermo, Italy, one year later). His eldest son, George, who also went into exile in 1924 when Greece became a republic, replaced Constantine. Shortly afterward, the military arrested six politicians, one prince, one general, and an admiral.[3] Ultimately, only the general and five of the politicians were chosen to pay with their lives for crimes against the state.[4]

The execution of the Six, however, was an aberration. Although coups and countercoups were part of the shuffleboard of Greek politics, they were relatively bloodless affairs. Mass killing, torture, and harsh imprisonment didn't become prevalent until later, growing out of the cult of ideology and fear that plagued Greek society during the civil wars in the 1940s. Prior to 1922, the wrong end of a political conspiracy usually meant loss of office and influence and the inability to reward the followers of one party or another with government largesse. However, these shifts in fortune were temporary and were rectified by the next election or coup. Albeit strong emotion and violence often accompanied major shifts in the power politics of the country, the prospect of death as a punishment for political failure represented a finality that few were prepared to countenance.

Indeed, most Athenians, including some of the officers who took part in this national exorcism, assumed or hoped that somehow external intervention would stay the execution. This sentiment stood in direct contrast to the demonstrations and headlines that, during the course of the trial, had screamed for blood and retribution. Yet, few Athenians believed that the executions would really take place. After all, foreign intervention had been an integral part of Greek political life since 1821. Many assumed that the omnipotent Great Powers, especially the British, would spare them the application of death as political revenge.

The creation of the Greek state in 1830 had been as much a result of the Greek War of Independence as of the intervention of the Great Powers, who forced the Ottoman sultan to concede the establishment of modern Greece in 1830. The Great Powers in 1875 had granted the Greeks more territory in the north and later the island of Crete and in 1913 the territories of Macedonia and Western Thrace. Foreign intervention was even enshrined in the Greek constitution, which assigned Britain, Russia, and France the role of protecting powers, a privilege they exploited in 1917 to remove King Constantine, when the monarch refused to drag Greece into the First World War on the side of the Entente. Now it only seemed fitting that the Great Powers would step in and spare the Greeks from their blood lust. For most, the verdict of capital punishment in and of itself had been sufficient to soothe the national conscience, but taking responsibility for the forthcoming execution was another matter entirely.

In 1922, there was further reason to believe that lives would be spared because Lord Curzon, the British foreign minister, had dispatched Commander Gerald Talbot to Athens to try to prevent the execution of the Six. Talbot had close ties to Eleutherios Venizelos, the most prominent

Greek politician and vehement opponent of King Constantine. Lord Curzon believed that Talbot could use that relationship with the revolutionaries (who looked on Venizelos as their spiritual leader) and convince them to commute the death sentences. Talbot arrived in Athens on 28 November, too late to stay the executions but just in time to save Prince Andrew of Greece (Constantine's son), also held responsible for the Asia Minor defeat.

Andrew had commanded the Second Army Corps in the Asia Minor campaign and during the Battle of Sakarya in 1921 had refused to execute a direct order. A military court had found Prince Andrew guilty of insubordination on 2 December 1921, and the British believed, as did most of the Greek royalists, that he, too, would face a firing squad. Since Andrew had ties to the British royal family, Lord Curzon had instructed Talbot to negotiate with the leaders of the coup. After a series of secret meetings between Talbot and these leaders, a compromise was reached. Instead of facing a firing squad, Andrew was condemned to perpetual banishment, and the prince along with his family, departed Athens on board the H.M.S. *Calypso*.[5]

Andrew's narrow escape and Talbot's intervention added further credence to the wide-held notion that the Great Powers—and the British, in particular—were the ultimate arbiters in Greek affairs.[6]

The army, or more specifically the officer corps, desperately needed to distance itself from the defeat in Asia Minor. As was the case with the military of the other Balkan states, the army officers saw themselves as the embodiment of the nation and the protectors of the state. Any stigma of defeat or humiliation had to be deflected and assigned to unscrupulous politicians or to the Great Powers. Consequently, the Greek military invoked a "stab in the back" excuse to explain their part in the 1922 defeat and to preserve the role of the army as the guardian of Greece.

However, this contempt for accountability only perpetuated a cycle of military interventions that frequently destabilized Greek society and guaranteed the army a disproportionate influence in the state. Consequently, the condemnation of the Six was simply another step in a self-serving process that enabled the military and the political opponents of the Six to avoid direct responsibility for the defeat. Although the disaster in Asia Minor was the immediate responsibility of the government in power, almost the entire Greek political and military establishment had played a part in bringing about this disaster. Tragically, the execution served to enshrine the political schism that had plagued Greek society almost from its inception, and later, a mutated form of this division would loom over the bloodletting of the civil wars in the 1940s.

The political, social, and economic divisions that fractured the Greek nation in 1922 were fundamentally the outcome of geography and history that had become part of the cultural baggage of the new Greek state in 1830. It was difficult to shed 500 years of Ottoman rule, which had exulted in absolute power and encouraged subservience. In effect, the Ottoman Empire had stifled political evolution and sustained an intellectual paralysis in most of the Greek communities in the empire. This condition was further compounded by the geographically scattered nature of Greek society, which, in turn, fostered regional social, economic, and cultural particularism. Effectively, the Ottoman sultans ruled over a collection of Greek communities on the southern Balkan Peninsula, in the Aegean islands, along the south coast of the Black Sea, and on the coast of Asia Minor in Turkey.

Life under an alien regime was often harsh, and the fate of individuals and groups depended on capricious sultans and, more often than not, on rapacious pashas. For the most part, the Ottomans were content to allow the Greeks a measure of self-rule. A good deal of what passed for indigenous regional government was exercised through the Greek Orthodox patriarch and his bishops, as well as by local notables, whose fortunes were hostage to the whims of the Ottoman administration. Consequently, over the course of five centuries, Greek political experience and the exercise of limited civic responsibility developed out of the peculiarities of the Ottoman system, which was predisposed to religion as the main catalyst for social and political organization. For the Christian subjects of the empire, the church was the primary mechanism for any degree of enfranchisement and access to the sultan's court. A financially powerful Christian (and predominantly Greek) aristocracy, based in the Phanar district of Constantinople, had evolved by the eighteenth century and assumed a predominant role in the affairs of the Orthodox church. Effectively, these men achieved through the church a significant but limited role in the affairs of the empire.

The Phanariots,[7] the collective name for this group of Ottoman Orthodox Christians, possessed linguistic and financial expertise as well as the mercantile networks deficient in the Muslim communities of the Ottoman Empire. Over time, the Phanariots secured almost exclusive control over Ottoman banking and trade; in addition they acquired a significant role in the diplomatic affairs of the empire. The sultans were grateful, and the Phanariots achieved considerable wealth and influence. Some became patrons of the arts, endowed schools, and built churches, but most of them focused primarily on amassing greater fortunes.

Traditionally, Phanariots administered the semi-independent principalities of Wallachia and Moldavia in Romania, which they exploited with a rapacious greed only matched by that of their Ottoman overlords. In the provinces and islands of mainland Greece, an equally small group of primates (Christian landlords, tax farmers, and ship owners) formed a powerful oligarchy that set them apart from the landless peasants and poor farmers. Both the Phanariots and the primates were an extension of the Ottoman regime and were not inclined to oppose a system that ensured their wealth and status. For most of these privileged few, the prospect of a Greek state, as defined by nineteenth-century nationalism, was an alien and dangerous concept, which they outright rejected.

The Ecumenical Patriarch of the Orthodox church, also a member of the Phanariots, was even less inclined to encourage a movement toward a Hellenic state or any movement that threatened the special relationship between the church and the sultan. The Ecumenical Patriarch had condemned the French Revolution and in 1821 excommunicated any Greeks who rebelled against the sultan. In practical terms the patriarch had little choice; the rebellion was concentrated in mainland Greece, while the center of Greek Orthodoxy was based in Constantinople in the heart of the Ottoman Empire. The revolutionaries could espouse the glories of an independent Greece, but the fact remained that three quarters of the Greek world was trapped within the Ottoman Empire and could not participate in the rebellion or join the prospective new state.

In addition to these practical considerations and potential liabilities, the church was opposed to the fundamental precepts of the French Revolution. During the first 200 years of Ottoman rule, the influence of the West and the ideas emerging out of the Renaissance were perceived as threats to the Orthodox church as an institution as well as to its dominion over Ottoman Christians. Until the czars of Russia presented an Orthodox alternative, the Ottoman Empire was the only bulwark against Western intervention and penetration of the Orthodox world. The Orthodox church was anti-Western and had rejected vigorously everything the Renaissance represented. According to L. S. Stavrianos, a historian of the Balkans, the Orthodox church was repelled by the "exaltation of reason in place of dogma, the turn to Greek antiquity. . . . In short, Balkan Orthodoxy opposed the West not only because it was heretical but also because it was becoming modern."[8] To the church, modernity threatened to unravel the monopoly of Orthodox theocracy over the Balkan Christian communities.

Five centuries of Ottoman rule had reinforced subservience to central authority, a concept inherited from the Byzantine period, while the anti-intellectual and antiscience attitude of Muslim clerics had also permeated the mind-set of the Orthodox hierarchy in the Ottoman Empire.[9] As a consequence, the Orthodox church did not encourage learning, nor did it develop teaching orders such as the Jesuits and Franciscans. The patriarchate in Constantinople was primarily concerned with survival, maintenance of the privileges of the clergy, and control over the secular affairs of the Greek and other Balkan societies.

The hegemony of Orthodox theocracy stagnated the intellectual development of Greek society. Literacy and education in general practically vanished in Greece during the Ottoman period. Most communities were reluctant to finance schools, and the church refused to fill the intellectual vacuum. The Patriarchical School in Constantinople, established in the sixteenth century, was the exception, but it primarily catered to the Phanariot elite and the families of the higher clergy in the Ottoman capital. At the end of the sixteenth century, the church began to fund new schools in several parts of Greece, but these were isolated examples and did not represent a network of education.

In contrast, by the eighteenth century the courts of the Phanariot princes of Wallachia and Moldavia, as well as their palatial homes in Constantinople, became centers of learning and the arts. In practice, this only benefited a small group of individuals, but the Phanariots also offered employment and protection for the handful of Greek professionals and artists who would have had to seek employment outside the Greek world. Later, some of these professionals, along with a few Phanariots as well as certain wealthy Greek merchants of the diaspora, represented part of the odd collection of revolutionaries who proposed rebellion against Ottoman authority and agitated for the creation of a Greek state. After the outbreak of hostilities in 1821, the Peloponnesian primates, the ship owners of the Aegean islands, and the bandits of mainland Greece and the Peloponnesus joined them.

Unlike the Phanariots and primates, the diaspora merchants did not constitute a collective entity and were exposed to the intellectual trends of their adoptive countries. Those in France and Britain were influenced by the liberalism of western Europe, whereas the Greek merchant communities in Russia were predisposed to the authoritative administration of the czars. The diaspora communities attempted to superimpose their political and constitutional ideas on the Greek independence movement, but in terms of influence, each group was limited to providing money and guns for the 1821 uprising. A few idealists traveled to Greece and participated in the war, but most remained in their adopted countries and used their influence to secure eventual recognition of the fledgling country. In this respect, the European diaspora Greeks in the nineteenth and early twentieth centuries became established as sources of finance and as informal ambassadors between Greece and the Great Powers.[10]

In contrast, the primates of the Peloponnesus and mainland had long roots in Greece but remained distinct from the ordinary peasants and shepherds who made up most of the population. Individually and as a group, the primates enjoyed considerable autonomy under the Ottomans and represented the wealthiest landowners in Greece. In addition, they augmented their wealth by engaging in tax farming and controlling the commerce of the region.[11] "The Peloponnesian Primates," writes John Petropoulos, "were very much a social class—self-perpetuating, cohesive and alike in their style of life."[12] Unlike the cosmopolitan Phanariots, the primates were conservative and to a degree reactionary. Although most of them eventually opted to join the move for Greek independence, they did so reluctantly and only after it became apparent that the Ottomans had lost control of mainland Greece and the Peloponnesus. However, these men understood that the new Greek state was to replace Ottoman absolutism with an indigenous and equally authoritarian regime.

Although the Phanariots and the diaspora elites provided the intellectual momentum and financial resources for the Greek War of Independence, they could not agree on the form or boundaries of the new state. Their views were influenced by their immediate environment and particular social and economic disposition. The Phanariots and the Greek diaspora merchants were physically and culturally removed from the primarily agricultural and pastoral communities of mainland Greece. The Phanariots, because of their position in the Ottoman Empire and their wealth, constituted a de facto aristocracy with direct participation in the center of an established empire. Cosmopolitan and sophisticated, they had little in common with the landless Greek peasants and shepherds. Most of them preferred a future in which the Ottoman regime would gradually give way to a secular and multicultural empire dominated by an economic elite. Some even believed that after the Muslim element was displaced, it would be only a matter of time before a Christian ruler assumed the sultanate and the Ottoman Empire followed in the footsteps of the Roman Empire and transformed into another Greek Byzantium.

The competition between the authoritarianism of Byzantium and the liberalism of classical Greece remained and later shadowed the political and cultural struggles in the modern Greek state in the twentieth century. The nostalgia for Byzantium and autocracy later served as an ideological base for dictators, monarchists, and any political faction in modern Greece that opposed liberal democracy. The Metaxas dictatorship of 1936–1941 not only defined itself as antiparliamentarian and anticommunist but proclaimed the dawn of a "Third Christian Civilization," implying a hazy succession from classical Greece to Rome and Constantinople.

For over half a millennium, Greek cities, towns, and villages lived under a flexible despotism that permitted a degree of local administration but at the discretion of the Ottoman sultan and his pashas. The only exception was the bandit groups in the mountains, which were a law unto themselves. Although during the War of Independence the bandits represented the foot soldiers of the uprising, only a small number of their leaders played any role in the new Greek state. The most prominent or notorious were pensioned off, but many simply resumed their former occupation. This was possible because after 1830 the authority of the Greek government was confined to large cities and towns. Large areas of the countryside and the mountains were beyond the reach of the state. Later, in the twentieth century, these isolated communities would become hostage to guerrilla armies and serve as both the staging areas and the battlegrounds of insurgencies opposed to foreign occupation and the political order in Athens. The bandits, however, remained a distinct element and one that could be harnessed to serve the interests of the political factions.

The Greek state that emerged after 1830 was dominated by the factionalism left over from the Ottoman period, the lawlessness of the bandits, and the division between the indigenous population and influx of refugees that had arrived in the aftermath of liberation. The inhabitants of mainland Greece and the Peloponnesus had been startled and disconcerted by the unexpected influx of refugees, along with Greeks of the diaspora (mostly idealists who had fought in the War of Independence) and some Phanariots, who had settled in Greece between 1821 and 1830. The indigenous population, concentrated around small and essentially isolated communities, was suspicious of any newcomers and viewed them as a foreign element.

Another factor in the evolution of the Greek state was that the Great Powers dictated boundaries and the constitution of the country. The Greeks had to accept a very small country and a foreign monarchy as the price for independence. Both concessions, however, contributed to a national restlessness that fueled irredentist ambitions and a polarized political environment exacerbated by an alien royal house.

A monarchy was thrust upon the Greek nation by the Great Powers to ensure that the new country adhered to the old regime in Europe that followed the defeat of Napoleon and the French Revolution. The concept of monarchical rule, however, did not fall on sterile ground, and some of the Greek revolutionary leaders were content to accept an authoritarian regime as long as they could form part of the new ruling elite. Others found the institution abhorrent, and once the dust of creating the new state settled, they proceeded to chip away at the powers of the crown, setting in motion a dynamic that engendered an ongoing political schism. For almost 150 years, the obsession with the constitution suffocated Greek society, sucking up all creative political energy at the expense of other issues.

In this environment, domestic and national interests gravitated between the king, a small coterie of hangers-on, and clusters of small political blocs. It is indicative of the period (1830–1864) that the Greek political factions that vied for the right to govern the Greek state not only lacked a party structure but were linked even by their names directly to the Great Powers. During the rule of King Othon, the first king of Greece, the political factions were labeled as the French, English, and Russian parties. To some degree, the leaders of these factions identified with or were strong proponents of British, French, or Russian influence in Greece with respect to the fulfillment of the Great Idea.[13]

Remarkably, foreign policy based on the mantra of the Great Idea dominated the discourse and policies of the competing factions. On a pragmatic level, the country's paucity of financial and natural assets left little room for domestic development and modernization. The Great Idea, on the other hand, was flexible, nonpartisan, and sufficiently intangible. As a concept, it fired the imagination of all Greeks regardless of political affiliation and provided a link with the unredeemed communities that were left in the Ottoman Empire. The only question that remained was how the Great Idea could be implemented, and the only realistic answer was that the unification of the Greek world could only come about with the help of one of the Great Powers.

The so-called Russian faction was convinced that if the Russian Empire did nothing else, it would assist Greek irredentism by simply waging war against the Ottomans. The French faction also assumed that France would facilitate the establishment of a greater Greece, but both groups were adamant in their opposition to Britain. This left the English party at a disadvantage since the British were not only occupying the Ionian Islands but insisted on maintaining the integrity of the Ottoman Empire. However, the English faction argued that Greece could not expand without British support, pointing out that the Royal Navy dominated the eastern Mediterranean and could intervene at will for or against Greece.

Regardless of the lofty ambitions for a greater Greece, independence from the Ottoman Empire did little to change the fact that the country was poor in resources and economically unviable. Furthermore, the rugged and mountainous terrain of Greece as well as poor communications concentrated the exercise of political power in Athens. With few exceptions, most political leaders either lived in the capital or had the resources to maintain a separate residence in the countryside—success in government was dependent upon wealth and establishing a political base in Athens. Consequently, the Greek political establishment, even in the twentieth century, was small and self-contained and fed from a complex system of clientage that revolved around an even smaller group of powerful individuals. Although the new Greek state had adopted European political institutions, the use of patronage, structural corruption, and servile (yet fickle) obedience to authority remained a legacy of the Ottoman Empire.

Accordingly, the dynamics of Greek politics in the 1920s and 1930s were shaped by the tumultuous events that had buffeted Greek society in the late nineteenth and early twentieth centuries. The course of Greek irredentism, launched successfully by Eleutherios Venizelos in the Balkan Wars of 1912–1913, and culminating with the Asia Minor disaster, came to an abrupt end during the summer of 1922. In the decades to come, notions of a greater "Greece" surfaced occasionally but were confined to the incorporation of Cyprus.[14] The rest of the decade was marked by military coups, the abolition of the monarchy, and the establishment of a short-lived republic from 1924 to 1935.[15]

The collapse of Greek financial institutions and the mass unemployment resulting from the Great Depression, as well as problems created by the influx of over a million refugees from Asia Minor, greatly undermined the credibility of the republic and hastened its demise. On 3 November

1935, after another attempted military coup, a fraudulent plebiscite led to the restoration of the monarchy. The return of King George II was less the result of increased popularity of the crown than a symptom of national malaise, brought about by the Depression, the never-ending political intrigues on the part of the major parties, and most of all the intervention of the military.

The revolution of 1922 not only forced the abolition of the monarchy but heralded a new era of direct intervention by the army in the making and unmaking of governments. Each coup, whether successful or not, was followed by a purge of the armed forces. In 1922, the royalists were drummed out of the military, but in the succeeding coups (1933 and 1935), the axe fell on mostly republican officers, so that by 1940 almost all antimonarchists had been forced into retirement.[16] As a result, control of the armed forces reverted to royalist officers, who, in conjunction with some members of the Populist Party, began to clamor for the restitution of the monarchy. After the Populist victory at the polls immediately following the March 1935 coup attempt, tremendous pressure was placed on Panagiotis Tsaldaris, the Populist premier, to bring about an immediate restoration of the monarchy.

Tsaldaris had promised a referendum on the issue of the monarchy, but following the landslide victory in the 1935 general election, many in his party, and primarily those senior army officers, demanded that he abolish the republic and invite George II to return to Greece.[17] When Tsaldaris refused, his government was promptly overthrown by the military. General George Kondylis, one of the conspirators, replaced him and upon assuming office, declared the end of the republic and advanced the date for the referendum on the monarchy to 3 November 1935. The results of the plebiscite were outlandish even to the most credulous supporters of the monarchy: Out of 1,492,992 votes cast, only a paltry 34,454 opposed the return of George II.[18] The restoration of the monarchy, according to one historian, "brought in a new and decisive factor, the King, who held the undisputed loyalty of the military."[19] Other factors, however, emerged that not only secured the position of the monarchy but even brought Greece closer to the totalitarian regimes of Germany and Italy.

The reinstatement of George II did not heal the fissures of Greek society, and the elections of 1936 showed this clearly by producing a parliament divided almost evenly between the Liberals and the Populists along with fifteen Communist deputies. Since the bitter divisions between the Venizelists and the monarchists made it impossible for the major parties to cooperate and form a coalition government, the other practical option was for one of the major parties to work with the communists. In 1936, the Greek Communist Party was on the fringe of the political scene. Although the communists did not enjoy widespread support, with the fifteen seats they had won they were in a position to hold the balance of power in parliament.[20] Both major parties initiated talks with the communists, and the Liberals actually managed to reach an agreement with them, but these efforts at political compromise were stillborn. When news of a possible Liberal-KKE coalition leaked out, Alexander Papagos, the minister of army affairs, with the support of the chiefs of the air force, navy, and gendarmerie, informed the king that the armed forces would not countenance a government that included communists.[21]

In the period preceding and following the election, Greece was undergoing labor unrest accompanied by strikes and violence, which occasionally led to serious casualties. On 8 May 1936, a strike in Thessaloniki by 6,000 tobacco workers broke down in violence, which prompted railway and tram workers to strike in sympathy. The government responded by deploying army units in support of the gendarmerie and issuing a decree mobilizing the railway and tram workers. These measures were ineffectual, and the number of strikers reached 25,000. The next day, the gendarmerie clashed with demonstrators around Government House, killing 12 and wounding 200 demonstrators.[22]

In the absence of a majority government or coalition, a caretaker government headed by Constantine Demertzis administered the country. Unfortunately, Demertzis died in April and Ioannis Metaxas, the deputy premier and the leader of a small right-wing party, succeeded him as head of the government. The death of Demertzis had been preceded by the demise of a number of other prominent political figures, including Kondylis, Venizelos, Tsaldaris, and Alexander Papanastasiou,

which at this critical juncture deprived the country of some its most influential and experienced leaders. The coincidence of the deaths of these
individuals and the labor unrest sweeping over Greece provided an opportunity for Metaxas, with the support of the king, to gain control of
the state. The Workers' Federation had declared a twenty-four-hour
general strike for 5 August, and on 4 August, Metaxas persuaded the
king to suspend certain articles of the constitution and declare martial
law in order to avert a communist revolution.[23] In effect, on 4 August
1936, King George II gave Metaxas the authority to establish a dictatorship that lasted even beyond Metaxas' death, until the exiled king reinstated the constitution in February 1942.

Unlike the totalitarian regimes of Germany and Italy, the Greek dictatorship was not based on a political party. Although supported by the
military, it was not given power by the army and did not develop a Fascist or Nazi ideology, beyond some vague references to the establishment of a "Third Greek Civilization."[24] According to Metaxas, the
Fourth of August Regime was "an anti-Communist Greek state" that
was totalitarian with an agricultural and labor basis and therefore an-
tiplutocratic. It did not depend on a political party but constituted the
whole of the Greek people, excluding the communists and reactionary
old political parties and factions.[25]

The dictatorship, in essence, included the king, Metaxas, and a small
devoted group of lieutenants propped up by the armed forces, whose
royalist officers depended upon the monarchy for their rank and to keep
out their Venizelist counterparts. In addition, an efficient security service quickly weeded out any opposition to the regime. Unlike Hitler and
Mussolini, Metaxas did not make a conscious attempt to distance himself from the military in order to avoid the appearance of relying on the
army for support, because the officer corps remained loyal to the king—
his authority remained entirely at the king's discretion.[26]

The leaders of the major parties failed to mount an effective opposition or make any serious attempt to challenge the dictatorship, and for
the most part, they did not pose a serious threat to the regime. Their activities were confined to written protests or trying to convince the king
that they could provide an alternative to the dictatorship.[27] There were

exceptions, most notably Panagiotis Kanellopoulos, but the noncommunist resistance effort came from those Venizelist officers purged after the 1930s coup attempts. With the exception of a single abortive rebellion in 1938, the efforts of these ex-officers were restricted to plotting future coups and printing illegal pamphlets.[28]

For Metaxas, the communists constituted the most serious danger, and immediately following the proclamation of the dictatorship, he outlawed the KKE.[29] Constantine Maniadakis, the minister of security, established a wide network of informants, and through communist renegades and police agents, he was able to infiltrate and ultimately dominate the local communist organizations.[30] Hundreds were arrested, imprisoned, or sent to internal exile on remote islands, while thousands more were coerced into signing declarations of repentance in order to avoid incarceration. Just before the Italian invasion in 1940, a proud minister of propaganda, Theologos Nikoloudis, claimed that 57,000 had signed declarations. Remarkably, these figures exceeded the total membership of the Communist Party, which did not surpass 14,000, and must be attributed to the excessive zeal of the police, who often seized individuals merely suspected of communist sympathies. Eventually, many of those unjustly arrested or condemned to prison drifted to the KKE.[31]

The tactics used by Maniadakis quickly undermined the communists, as most of their leadership ended up in prison, while the few who managed to escape were forced to live a clandestine existence that proved invaluable during the occupation.[32] In addition to the use of informants and infiltration of police agents into communist organizations, Maniadakis created a government-controlled KKE central committee as a counterweight to the existing central committee, which, along with the numerous declarations of repentance, came close to destroying the KKE. Throughout this period, the police, the gendarmerie, and the security service were the primary instruments of the dictatorship and in the war against the communists. The army remained exclusively loyal to the king despite Metaxas' efforts to gain the wholehearted support of the officer corps.[33]

Aside from the persistence and audacity of its loyal cadres, the continued survival of the Communist Party is partially attributable to Zachariadis' policy of decentralizing some of the KKE's underground into independent, self-contained cells.[34] Although many of these units were penetrated by the Metaxas security services, enough survived to provide a core for the party's reorganization after 1941.[35] Another important, albeit inadvertent, contribution was made by the policy of the Metaxas regime in keeping arrested communists together in special political prisons and islands of exile. The imprisoned communists transformed their incarceration into useful activity by conducting classes on Marxism and training the less experienced cadres in clandestine work.[36] To some extent these factors explain how the KKE, although seemingly at the point of extinction during the Metaxas period, was capable by the autumn of 1941 of beginning the organization of a wide and effective underground.[37]

However, despite the vigilant efforts of the dictatorship's security services, some opposition remained, and communist cells and groups of Venizelist officers continued to work underground. Their survival and reemergence during the occupation would play a pivotal role in the resistance. Each year, however, the Metaxas regime tightened its grip on the country and it became progressively more difficult for anyone to organize effective opposition. The general population continued to remain indifferent to the dictatorship, particularly as the Fourth of August Regime provided a number of reforms, which, if they did not inspire popularity for the dictatorship, assured it of benign toleration.

For most of the 1920s and 1930s, Great Britain, the foreign protagonist in Greek affairs, had little interest in the small Balkan country. The Greek debacle in Turkey had been a major setback for British ambitions in the Near East, and after 1923, the British had to reconsider their policy toward Greece, Turkey, and the Balkans. On 14 October 1922, Britain's chiefs of staff, in a memorandum to the Foreign Office, recommended closer ties between Britain and Turkey, rather than between Britain and Greece.

Consequently, within this new geopolitical context, Greece ceased to be the focal point of British policy in the eastern Mediterranean. The British government regarded the internal political situation in Greece with indifference and for the most part lost all interest in Greece. According to Sir Robert Vansittart, "Those who helped Greece into a mess did nothing to help her out."[38] During the next sixteen years (1923–1939),

British-Greek relations remained dormant except for the occasional disturbance by the Greek population of Cyprus.

The reaction of the British government to the Metaxas dictatorship was mixed, and for the most part the British reconciled themselves to the new order. The appraisal of Sir Sydney Waterlow, the British ambassador in Athens, of the political situation in August 1936 played down the abolition of parliamentary democracy and stressed that the king was in control of the situation; the dictatorship, he argued to the Foreign Office, was advantageous to British interests.[39] Privately, Sir Sydney had reservations.

Metaxas, for his part, went out of his way to assure the British that he would maintain the traditional Anglo-Greek friendship. He informed Waterlow in December 1936 that Greece "was irrevocably and unreservedly devoted to the British connection."[40] In the same vein, Metaxas, in the aftermath of the Czechoslovakian crisis in 1938, attempted to placate the German ambassador in order to preserve Greek neutrality. During the course of a meeting with the German minister, Prinz zu Erbach, in early October 1938, Metaxas admitted that the king would oppose a pro-German policy and that any movement in the direction of Germany would lead to the downfall of his government. At the same time, Metaxas told Erbach that if Greece sided with Great Britain, the Venizelists would use this opportunity to take control of the state.

As he indicated to the German ambassador, Metaxas had to tread very carefully with respect to Greek foreign policy since he required the goodwill of the king, and the monarch insisted upon close ties with Britain. Metaxas had to maintain at least a veneer of pro-British sentiment. He feared that the British did not like the dictatorship and that they harbored strong misgivings about his past affiliations with Germany as well as his loyalty to King Constantine. On 12 March 1939, Metaxas wrote in his diary that he suspected that the British would try to remove him, and as late as April 1940 he was still suspicious that there were British intrigues against him.[41]

After the outbreak of war in September 1939, the Foreign Office requested from the Committee of Imperial Defense (CID) a strategic analysis of Greece. The CID was to determine what possible support Britain could provide the Metaxas government should circumstances bring the Greeks into the conflict. According to the chiefs-of-staff:

> It will be to our advantage for Greece to remain neutral as long as possible, even if Italy declares war against us. As a belligerent she will undoubtedly prove to be a liability and will tend to absorb allied resources which could be used elsewhere. It has already, however, become apparent that the use of Suda Bay for our patrols engaged in interrupting German sea-borne trade would be an advantage. If Turkey comes in on our side this need would be obviated since contraband control could be more effectively exercised from the Bosporus. If Turkey, however, remains neutral or even becomes hostile the use of a Greek harbor may become necessary. In this event Greece might submit to "force majeure" while remaining neutral in the best interests of the allied cause.[42]

Metaxas, however, was determined at all costs to keep Greece out of the war. He confided in his diary that the interests of Greece, as far as the major powers were concerned, received a very low priority. The only option for his country was to become self-sufficient and maintain its neutrality.[43] At the same time, the British policy of keeping Greece neutral enabled Metaxas to avoid a possible showdown with the king should the latter press for Greece to enter the war on the side of Great Britain. Despite Metaxas' repeated displays of friendship for Britain and his maintenance of a strictly formal relationship with Germany, the British always had doubts about the Greek dictator. However, they accepted the situation because they could do little else under the circumstances and because they could count upon the pro-British attitude of King George II.

On 28 October 1940, Mussolini issued an ultimatum to the Greek government, which, if accepted, would have reduced Greece to the status of an Italian satellite. The immediate and uncompromising refusal of Metaxas to accept the Italian demands led to war. The Greek dictator's strong stand against Italy alleviated any doubts that the Foreign Office had about Metaxas' potential Axis sympathies, at least as far as

Italy was concerned. There was still the question of Germany, and the British were particularly sensitive to the possibility that Metaxas could turn to Germany for mediation and support. Germany, however, remained neutral.

The surprising victories of the Greek army over the Italians in Greece and Albania reinforced the British policy of support for Metaxas, despite pressure from the Foreign Office to encourage the Greek government to release political prisoners and cooperate with the opponents of the regime.[44] By December 1940, the Special Operations Executive (SOE) already had an agent in Athens. He was attempting to secure the return of the exiled politicians, encourage the Venizelists to support Metaxas, and make known to the Greek government the undesirability of having two pro-German ministers in the government. The Foreign Office had serious doubts about the use of such activity, and the SOE had to ensure that its representative would not undertake any major action without the express approval of the British embassy in Athens.[45]

In fact, the newly created SOE had very little contact with the intelligence services, ministries, or individuals close to the Metaxas government. Its raison d'être was to prepare for and create sabotage and resistance—in Winston Churchill's often-quoted phrase, to "set Europe ablaze." Its role in Greece was to organize a network of agents to conduct such activity in anticipation of a possible Axis occupation. Despite the assurances given to the Foreign Office by the London SOE, SOE officers in Athens began to make contact with Venizelists, communists, and other opponents of the Metaxas regime since, as will be illustrated below, the SOE believed that such groups were capable of the type of underground work required to pursue its objectives in an occupied country. As a result, after the occupation of Greece the SOE's contact was mainly with Venizelists and communists who were still opposed to the Greek monarchy, which effectively was the Greek government-in-exile. On the other hand, the Foreign Office and the British government were committed to the Greek king, and the traditional British intelligence services, such as MI6, had contacts in Greece with monarchists and with individuals who had been a part of or were in sympathy with the Metaxas regime.

The continued success of the Greek armies against the Italians in Albania and the appearance of British forces, even of token strength, on the Greek mainland and Crete made a German invasion a distinct possibility. As early as 4 November 1940, Hitler had decided that some kind of intervention in the Balkans was necessary to rescue Italy, his only ally, from a humiliating defeat. On 12 November, Hitler directed the commander-in-chief of the German army to make preparations for the occupation of the Greek mainland north of the Aegean, should it become necessary to attack British air bases in Greece.[46]

Although he had not yet decided on the outright occupation of Greece, he was contemplating the seizure of bases for the German air force in order to dominate the eastern Mediterranean. His main concern, according to Directive 20, the operational order for the attack against Greece, was to frustrate British designs against the Ploesti oil fields, and for this reason, he ordered a plan for the invasion and occupation of northern Greece alone. Nevertheless, if necessary, he was prepared to overrun the entire Greek mainland.[47]

After the Italian attack against Greece, the Greek government was less reticent about receiving British military aid but still wanted such support kept secret, for the Metaxas regime did not wish to antagonize Germany.[48] In addition to formal contacts between Greek and British military representatives, Military Intelligence Research (MIR) and Section D, the forerunners of the SOE, began preparations for the organization of clandestine networks in anticipation of a German occupation of Greece. Agents of Section D managed to procure substantial quantities of small arms, ammunition, grenades, and incendiary bombs and hide them in the British Consulate in Athens. In addition, sabotage kits were manufactured out of four-gallon petrol cans; they included explosives, a saboteur's handbook translated into Greek, 100 pounds in Greek currency, two pistols and ammunition, and a few knuckle-dusters. At the same time, as many as 300–400 potential saboteurs were trained.[49] MIR worked closely with the Greek General Staff, but Section D activities were kept secret from the Greek authorities, since these efforts involved the organization of underground cells staffed by Greek subjects hostile to the government as well as to the monarchy. Another consideration for secrecy was that post-occupation planning might have undermined the will of the Greek military, implying the defeat of Greece was inevitable.[50]

Eventually, the British secret services employed communists and republicans because they were willing and able to function underground. In contrast, individuals loyal to the Greek government and to the king were not interested—they were content with the political situation in Greece. Some even believed in an ultimate Axis victory or sympathized with the regimes of Germany and Italy. C. M. Woodhouse, a man who played a pivotal role as head of the SOE's mission in Greece and one of the principal historians of that period, claims that "the right wing and the monarchists were slower than their opponents in deciding to resist the occupation, and were therefore of little use to the Allies until it was too late."[51]

Nicholas Hammond, a member of Section D and later of the SOE, states that the rationale for using communists and republicans as agents prior to Greece's entry into the war "was that the Greek King and the Government, headed by General Metaxas, who had been trained as an officer in Germany, would side with the Germans, who [the Germans] had cleverly remained neutral and were disregarding the war of their ally, Italy with Greece."[52] According to Richard Clogg, many senior Venizelist officers became willing agents of the SOE in the fall and winter of 1940–1941 because the Metaxas regime had refused them permission to fight the Italians. Clogg writes that these men were "almost by definition pro-British. . . . With British contacts going back to 1916, this group of officers was eager to contribute to the war effort but condemned by Metaxas' vindictiveness to kicking its heels in Athens."[53]

On the other hand, the *Report on SOE Activities in Greece and the Islands of the Aegean Sea,* composed on 27 May 1945, clearly states that the premise for SOE dealings with left-wing organizations was that "subversive activities must be based on a political concept. Effective sabotage and or guerrillas [*sic*] can only thrive if a revolutionary atmosphere has been created previously through political organizations."[54] This report was written after the war and with the benefit of hindsight. Its anonymous author further states: "The fact that resistance movements and eventually guerrilla warfare had to be built on left-wing political elements was well known to all concerned, and accepted in the SOE directives of the Chief-of-Staff for 1943 and by the Prime Minister in his directives on our policy to Greece."[55]

Initially, British strategy toward resistance in occupied Europe was to form secret armies inspired by revolutionary zeal. Although the concept of secret armies was not implemented, it continued to influence SOE policy toward resistance throughout the war.[56] Given this context, it is not surprising that Section D in 1940, and later the SOE, turned to the more radical elements in Greece for its recruits. Equally relevant, for many Greek nationals, employment in the secret service of a foreign power could be construed as an act of treason. At least this would have been the case up until the German attack against Greece. The communists and many republicans did not consider the monarchy and the Metaxas regime the lawful representatives of the Greek state and welcomed support from the British secret services to organize an underground that eventually they could use to achieve their own political ends.

On 29 January 1941, Metaxas unexpectedly died from tonsillitis, which left King George II in control of the Greek state, but the Greek monarch could not bring himself to dismantle the dictatorship. Instead, he appointed Alexander Koryzis, the governor of the National Bank of Greece, as Metaxas' replacement. Sir Michael Palairet, Waterlow's successor, urged the king to take provisional control of the government rather than appoint a nonentity figurehead, because Sir Michael feared that the death of Metaxas would cause internal dissension. Metaxas, Palairet commented, was "unfortunately irreplaceable."[57] The king, however, was reluctant to take such a step. Koryzis became president of the council, and control of the army was left to the commander-in-chief, General Alexander Papagos. The Greek general was an Anglophile and even before the death of Metaxas had made his pro-Allied views known to the British military attaché in Athens, who reported that Papagos "definitely considered himself and Greece as being our allies in all except word."[58]

The continued defeats of the Italians in Albania, North Africa, Ethiopia, and the eastern Mediterranean and the presence of British forces in Greece, however, forced Hitler to intervene. On 22 March 1941, Hitler ordered Operation Marita, which included the occupation of the entire Greek mainland as well as all the islands.[59] The only changes in Hitler's plans came as a result of the coup in Yugoslavia on the evening of 26–27 March, which caused the resignation of the regent, Prince Paul, and the fear that Yugoslavia would withdraw from the Tripartite Pact with Germany. This situation required the transfer of additional forces to participate in attacking Yugoslavia as well as Greece. The Yugoslav coup expanded Hitler's strategic options for Operation Marita by simplifying the logistical and transportation difficulties that an invasion of Greece would involve. The Yugoslavs had inherited their railroad system from the Hapsburg Empire, and it connected Austria, Hungary, Romania, and Greece. Thus, rather than having to attack via their ally Bulgaria, the German army had a direct approach to Macedonia.[60]

On 6 April 1941, the German armies launched their offensive and quickly overwhelmed the Yugoslav forces, reaching the Greek frontier within days and not weeks, as anticipated by General Papagos. Meanwhile, the deployment of the Greek army and the British Expeditionary Force (BEF) was, according to historian Martin Van Creveld, "suicidal."[61] Papagos had dissipated his limited forces by keeping four divisions along the Metaxas Line, which protected eastern Macedonia and Thrace, but allocated only three divisions to join the BEF and defend the Aliakhmon Line a hundred miles to the rear.[62] These dispositions created three defensive positions, which depended for their security on the Yugoslavs' holding their ground against superior German forces and equipment. Papagos' plan was not what the British had agreed to when General Sir Archibald Wavell had discussed with the Greek general the role that the BEF would play in the defense of Greece; rather, it was the result of misinterpreting Yugoslav intentions and political expediency.[63]

This situation was particularly disheartening for the British, especially since the decision to send troops to Greece had been made over the objections of the chiefs of staff and the commander-in-chief for the Middle East.[64] Aid to Greece was less motivated by military considerations than by Churchill's enthusiasm for supporting a "gallant" ally. In

addition, there was the faint hope that this aid might result in a significant setback for the Germans; then there was the fear that if Britain did
not support Greece the result would be grave repercussions on relations
with Yugoslavia and Turkey.[65] The chiefs of staff finally agreed to send
help to Greece, but they cautioned that if British forces were to have
any effect, they had to be dispatched as soon as possible. The strategy of
holding the Aliakhmon Line with the Greek forces withdrawn from
Thrace and Macedonia, they concluded, would have the only chance of
success.[66]

The military situation, however, deteriorated within a matter of
weeks, followed by the near collapse of the Greek government. On 9
April, the Germans routed the Yugoslav army and captured the Metaxas
Line. Once they had achieved this objective, they were able to turn the
left flank of the Aliakhmon Line and advance into central Greece, while
a detached force outflanked the Greek position in Albania.

The Greek forces in Albania held their ground despite an Italian attempt to mount an offensive to coincide with the German attack, and
the Italian army ultimately failed to achieve a breakthrough. The
British, on the other hand, did not have the opportunity to offer serious resistance, since each defensive position they took deteriorated rapidly, thanks in part to German superiority in equipment and airpower.
Once their position on the Aliakhmon Line was outflanked, they fell
back from one position to another until the Royal Navy rescued
them.[67] The commander of the First Greek Army in Albania, General
George Tsolakoglou, realizing that his forces were cut off, decided on
his own initiative to surrender to the Germans rather than give the Italians a victory they did not deserve.[68]

Koryzis tragically took his own life on 18 April 1941, and the king appointed a new premier, Emmanouil Tsouderos. On 21 April, General
Papagos recommended that the British begin evacuating their forces
from Greece.[69] On 23 April, the remnants of the BEF, the king, and his
government were evacuated to Crete. The island, however, provided
only a temporary respite, and once again the Royal Navy had to rescue
the British forces, the king, and his ministers and take them to Egypt.
From this point on, the Greek government was a government-in-exile

under circumstances that would impede its credibility with the general population of occupied Greece.

Ultimately, in the hectic weeks before the collapse, George II lost another opportunity to establish a national government that might have enjoyed the confidence of his people through the dark years of occupation. Instead, with the exception of Tsouderos, the monarch surrounded himself with a camarilla of ex-Metaxas ministers and some Venizelists, who hardly qualified as true representatives of the Greek people. Meanwhile, some members of the Greek political and military leadership who remained in occupied Greece collaborated with the Axis powers, as was the case with Tsolakoglou, but most of the traditional political elite remained on the sidelines, following the lead of Papagos.[70]

The government-in-exile contained no outstanding personalities, with the exception of Admiral Alexander Sakellariou, who had managed to evacuate part of the Greek fleet to Alexandria, and Tsouderos, who had been governor of the National Bank of Greece until Metaxas removed him.[71] Although the Foreign Office suggested that the Greek king and his government remain in Cairo, at least until the Battle of Crete was over, it reconsidered after the Egyptian government refused to allow the Greek government to stay in Cairo. Eventually, the Foreign Office decided that it was more convenient to have the Greek monarch in England. Thus London became the base of the exiled government, as was the case with all other exiled governments. London, however, offered one serious drawback: It isolated the king from almost any contact with other Greeks, who continued to make their way to the Middle East throughout the occupation and could have given him a realistic picture of the political situation in Greece.

The Greek government-in-exile attempted, at least superficially, to distance itself from the Metaxas regime, but it was reluctant to grapple with the problem of constitutional changes. The king and Tsouderos did not consider the constitutional issue critical or immediate; the primary preoccupation of the government was the war. According to Tsouderos, only after liberation should the king and the government introduce constitutional changes.[72] The top priority of the Greek government was the organization of the Greek forces in the Middle East, followed by Greek claims to acquire northern Epirus, the Dodecanese, and Cyprus. The premier also argued for an adjustment of the frontiers with Bulgaria and Yugoslavia and for massive Greek immigration to the Italian colonies of North Africa. In addition, if Turkey were to follow a hostile policy toward Britain, Greece should demand the accession of Eastern Thrace and insist that Istanbul become a free city, with Greece participating in its administration.[73]

However, much as he tried, Tsouderos could not bypass the problem of the constitution, and to avoid the appearance of bowing to British pressure, he encouraged George II to terminate officially the Fourth of August Regime. The king issued a decree ending the Metaxas regime in October; four months later, in February 1942, he signed a new Constitutional Act revoking Metaxas' legislation of 4 August 1936 and reestablishing the constitution of 1911.[74] It is not evident from the extant sources whether this move was either the result of British pressure, as an attempt to placate the resurgent republican sentiments of the Greek political parties, or simply a response to the fact that, as Tsouderos had pointed out on 25 January 1942, the death of Metaxas had ended the dictatorship.[75]

The lack of popular support for the Greek monarchy in Greece left the king in a position of weakness when dealing in matters of Greek foreign policy and territorial claims. The problem for the Greek government-in-exile was complicated further by the fact that all Greek political leaders, with a few exceptions, had turned their attention to the constitutional question, while Greek territorial interests took second place.[76] This not only affected questions of foreign policy but created a political vacuum in occupied Greece that enabled the communists to dominate the resistance movement. Indeed, the first approach by the KKE to the Greek republican parties to form a common front with the aim of organizing resistance was a failure.

The leading figures of the Greek political parties were obsessed with the constitutional issue and regarded the establishment of resistance organizations as premature or as an unnecessary hardship for the Greek people, who had done more than enough for the Allies in the campaigns of 1940–1941.[77] As a result, the king and his government were under constant attack by their opponents in Greece as well as by many of those living in exile who challenged their right to represent the Greek nation. Under these conditions, it was extremely difficult for the Greek government-in-exile to pursue a policy of reclaiming Greek territory. Even more difficult was the prospect of organizing a resistance movement, which, because of the political climate in Greece, would be beyond their control and would eventually be manipulated to oppose the return of the monarchy.

The first major problem for the Greek government-in-exile, however, was not opposition but the growing famine in Greece. The king and Tsouderos had to persuade the British to lift the blockade, if only temporarily.[78] The crisis placed the Greek government-in-exile on the horns of a dilemma. Tsouderos understood the utility of the strategy of blockade as a measure of war and as a means of defeating the enemy.[79] However, the question was one of degree: Depriving the occupation forces of external food supplies was one thing, while accepting a full-scale famine was entirely another. Tsouderos bombarded the British government with appeals and memoranda desperately pleading for the lifting of the blockade, but the interests of the Greek government-in-exile had very little impact on the British.[80] The British government did authorize the shipment of grain from Turkey, but the amounts were negligible and the grain had almost no effect on the food crisis that developed in the winter.[81] According to Elias Venezis, in the winter of 1941, the British ambassador had assured the Greek premier, Koryzis, that in the event of the occupation of Greece, the British would permit the importation of 30,000 tons of grain per month. After the collapse of Greece, the British failed to honor this agreement.[82]

For the British the famine in Greece had other implications. Lifting the blockade for the Greeks would set a precedent for other countries experiencing hardship in occupied Europe.[83] Another consideration was that food shortages could have the effect of inciting the population to a greater degree of resistance against the occupation forces. The role of the blockade, writes W. N. Medlicott, was to weaken the Axis by draining their personnel: "By maintaining the health of Axis-occupied territory the Allies would be providing ample resources of extra manpower for

Axis economy, in addition to diverting shipping and supplies from Allied users." He adds, "The Axis Governments would also be spared the dangers of pestilence and revolution in the occupied areas; this would reduce the need for occupation forces, and [be] one more deterrent against future conquest."[84]

The famine caught the attention of the world press, and the added pressure of the international community threatened to affect adversely world opinion of Great Britain.[85] Ultimately, the War Cabinet relented and lifted the blockade, but only after strong signs of American disapproval.[86] In the interim period thousands starved to death as the British grappled with strategic and moral dilemmas as well as the impact of starvation on subversive warfare. While the British government debated whether death by starvation of a substantial number of Greek people was necessary to the war effort, these same Greeks were risking the death penalty from the occupation authorities by hiding British soldiers.[87]

Concurrent with the problem of the blockade was the attempt by the Greek government-in-exile to implement a foreign policy based on a postwar political alliance with Britain that would be instrumental in addressing Greek territorial demands. On 29 September 1941, Tsouderos proposed to Alexander Cadogan, Permanent Under Secretary of the Foreign Office, a Greek-British alliance and offered the British naval and air bases in Greece. Cadogan responded favorably to the Greek proposal but assumed that such an agreement would also involve Greek territorial claims.[88] For this reason Edward Warner, the head of the Southern Department, was reluctant to endorse an alliance that included any postwar territorial revisions in the Balkans and the eastern Aegean. He proposed instead a military alliance along the same lines as that concluded with the government of Norway and suggested that the question of British bases and Greek territorial claims could be discussed later, without any current formal commitments.

On 25 November 1941, Anthony Eden, the British foreign secretary, met with Tsouderos and proposed the formation of an Anglo-Greek military alliance. He pointed out that any territorial and political agreements could be considered only after the end of the war. Tsouderos had little choice but to accept Eden's offer, and after Tsouderos received the king's agreement, a military alliance was concluded on 9 March 1942, which gave the British operational control of the Greek forces for the duration of the war.[89]

The British government supported the exiled king and his government in the expectation that he would be welcomed back in Greece after the end of hostilities; only then, the British assumed, could demands for constitutional change be addressed in an orderly manner and through free elections. British policy, according to Sir Llewellyn Woodward (the official historian of British foreign policy during the Second World War), "could not have been based on any other assumption, but such a policy of moderation and common sense assumed a higher level of political education and restraint than was the case in the predominantly peasant countries of Yugoslavia and Greece."[90]

Prior to the war neither of these countries had popular or democratic governments, and during the occupation the left-wing underground in both states gained control of the resistance, leaving the British little choice except to cooperate, as military necessity dictated, with the communist resistance organizations.

British policy in Greece between the beginning of the Axis occupation and liberation was characterized by two uncompromising principles. First, the Greek king and his government were the legitimate representatives of the Hellenic state, and second, Britain could neither sanction nor impose any political change during the war. Within these guidelines, British policy was adapted and stretched to accommodate the Greek resistance groups in order to encourage them to play a useful military part in the overall efforts of the Middle Eastern Theater of Operations in the Mediterranean. In his first book, *Apple of Discord,* C. M. Woodhouse defines British policy toward Greece as taking shape in an ad hoc manner and excludes the notion that the British government maintained any fixed policy:

> There was no such thing as His Majesty's Government policy towards Greece, in the sense of a fixed set of objectives laid down in advance. British foreign policy has never been something that is laid down in

advance, to be achieved regardless of what may happen between its for-
mulation and its execution; it is rather an emergent character which can
gradually be detected amongst the welter of *ad hoc* discussion.[91]

As far as the British government's support of the Greek monarchy
was concerned, Woodhouse explains this was a commitment to the person of King George II. The motives for Britain's loyalty to the Greek
king, Woodhouse writes,

> sprang hardly at all from the consideration that the restoration of the King
> would ensure the friendship of Greece towards England, because as a matter
> of plain fact almost any Greek government that was not communist would
> be friendly to England; they sprung almost entirely from gratitude and loy-
> alty to the man who had stood with us when everything seemed lost.[92]

A better question surely is whether the British had any other alternative. The king and the Greek government-in-exile were the internationally accepted representatives of the Greek state. Consequently, British
denial of the legality of the Greek government would have given some
credibility to the puppet regime in Athens.

During the course of the occupation, 1941–1944, British policy alter-
natives in Greece fell between military expediency, using resistance
groups to hamper and cause damage to the Axis forces in Greece and
thus indirectly to support the war effort in North Africa, and a political
agenda that strove to keep postwar Greece in the British sphere of influence. To ensure the latter, the Foreign Office remained loyal to the king
of Greece. In addition, Churchill maintained a sense of gratitude to
George II for his allegiance to Great Britain in 1941,[93] but he was less
eager to maintain the Greek monarchy than to preserve an orderly transition from occupation to liberation. In a statement to Rex Leeper, the
British ambassador to the Greek government, Churchill outlined his
policy regarding the Greek monarchy:

> The King is the servant of his people. He makes no claim to rule them.
> He submits himself freely to the judgment of the people as soon as nor-

mal conditions are restored. He places himself and his Royal House entirely at the disposition of the Greek nation. Once the German invader has been driven out, Greece can be a republic or a monarchy, entirely as the people wish.[94]

The underlying factor influencing British foreign policy was that the Greek monarchy represented legitimacy. From the beginning of the German hegemony over Europe, Churchill had resolved that during the war Great Britain would resist any changes that altered the internal political structures of the occupied states.[95] He was resolute in this policy and only gave way in the face of new realities, as was the case in Yugoslavia, France, and Poland; where possible, Churchill remained steadfast to the concept of legitimate authority. Within these parameters, however, the British government had to pursue a military strategy that in some theaters of operations required the cooperation of resistance groups with paramilitary organizations such as the SOE. In these circumstances it was necessary to ignore temporarily the overall guidelines of British policy in order to satisfy military expediency. Accordingly, throughout the war, the perceived usefulness of resistance organizations to military strategy had to compete with the policy objectives set by the Foreign Office.

British policy toward carrying on the war in occupied Europe was to be carried out by guerrilla forces inspired by revolutionary fervor and not by the secret armies of patriots originally envisaged by the chiefs of staff. Although the British government did not adopt the secret-armies strategy, it was incorporated into the idea of guerrilla forces and was adopted as part of the mandate of the SOE. The very concept of revolutionary upheaval, however, was anathema to the Greek government-in-exile as well as to the political establishment in Greece. Ultimately, the Greek government-in-exile had to accept responsibility for the consequences of the occupation of Greece. For George II and Tsouderos, instigating an organized resistance movement held the prospect of considerable reprisals and the devastation of the country, but to what end? In 1941–1942, the British were not in a position to attempt an invasion of the Greek mainland; they were barely holding their ground in

North Africa. However, once the king and his government left Greece, they were out of context. The brutality of the occupation forces and the ensuing misery that descended on the population proved the primary catalyst for resistance.

In the first days of the occupation, the German army behaved with almost extreme courtesy toward the Greek public. German soldiers paid for anything they bought and were particularly well mannered in encounters with Greek officers. Hitler, on the recommendation of Field Marshal Wilhelm List and Günther Altenburg, the Reich plenipotentiary, had ordered the immediate release of all Greek officers and other ranks who had been taken as prisoners of war.[96] In fact, during the German invasion of Greece, Hitler had instructed the Wehrmacht to treat all captured Greek officers with military courtesy and permit them to retain their personal swords.

The hastily formed government of Tsolakoglou, a creature of the Axis, attempted to be as accommodating as possible and believed that Hitler could be prevailed upon to keep out the Italians. One of Altenburg's first reports from Greece was to pass on a message of thanks from the Greek government, supported by telegrams from medical and professional associations, with the request that Hitler take Greece under his protection.[97] Symbolic gestures made by the Germans such as maintaining the Greek flag on public buildings and the honor guard at the Tomb of the Unknown Soldier made a positive impression during the first weeks of the occupation.

However, it is extremely difficult to determine the attitude of the average Greek toward the Germans at the time. According to the Nazi press, the Wehrmacht was greeted with flowers and overwhelming enthusiasm, while the Greek underground press contends that from the beginning the population displayed its outright hatred toward the Nazis.[98] Between these two extremes, it is almost impossible to gauge the sentiments of the average Greek. The onset of the German occupation found a population that was war-weary and numb, one that felt Greece had fulfilled its duty to the Allied cause.[99] Between the entry of the German troops into Athens and the end of the Battle of Crete, most people, with the exception of opportunists and some old supporters of King Constantine, maintained an attitude of passive resignation toward the Germans.[100] In a report to King George II, Prince Peter stated that the Germans, unlike the Italians, initially were not hated. On the contrary, some, especially the upper class, sympathized with and even admired Germany.[101] After the Battle of Crete and the entry of the Italians into Greece, the public attitude toward the Germans quickly hardened into hatred.

The early gestures of the Wehrmacht, aimed at softening Greek attitudes toward the new order, were negated by acts of symbolic oppression, which, coupled with the presence of the despised Italians, quickly convinced most Greeks that the Germans were not likely to treat them with any measure of respect and honor. Simple irritants, such as the way the Germans indulged themselves in numerous baths and wasted water to wash their automobiles despite a chronic water shortage, as well as more disturbing behavior, such as confiscating automobiles, villas, and any other valuable possessions, drastically changed people's attitudes.[102] The Germans confiscated numerous houses and apartments in Athens as well as in other parts of Greece. Usually, they simply gave the unfortunate owners a receipt from the Wehrmacht. In some cases, they requisitioned part of a house and relegated the previous occupants to a few small rooms. The new German occupants also took possession of all the furniture, but occasionally they either paid a small sum or allowed the owners to take with them some of their belongings.[103] German domination and insensitivity were also reflected by the double standards in restaurants, which permitted German soldiers to have access to meat, beer, and other commodities denied to the Greeks.

In addition, the curfew was extended, and Athenians were not permitted outdoors after 10:00 P.M.; Greek households were forced to keep their shutters closed day and night despite the oppressive heat of the summer.[104] Furthermore, the Wehrmacht in Greece purchased everything with freshly printed occupation currency that immediately became worthless. At the peak of the famine that gripped Athens in the winter of 1941–1942, German soldiers were permitted to send food to their families in Germany, while the occupation authorities requisitioned foodstuffs in quantities that exceeded their needs and sold the surplus at prohibitive prices.[105] The German authorities took over most transportation and all communication networks as well as imposing a strict press censorship. The former was particularly significant, since not only did it inconvenience the public, but the confiscation of all public and most private transport also made it almost impossible to supply Athens with foodstuffs from the islands and the countryside.[106]

The Greeks showed where their sympathies lay by their attitude toward British prisoners of war. Whenever the Germans transported these prisoners through the streets of Athens, people cheered the British and gave them cigarettes and food; from a population that now faced extreme deprivation of all such items, these were not merely symbolic gestures. Attitudes on both sides hardened considerably during the Battle of Crete, and then at the end of May 1941 two young men scaled up the Acropolis and took down the German flag.[107]

This nonviolent and symbolic act caused the Germans to overreact. On 31 May 1941, the German authorities issued a proclamation that clearly exposed the oppressive and brutal nature of the occupation, although it attempted to shift responsibility for the new policies to the Greek population. According to this decree, the harsh policies that the Germans were adopting had resulted from the recent attitudes and reactions of the Athenians toward the occupation forces. The taking down of the German flag and similar acts of symbolic and sporadic resistance in the first months of the occupation were either benign or ineffective. The response of the occupation authorities, however, escalated in severity and acted as a catalyst for more organized and violent acts of defiance that within a year led to the creation of guerrilla bands in the Greek mountains.

By the end of the summer of 1941, the combination of the approaching famine and the increasing brutality of the occupation forces resulting essentially from minor and insignificant acts of defiance provided additional incentives for the Greeks to commit acts of violence against the Germans and Italians. On 19 June 1942, Archbishop Damaskinos, the head of the Orthodox church in Greece, met with Günther Altenburg, the Reich plenipotentiary, to protest the execution of hostages by the German authorities. The Greek cleric pointed out to Altenburg that it was unjust to kill innocent individuals as a reprisal for acts of sabotage committed by unknown parties. The Greek people, Damaskinos added, expected better treatment from the Germans. They believed that Germany would protect Greece from the despised Italians and were prepared to accept a German occupation. However, after the executions and other acts of reprisal, the Greek people, including the Germanophiles, looked upon the German occupation forces with hatred.[108]

Despite the burgeoning and progressively violent opposition to the Axis, the Greek government-in-exile was reluctant to instigate organized resistance and remained on the sidelines until it was forced to react to events. According to the British ambassador to the Greek government-in-exile, Sir Michael Palairet, Tsouderos and the king were more anxious to consolidate their power against the encroachments from the Venizelist and antimonarchist exiles than to help form a resistance.[109] Just after the occupation, the former commander of the Greek forces in Crete, General Christos Kitsios, returned to Athens and advised Greek officers that it was the monarch's wish that they should avoid getting involved in politics and should make sure that the younger officers did likewise. John Hondros, a specialist on the history of the German occupation in Greece, interprets "involvement with politics" to mean that the king and his government were against the idea of resistance.[110]

Edmund Myers, who led the first British sabotage mission in Greece, writes, "There were indications that the majority of influential Royalist officers had been ordered by the Greek government-in-exile to remain in Athens, to have nothing to do with the Republican resistance movements and to await the return of the Royalist Government."[111] Ultimately, the Greek government-in-exile was not so much opposed to attacking the enemy within Greece as to the concept of mass resistance, which meant that the Greek population would have to sustain terrible casualties, since in 1941–1942 there was little hope of an Allied landing in Greece.

During the first year of the occupation, the defeat of the Axis was a remote possibility. Essentially, the Greek government-in-exile and its supporters in Greece had to accept, at the very least, a long occupation period and a possible German victory. Both outcomes would have dire consequences for Greece. A mass resistance, in any case, was beyond the capabilities of the Greek government-in-exile to control. It also had the potential of devastating the country. Britain on her own could not support the Greek army in 1941, let alone arm and supply a large resistance organization in Greece. Although the situation changed in late 1942, the king and his ministers had to assume that their priorities were to keep the country intact so that if and when the Allies won the war, they could return and reestablish the former political and social status.[112]

Ironically, the puppet governments of occupied Greece adopted a similar policy. From Tsolakoglou, the first quisling prime minister, to Ioannis Rallis, the last head of the occupation government, the main objectives of these regimes were to prevent the disintegration of the country and maintain the prewar social and political fabric of Greece.[113] Tsolakoglou was convinced that the Germans were winning the war and that Greece had to make the most out of a bad situation. The second puppet prime minister, Constantine Logothetopoulos, had expectations of a profitable career, while Rallis claimed that his motives were to keep Greece under control in the wake of the anticipated German withdrawal and to hand over the country to the Greek government-in-exile, thus preventing chaos and a possible communist takeover. All the puppet regimes as well as the Greek government-in-exile assumed that the officer corps would be instrumental in accomplishing these ends.

The obvious leaders of a Greek government-sponsored resistance would have been the veterans of the Albanian campaign, but the officers who had led the victorious Greek armies against the Italians also bided their time and were slow to react to events as a professional body. The professional officers of the Greek armed forces who had served during the campaigns of 1940–1941 formed a distinct group and, to a degree, identified with the established social and political order.[114] Another group included the purged officers from the 1930s who had remained loyal to the cause of Venizelos and continued to oppose the restoration of the monarchy.[115]

At the beginning of the occupation, there were approximately 4,391 professional and 8,700 reserve officers.[116] The initial reaction of these officers to the occupation, as far as it can be determined, was resignation. At first, some Greek officers participated individually in several small underground organizations formed in the autumn and winter of 1941–1942. Later many officers joined or helped to establish various resistance groups, while others escaped from Greece to fight with the forces of the Greek government-in-exile. One major difficulty for the officers was that the Greek government had not left any instructions to the military regarding the organization of resistance. At the same time, a large percentage of the senior officers believed that opposition to the Axis was futile; they assumed that Germany, because of its superior weapons and forces, would win the war. At any rate, this was the perception until the Battle of Stalingrad in 1942.[117] Another obstacle was that no one in Athens was authorized to speak on behalf of the Greek government-in-exile and to maintain contact with the officer corps.

The initial policy of the Greek government-in-exile was to encourage its followers, particularly those in the officer corps, to focus on espionage and sabotage as a means of continuing the struggle in occupied Greece. Another consideration, which had important consequences for the future, was access to and control of information concerning the situation in Greece by the British and Greek authorities in the Middle East. In the first year of the occupation, information about Greece came essentially from Allied soldiers who had avoided capture and had made their way to the Middle East. Another source was Greek politicians, businesspeople, professionals, and military officers who had left Greece because they were wanted by the occupation authorities or had decided to join the forces raised by the Greek government-in-exile. Finally, the clandestine groups organized by MI6 and SOE provided an abundance of intelligence on the political conditions in Greece, especially on the resistance groups, but that information was heavily censored before it was passed on to the Greek authorities in the Middle East and in London.

The Tsolakoglou regime also attempted to control the officer corps or at least keep it neutral by maintaining a ministry of defense, even though the occupation authorities did not permit the existence of armed forces. Greek generals, many of whom were heroes of the Albanian campaign and exercised considerable influence over the senior and, to a lesser extent, the younger officers, headed the ministry. For the most part, these officers either were royalists or had been followers of the Metaxas regime. Despite the generals' influence, hundreds of Greek officers made the perilous journey to the Middle East to join the armed forces of the Greek government-in-exile. The tendency of the ministry of defense of the Greek government-in-exile was to employ officers who had royalist and conservative credentials. In some cases, "reformed" Venizelist officers were readmitted into the Greek army, but despite their newfound allegiance to the monarchy, their presence caused considerable resentment among the royalist officers and eventually led to several mutinies in the Middle East.[118]

The officer corps continued to maintain its two broad divisions— royalist and republican—which had the effect of marginalizing the institution in the covert and guerrilla war against the Axis in Greece. Furthermore, many of the younger and middle-rank officers either found their way to the Middle East or joined the resistance groups that started to develop in early 1942. Both trends undermined the control that senior officers exercised over their junior colleagues and weakened the cohesiveness of the officer corps. In the Middle East, the monarchist-republican rivalry continued to cast a shadow over the Greek armed forces. In Greece, however, the old schism underwent a metamorphosis that galvanized the country into pro- and antileft coalitions, which quickly took on the labels of *communist* or *nationalist*. It was this new division in the Greek population that later defined the battle lines in the civil war.

2

THE POLITICS OF VIOLENCE: FROM RESISTANCE TO CIVIL WAR

So now what will become of us, without barbarians? Those men
were one sort of resolution.

﹪CONSTANTINE P. CAVAFY
Waiting for the Barbarians

FOR GREEKS TODAY, OCCUPATION, RESISTANCE, AND CIVIL WAR
invoke a parade of images—some magnificent, others outrageous—all
cataloging a painful period in their recent history. The Athenians define
the occupation as the period of darkness. Most remember the first day, a
glorious Sunday on 27 April 1941. The capital basked under a cloudless
rich blue sky, over the Acropolis as well as the bone white marble of the
Parthenon, the centerpiece of ancient and modern Athens. During the
morning, the Germans, in a solemn ceremony, raised the red and black
swastika on the Acropolis. At 11:00 A.M., the German commandant of
Athens ordered the Greek Evzone, a soldier of the unit that traditionally
guarded the Tomb of the Unknown Soldier and took part in official

ceremonies, to lower the Greek flag as a special tribute to Hitler. The
Evzone, dressed in the traditional kilt of the revolutionary soldiers of
1821, refused the command, and then, as the Germans watched in aston-
ishment, he threw himself over the wall, plummeting to his death 500
feet below, in the foothills of the Acropolis.[1]

Three days later, on a moonlit May evening, two young men, Manolis Glezos and Apostolos Santas, scaled the Acropolis and climbed over
the barbed wire enclosing the Parthenon. They were determined to
bring down the swastika and thus for a brief moment leave the
Parthenon free from the stain of the Third Reich's battle flag. At a few
minutes past midnight, the young men reached their objective and with
some difficulty managed to pull down the swastika. The Athenians were
jubilant. Word spread quickly: Enough people had noticed the absence
of the swastika from the Acropolis and passed the news by word of
mouth. The German response was disproportionate to the deed and a
hallmark of the German administration of Greece. They imposed a
10:00 P.M. curfew to punish the Athenians and declared the Acropolis
off-limits to all Greeks.

During the first month of occupation, the issue of flags on the Acropolis almost became an obsession with the Axis. The Italians, a few days
after they arrived in Athens on the heels of the German army, raised an
immense Italian flag on the Acropolis, dwarfing the swastika. By noon,
the wind had shredded the Italian flag, which was promptly replaced
with a much smaller one. A few days later, the Italian authorities raised
yet another flag, this one merely three times as large as the swastika. The
Germans responded by replacing their flag with one significantly larger
than the Italian one. Twenty-four hours later, the wind tore the swastika
to pieces. The Germans then raised a smaller version, but one still larger
than that of their Italian allies.

The comic relief of the battle of the flags soon gave way to a harsher
reality. The Germans commandeered all Greek hospitals, still overcrowded with the wounded of the Albanian war. The Greek soldiers,
many with amputated limbs, had to leave regardless of their condition.
Some lucky few had means of transportation; however, most had to
make their way on foot. For several days, Athens was awash with thou-

sands of wounded soldiers making their way home. Shortly, a new creature appeared in the capital: the pro-Nazi-pro-Fascist Greek.

The collaborators emerged almost immediately, a motley collection
of businesspeople, husbands of German spouses, petty criminals, members of the extreme Greek right, and, sadly, some of the senior commanders of the Greek army. General George Tsolakoglou, a corps
commander on the Albanian front, agreed to form a government under
Axis tutelage and served as the first in a succession of puppets to dance
to the tune of the occupation authorities. Other collaborators assumed
more humble tasks, such as translators in the unspeakable horrors of
Gestapo and SS interrogations, while the lowest form of Axis lackeys
served as double agents and informants. During the occupation, they
strutted about like peacocks in their leather coats, impervious to the
suffering around them and protected by their German-issued identification cards.

Civil war was the price that the Greeks had to pay for mass and organized resistance against the Axis. The causes reached back to the inception of the Greek state in 1831, but occupation and resistance
spawned the culture of violence that made civil war almost certain. The
forces that spiraled the country into fratricide during and after the occupation, however, resulted from the convergence of several factors, each
of which played havoc with Greek society. First, the demobilization of
the Greek armed forces by the German occupiers provided a large pool
of trained men for guerrilla war. Second, the British strategy of instigating mass resistance, sabotage, and subversion prompted the newly established SOE to sponsor republican and left-wing clandestine networks in
Greek cities and towns as well as guerrilla bands in the mountains. In
sharp contrast, the British Secret Intelligence Service and the Foreign
Office continued to support the royalist cause in Greece, thereby back-
ing the sworn enemies of the major resistance organizations working as
the SOE's preferred allies. At first, the exigencies of war overshadowed
the divergence in British policy toward Greece, but over the course of
the occupation, this situation contributed to the right-left polarization
of the Greek resistance. Finally, the famine in 1941 brutalized the urban
population and shattered any illusions that the Greeks may have had

about their security and survival under Axis rule. The failure of the Axis to prevent, or even try to address, the disastrous effects of the famine fueled resentment and swelled the ranks of the resistance organizations.

The vast majority of the Greek population during the late summer of 1941 was still recovering from the shock of defeat and anxiety and fear for their lives under foreign occupation. Greek society was in a state of reshuffling, and almost the entire country was on the move. Anxious people yearned for the security of familiar surroundings and sought comfort in old neighborhoods or found a way out of the cities. The fortunate ones could return to ancestral villages and islands to weather the storm, but a great many, especially parents, spouses, and children of soldiers, had to stay put, waiting with apprehension for the return of the men who fought in the war. The postal network between Albania and Greece was practically nonexistent, and the few prewar telephone and telegraph lines had disintegrated during the course of the fighting. The tens of thousands of demobilized soldiers (the future resistance fighters) were slowly making the arduous trek home and had no ready means of communicating with their families. Long columns of bone-weary men— some wounded, all gaunt—snaked around the few mountain roads in southern Albania as they headed back toward the Greek frontier.

For almost a year, they had fought with grim determination, relentlessly hounding the Italian army out of Greece and forcing it back to the bleak mountains of southern Albania. In the winter of 1941, the fighting was bitter and waged under the harsh mountain conditions of northern Greece and southern Albania. Greek soldiers, suffering from frostbite and unattended wounds, were tormented by lice, worn down with fatigue, and handicapped by dwindling critical supplies. Cold and hungry, they mounted bayonet charges in blizzards and fought hand-to-hand, when they ran out of ammunition, but all to no avail. In the spring, a German army of mechanized and armored divisions poured over the northwestern frontier to rescue Hitler's vanquished Italian ally.

It was over in less than three weeks. The Greek soldiers in Albania were outflanked when the British Expeditionary Force fell back from the German onslaught and, for the second time in the war, had to be rescued by the Royal Navy. Mussolini, with the false bravado of a cheat, insisted on a final Italian offensive in Albania to take advantage of the German victory, only to face yet another failure. The Greek lines held because the Greek army refused to concede defeat to a vanquished foe. In the early summer of 1941, the heroes of the Albanian campaign were just anxious to go home and protect their families from the uncertainties of occupation. The Germans, in a rare gesture of compassion, did not intern the Greek army; the soldiers were simply given indefinite leave and sent home. Tragically, the arrival of thousands of hungry men further aggravated the critical shortage of food supplies and accelerated the progress of mass starvation.

The famine remains as the darkest legacy of the occupation and was the incubator of hatred that inspired mass resistance against the Axis. Starvation pervaded every city and town in Greece, consuming its victims at an alarming rate. Thousands succumbed to the debilitating effects of malnutrition or died from the onset of disease triggered by the famine. More than 100,000 died of starvation and associated diseases in Athens alone, and thousands more in other cities and towns. For many, survival hinged on the drudgery of waiting in long lines to collect a bowl of watery soup delivered daily by the Greek Red Cross. People sought every means possible to survive. They sold whatever they had of value to purchase a loaf of bread, a couple of eggs, or any form of vegetable. Cats and dogs became a rare delicacy, and when these were not available, rodents had to suffice.

Every morning vans collected a fresh crop of the famine's victims and headed to the outskirts of Athens, disgorging their grizzly cargo into open pits that served as makeshift graves. Soon lack of fuel curtailed these grim convoys, and the backlog of decaying bodies posed a new hazard for the beleaguered Athenians. For many survivors, images of emaciated children standing vigil over a dead parent and small piles of corpses stacked by street corners are some of their haunting memories of the famine.

Mass starvation was inevitable. The Germans had descended like locusts upon Greece, consuming or conscripting everything of value and paying for it with useless occupation currency. The Nazis awarded

Macedonia and Thrace to their Bulgarian allies, who promptly seized
the wheat fields and denied any supplies to Greece, which exacerbated
the critical food shortage. The Axis also mined Greek waters and appro-
priated most of the fishing fleet, allowing only a handful of boats to
supply the mainland. In addition, the confiscation of all locomotives
and rolling stock, trucks, cars, motorcycles, bicycles, horses, donkeys,
and mules by the Axis severed the connection between the countryside
and the cities for the duration of the occupation.

Before the war, the small mountain towns and villages in the hinterland constituted distinct societies, self-contained and remote from the
political and social changes that buffeted the rest of Greece. For centuries, the only common denominator between the villages and the
cities had been religion, and trade remained as the primary mode of
communication. The villagers and farmers supplied the urban centers
with the basic staples of olive oil, dairy products, beans, wheat, and so
on in exchange for essential products such as tools, plows, knives, shoes,
fabrics, and glass, as well as a few luxuries. Nonetheless, centralized authority was the primary feature of the Greek state, and power radiated
from the city and dominated the village. Because of the famine and the
guerrilla forces in the mountains, the roles were reversed: Legitimate
Greek political authority shifted to the village.

The famine also disintegrated civil society in Greece and discredited
the authority of the state. Whatever limited influence over events the
first occupation government (headed by General Tsolakoglou) may have
had, the famine exposed the effectiveness of the first German-sponsored
quislings as a cruel joke. It was nothing more than a collection of ex-
soldiers and politicians addicted to the exaggerated pomp of petty bu-
reaucracy. The regime had only limited currency in larger towns and
cities, and even there it simply adjudicated trivial matters of state or
cases of petty crime. Issues of organized crime, such as the black market,
homicide, and other serious offenses, came under the jurisdiction of
Axis-controlled law enforcement. Under these circumstances, the police
and gendarmerie too often were identified as the instruments of occupation, and regardless of their contribution to the resistance, both officers
and men were eventually tainted with the stain of collaboration.

In the countryside, and particularly in the mountain regions, the presence of the Axis was limited to towns near strategic mountain passes, major bridges, and viaducts that serviced major communication networks. The remaining villages strung along the naked mountain ranges of the rugged Greek hinterland provided the ideal setting for the organization of paramilitary bands. The mountains of Greece had historically nursed the forces of armed insurrection; indeed, the Hellenic and Christian warrior descending from snow-covered peaks to vanquish the Turk was part of the cultural identity of the modern Greek state.

The embryonic guerrilla bands that took to the mountains in the spring and summer of 1942 were aware of the power of history, and even more of mythology, and they attempted to link themselves with the glories of the past. The Greek partisans, or Andartes, adopted the dress and style of the bandit freedom fighters who had fought in the War of Independence. It was common for some of these men to wear thick beards and hair in long ponytails, occasionally sporting the traditional woolen kilt and stockings. The appeal to history was less for the benefit of city folk and more a means of forging a bond with the simple villagers and shepherds, who could be exploited for provisions and recruits needed to sustain the guerrillas in the field.[2]

Nevertheless, during the first year of occupation, opposition against the Axis was spontaneous and disorganized. The early resistance consisted of minor acts of defiance such as writing graffiti on public buildings, puncturing the tires of Axis military vehicles, and cheering Allied soldiers led to captivity by the Germans. When some of these Allied troops managed to escape, they found refuge in the homes of people willing to risk, at minimum, imprisonment in a concentration camp. In time, hiding and assisting the escape of British troops served as the initiation for many into the hazardous world of clandestine work. Dozens of small networks sprouted overnight to facilitate the transportation of these men to Turkey or the Middle East.

However, lack of skill in intelligence tradecraft resulted in arrest as well as instant reprisals by the occupation authorities and quickly deflated the enthusiasm of these early resistance groups. Those who survived did so because they found employment and rudimentary training

with the British intelligence services or with left-wing or republican resistance groups, and in some extreme cases even with the Axis authorities. Nonetheless, the covert groups in the cities, more than the partisan
bands in the mountains, attracted a strange assortment of individuals
from the fringes of society. Left-wing radicals liberated from the grip of
the Metaxas security apparatus, disenchanted army officers, smugglers,
communist renegades, police informants, displaced persons, prostitutes,
thieves, and bandits gravitated to clandestine warfare like moths to
light. Some were compelled by adventure, others by patriotism; most
joined because hiding from the authorities had become as much a
lifestyle as a means of survival.

A somewhat similar situation prevailed among the ranks of the
British intelligence services: For the duration of the war, espionage, sabotage, and subversion were the domain of the gifted amateur, the ro-
mantic eccentric, the reckless volunteer, and the downright scoundrel.
After the First World War, the traditional disdain for espionage, along
with skepticism about its value, led to deep budget cuts, which had left
the British intelligence community small and with few active agents, let
alone networks, in Europe. The SOE had managed to organize a few
clandestine groups in Athens and Thessaloniki and equipped one of
them with a radio transmitter before the debacle in Greece, but it could
not establish contact until much later, in the fall of 1941.[3] The other
British intelligence services fared even worse. The Secret Intelligence
Service (SIS) as well the Military Intelligence Directorate (MID) also
had organized clandestine groups and equipped them with radio sets,
but within a week the Germans arrested all the operators because these
British services had divulged the names of the agents to the Greek government.[4] Information about Greece came from the trickle of British
and Greek soldiers as well as from civilians who had succeeded in reaching the Middle East (but the information was not reliable and most often dated) and from a handful of agents who managed to travel back
and forth between Greece and Cairo.

The principal SOE operative and key link with the republican and
left-wing groups in Athens and Thessaloniki was Gerasimos Alexatos,
appropriately code-named Odysseus, because of his native cunning and

appetite for danger.⁵ Alexatos was an enigmatic Zorba-like character, hovering on the edge of society, and a minion of the murky eastern Mediterranean underworld. In 1940, he volunteered to work for the British and graduated from the SOE's makeshift training school, which operated out of a semiruined Venetian castle on the island of Crete. For the fledgling SOE intelligence directorate in Cairo, Odysseus was a godsend. As an accomplished smuggler, he was familiar with the "back alleys" of the eastern Mediterranean—small islands with natural harbors and deserted coastlines endowed with secret coves—that provided surreptitious transit in and out of Greece.⁶

It is somewhat a mystery why this middle-aged smuggler decided to risk his life for the Greek resistance. On the other hand, he did manage to combine espionage with smuggling and on occasion was caught sneaking precious gems past the customs officials in Greece and the Middle East. Equally baffling is why this barely literate man sympathized with the left, which played no small part in convincing the SOE that only radical republican groups and the communists had the desire and aptitude to organize a resistance. After the war, he vanished into obscurity. In 1955, Michael Ward, a former member of the Greek section of the SOE in Cairo, saw Odysseus walking ahead of him on a street in Piraeus. Ward fondly recounts, "Walking up behind him I tapped him on the back, saying 'Odysseus my friend' when he jerked his head over his shoulder, took one suspicious look at me and beat a hasty retreat round the nearest corner. One thing was certain: he was up to his old tricks."⁷

In the first months of the occupation, when the SOE had no contacts or agents in Greece, Odysseus laid out the secret routes between Turkey and the Greek islands that later enabled the SOE, as well as other British intelligence agencies, to smuggle people and weapons in and out of Greece. By November 1941, Odysseus had managed to bring to Athens the radio codes for the transmitter of Prometheus II, the only underground group that had survived the Axis invasion and the primary liaison between the SOE and the Greek resistance. For the next two years, Odysseus served as courier, saboteur, guerrilla fighter, and, perhaps, the most important link between the SOE and the KKE. Certainly, he was the SOE's main source on Greece, and his reports influenced the opinion of the British intelligence organization in Cairo in favor of the left.[8] In part, thanks to him, as early as February 1942 the SOE Greek desk had become convinced that "the Royalist cause in Greece was as good as lost, and that when the country was liberated we should find Republican sentiment too strong to be imposed upon. We did however differ somewhat in our estimate as to what type of Republicans we should find rampant when liberation came."[9]

According to one historian, the information from Greece convinced the SOE Greek experts in Cairo that "preparation for resistance or acts of resistance were the work of the left, of Venizelists or of Communists."[10] To some extent, the information collected and passed on was selective and occasionally colored by the bias of the individual SOE officer. It can also be argued that an equal number of reports from Greece warned of the danger posed by the National Liberation Front (EAM) and described the resistance activity of organizations that were prepared to accept the government-in-exile and to deal with the constitutional problem after the war.

In contrast to the experience of the SOE with Greek agents who opposed the Greek monarchy and the government-in-exile, the few operatives of MI6 either sympathized with King George II or were not concerned about the constitutional issue. As was the case with the SOE, potential Greek agents made contact with the Secret Intelligence Service on their own initiative, and some did so by chance encounters. Others, such as Greek loyalists, had access to representatives of the British Foreign Office—namely, consuls and ambassadors—and these officials led them to the SIS.

In the late summer of 1941, the British were desperate: The war was not going well, the Germans had overrun Europe, the Americans were committed to neutrality, Stalin and Hitler were allies, and the campaign in North Africa was heading for another defeat. Covert action was one of the few methods available to slow down the German Africa Corps by cutting off its supplies from Greece. Few British political or military officials in London and in the Middle East had much faith in clandestine operations, yet they could not afford to ignore any means of striking at the enemy. In this atmosphere of desperation and doubt, the SOE had to undertake in Greece, almost from scratch, the complex business of espionage, sabotage, and guerrilla warfare. By so doing, the organizers of the SOE contributed to the radicalization of Greek society because circumstances ultimately left the British little choice but to work with individuals and groups opposed to the established order. This was partly the result of the SOE's reliance on only a handful of agents for information concerning the Greek resistance and partly the tragic outcome of the first major covert mission in Greece. The first skewed SOE policy in favor of the left; the second, by fatally damaging the moderate elements in the Greek underground, practically ensured that left-wing organizations would dominate the resistance movement.

The precise details of this event remain shrouded and involve the tragic story of John Atkinson, a junior officer and the key protagonist of the drama.[11] Atkinson was one of the many soldiers captured after the British withdrawal from Greece in April. However, he managed to escape the Germans with the help of Alexander Zannas, the head of the Greek Red Cross and one of the leaders of the nascent resistance movement.[12] For months, Atkinson shared an apartment with a Greek family, who also had to provide room for an Italian colonel. Despite serious obstacles, Atkinson left Athens and reached Alexandria possibly in early October 1941. He volunteered his services to the SOE, which turned him down, but he eventually went to work for Section N of MI9, the British service responsible for assisting the escape of prisoners of war.[13] By early fall, Atkinson had returned to Greece and was operating a secret cell on the island of Antiparos for the purpose of establishing escape routes to the Middle East for Allied soldiers and civilians.[14]

In late October or early November 1941, the British agent met Zannas in Athens and through him acquired intimate knowledge of the clandestine networks that had initially been set up to help escaped British soldiers; by now, these organizations had expanded to espionage and sabotage activities.[15] As a member of Athenian society, Zannas was able to use his influence and position to support these groups as well as to recruit other prominent individuals to work against the occupation forces.[16] During their discussion, however, Zannas noticed that Atkinson was keeping notes of everything discussed, including the names of those involved in clandestine activities.[17] When Zannas objected, Atkinson promised that he would later destroy his papers.[18] Atkinson, with Zannas' help, set up an escape route that ran from Athens to Antiparos via the small island of Anavysos and then by submarine to Egypt.[19] Indeed, shortly after this meeting, twenty-two British and five Greeks were able to leave Greece using that route.

It is not certain, but in addition to organizing escape routes, Atkinson ventured into espionage and sabotage work. His first breakthrough came when he acquired the services of an Italian sergeant, Bero Likeri, a member of the Italian garrison of the nearby island of Paros. Likeri was able to give Atkinson and his group advance warning of Italian or German search parties coming to the island as well as to provide information on the Paros garrison.[20] With Zannas' assistance as well as with the help of local fishermen, who were all anxious to play some role in the struggle against the occupation forces, Atkinson was able to establish an intelligence network that provided information about Axis naval movements in and out of the Cyclades islands.[21]

Early success, according to one account, encouraged Atkinson to extend his activities to sabotage, and he undertook to destroy two German tankers anchored at the island of Milos.[22] In November 1941, with help from a local fishing-boat captain, Georgios Anyfandis, and two of his men, Atkinson sailed to Milos and planted explosive charges against the hulls of the tankers. In the early hours of the morning, the explosives went off, sinking both ships.[23] The sabotage of the German ships increased Atkinson's prestige with the islanders and encouraged more volunteers to help with information and escape work, but the increasing level of activity also attracted the attention of the Italian garrison at Paros.

In early January 1942, Likeri, Atkinson's Italian accomplice, warned him to leave the island as soon as possible, but for some reason the British officer delayed his departure.[24] On 6 January, the Italians surrounded the whitewashed house that served as the base for the clandestine group, and within minutes, the barking of automatic weapons shattered the tranquility of the island. As the Italians burst through the front door, Atkinson shot the first man, who managed to toss a grenade before collapsing on the floor. Fragments from the grenade struck Atkinson, ripping through both his legs. A few minutes later, the entire group was taken prisoner.[25] To make matters worse, the Italians found Atkinson's code book, a list of current and potential agents indicated by their initials, a seventeen-page report on possible contacts in Athens prepared by the Greek embassy in Cairo, $10,000 and £500, Atkinson's notes from the meeting with Zannas, and a diary of his activities in Greece.[26]

Atkinson was in a terrible physical state, and one of his legs had to be amputated. Although the Italians treated the British officer well, he suffered considerably when they moved him from Antiparos to Athens. The other members of his party were less fortunate. One man was beaten every day and another tortured by being subjected to long periods of starvation. Perhaps depression over the loss of his leg, the loss of blood, and the pain of recovery served to undermine Atkinson's morale, and after only a short time he broke down and confessed. The Italians, according to all accounts, did not apply torture to him. Atkinson just gave up and provided his captors with names, organizations, and a list of all his collaborators.[27] Atkinson's disclosures dealt a crippling blow to the burgeoning Athenian resistance groups and to those who had been involved with his network in the Cyclades.[28]

The Italians arrested at least fifty individuals, including some of the most prominent Athenians involved with the underground, who had given Atkinson refuge in the course of his first escape.[29] Atkinson's confession spared no one, including himself. Initially, the Italians were inclined to spare the British spy, but their German allies demanded the death penalty for Atkinson and for all the members of the Antiparos group. A few months later, on 24 February 1942, at the crack of dawn, the hapless British officer joined the other four men marked for execution in front of a firing squad. He had to be carried on a stretcher and then tied to a chair because the extent of his injuries made it impossible for him to stand up. Atkinson asked and received permission to say a few last words, and looking up from his chair, in broken Greek, he pleaded, "Please forgive me so that God can also grant me forgiveness."[30]

The arrests and subsequent trials astonished the Athenians almost as much as the fact that those apprehended were involved in espionage.[31]

This event represented the first major success of Italian counterintelligence and a significant setback for the Athenian underground, particularly for those groups made up of individuals loyal to the Greek government-in-exile or, at any rate, those opposed to revolutionary change. Some who styled themselves republican members of these organizations represented the more conservative wing of the Greek Liberal Party, but they would have accepted a constitutional arrangement that included the Greek king. In their absence, control of the Athenian underground passed to less-well-known individuals and fanatical opponents of the monarchy as well as to the left.

In the critical period 1941–1942, when the resistance was being organized, the absence of moderates such as Panayiotis Kanellopoulos, one of the few prewar politicians willing to participate in a resistance movement and prepared to accept the Greek government-in-exile, left the initiative to the Greek communists and the more radical republicans.[32] Kanellopoulos' name was among the papers captured with Atkinson, and the Greek politician fled to the Middle East. Although a royalist, Kanellopoulos had opposed the Metaxas regime and was in the process of creating a large resistance group that could have served as a counterweight to the left-wing organizations established by the KKE. After his departure, the group fell apart, since there was no one with his stature to fill the void. In the Middle East he joined the Greek government-in-exile as vice-premier but quickly became marginalized.

Thus far, with the exception of Kanellopoulos, the response of the traditional Greek political leaders to the occupation had been at best passive and in some cases outright defeatist. The leaders of the Liberal and Populist Parties, as well as of the factions that existed within these organizations, viewed the prospect of resistance as premature and did not entirely trust the former republican officers to lead such an endeavor.[33] The smaller parties either believed in an ultimate Axis victory or preferred to follow the lead of the communists in the creation of the EAM.

The Greek government-in-exile, however, did make one attempt at coordinating the underground organizations and resistance groups, but it ended in failure. The effort collapsed partly from the carelessness of the officer in charge of the operation, but also from the policy of the SOE of establishing and maintaining exclusive control over the Greek resistance. The Greek government-in-exile had had contact, mainly through MI6, with a group of Greek officers known as the Committee of Six Colonels, who were planning to organize resistance and sabotage activity in Greece. The Six Colonels, led by General Panayiotis Spiliotopoulos, the former head of the gendarmerie, had links with most of the senior Greek officers who had fought in the Albanian campaign as well as with Kanellopoulos, now serving as a minister in the government-in-exile.[34]

In the spring of 1942, the colonels, through the efforts of Epaminondas Tsellos, a close associate of Kanellopoulos, had obtained a radio transmitter and attempted communication with the Greek government-in-exile.[35] Kanellopoulos believed that the Six Colonels with adequate support could instigate sabotage and guerrilla warfare in Greece and proposed the creation of an action committee based in Athens directed by these officers. At about this time (July 1942) the SOE was planning a sabotage mission to block the Isthmus of Corinth as well as destroy a bridge in Lamia. Although it was not common practice to notify the Greek government-in-exile of their plans regarding operations in Greece, the SOE on this occasion required the use of a senior Greek officer and approached Kanellopoulos.[36]

Kanellopoulos not only agreed to loan the SOE a Greek officer, Ioannis Tsigantes, but saw this as an occasion to set up an organization to coordinate the resistance under the direct control of the Greek government-in-exile. The SOE in Cairo accepted Kanellopoulos' proposal and agreed that the Tsigantes mission, in addition to the sabotage operations, would also get in touch with the colonels in order to set them up as the coordinating committee for the resistance.[37] This was a major breakthrough for Kanellopoulos in his goal of developing the resistance, since he had had serious reservations about the isolation of the Greek government-in-exile concerning events in Greece. He confided (in his diary) that the British intelligence services controlled all access to the underground groups in Greece and were basing their estimates of the situation there exclusively on reports from biased Greek and British agents.[38] The Greek government-in-exile, consequently, could not ascertain the political developments in the country independently or have any say over the resistance.[39] He believed that by cooperating with the SOE, he could achieve a relationship of trust between the Greek government-in-exile and the British intelligence services and could thus have some influence on the Greek resistance organizations.[40]

Three months later Kanellopoulos' efforts had born fruit: An Anglo-Greek committee was set up to oversee and direct all intelligence and guerrilla warfare operations in Greece. For a short period, the committee was kept informed about most intelligence and resistance activity in Greece, including the establishment of a British military mission in the Greek mountains in the fall of 1942. But after the resignation of Kanellopoulos from the Greek government-in-exile, the effectiveness of the committee diminished, and it became simply a propaganda outlet for the SOE.

The team assembled by the Cairo SOE, code-named Midas 614, included Colonel Tsigantes, who was placed in charge of the operation, along with eleven other officers and enlisted men trained for sabotage and espionage. The mission was subdivided into several groups, each assigned a specific task. One team was to block the Isthmus of Corinth, another to destroy a bridge near Lamia, and a third to bring supplies to an alleged resistance group in the southern Peloponnesus called Philiki Etairia Stratou Eleftheroseos (PESE), which the SOE mistakenly believed had over 3,000 members. A fourth team was to organize the transport of Allied troops who had evaded capture, while the rest of the mission, among them Tsigantes, was to go to Athens and assist in the organization of a center to coordinate all resistance activity, provide information on the food crisis and the intelligence and counterintelligence services of the Axis forces, and implement sabotage and subversive operations.[41]

Although all the members of the team were Greek, they represented different intelligence agencies stationed in the Middle East, which included the SOE, MI6, MI5, and the Hellenic Intelligence Service.[42] Midas 614 left Alexandria aboard the submarine *Proteus* and reached Mani on the southeastern Peloponnesus on 1 August 1942. There they hid in a cave for ten days while one member of the team, Panagiotis Rogakos, attempted to make contact with the PESE—only to discover that the resistance group did not exist. His efforts to find the phantom organization, as well as to secure a means of transportation to Athens, alerted the Italian authorities; the group managed to leave the region just ahead of the Italian security forces. On 12 August, Tsigantes divided his team into two sections, and each made its way to Piraeus by separate boats. From the harbor, they made their way to Athens individually or in groups of two or three.[43] Tsigantes had decided to trust the owner of the boat and left behind one of the radio transmitters and most of the explosives. All the members of Midas found accommodation in the homes of family or friends, but they had to keep changing locations to avoid detection by the occupation authorities.

The situation, however, began to unravel almost from the beginning of their presence in Athens. The boat, on which Tsigantes had left a good portion of their supplies, was seized by the Italians, and to make matters worse, the second group, along with the only other radio, failed to make contact. However, eight days later another boat arrived with the rest of the Midas team. Tsigantes began to initiate contact with old associates and slowly set up groups to gather intelligence on the Axis forces in Greece. Nevertheless, his main preoccupation was to organize a center to coordinate the resistance.

The other priorities for the Midas teams were to block the Corinth Canal and to destroy the bridge at Karyon near Lamia (central Thessaly), thus disrupting the only rail link between Athens and Thessaloniki. Tsigantes dispatched Spiros Kotsis to survey the bridge, but after close examination, the latter reported that the bridge was too narrow and well defended: Its destruction would cause minimal delays since repairs could be effected quickly. He suggested that the Gorgopotamos viaduct presented a much better target: It was 215 meters in length and supported by six piers, four of stone and two of steel. Tsigantes agreed with Kotsis and recommended to SOE headquarters in Cairo the destruction of the viaduct, requesting the supply of appropriate explosives. In the meantime he organized, with the help of Dimitris Psarros, a team of former Greek officers who would undertake to attack the garrison of the bridge while the explosives were set.[44] However, this step was as far as Tsigantes got in organizing the sabotage of the bridge or the attempt to coordinate the resistance movement. The Greek officer could not resist getting involved in the political intrigues and machinations of the Athenian party factions as well as establishing a lavish lifestyle. Soon both the SOE and Kanellopoulos had lost confidence in him. On 15 January 1943, an anonymous woman tipped off the Italian authorities on the location of Tsigantes' hideout. In the ensuing gun battle the Italians shot and killed Tsigantes, but not before he managed to destroy his papers. However, even before his demise, the SOE had dispatched a British team to Greece, the Harling Mission, which undertook the destruction of the Gorgopotamos viaduct and took over the effort to direct the development of guerrilla warfare.[45]

From this point on the plans for both the direction of the underground in Athens and the organization of resistance, as envisaged by the Greek government-in-exile and the SOE, went in opposite directions. Kanellopoulos wanted to establish an organization in Athens that would coordinate all major sabotage activity in Greece and organize the deployment of guerrilla bands. The key objective of the Tsigantes Mission, from Kanellopoulos' perspective, had been to establish an organization made up of Greek officers loyal to the Greek government-in-exile and moderate in political outlook.

A significant act of sabotage such as the destruction of a major communications link would have given Kanellopoulos' proposed organization tremendous political and moral authority in occupied Greece. Instead, the credit for this accomplishment went to the two organizations, the National Republican Greek League (EDES) and ELAS, whose policies were contrary not only to the Greek government-in-exile but also to the British Foreign Office. Indeed, the arrival of the Harling Mission represented a critical turning point in the evolution of the resistance movement and the road to civil war. The SOE, by destroying the Gorgopotamos viaduct, demonstrated to the satisfaction of the British government and the military chiefs the possibilities of large-scale partisan operations in Greece. The SOE, however, accomplished the first major act of sabotage in occupied Europe with the support of the fledgling left-wing and republican guerrilla bands.

For the communists and radical republicans, the Gorgopotamos operation was a remarkable opportunity to demonstrate to the Greek people that the left-wing resistance was working in tandem with the British in order to liberate Greece. The communists, from the onset of occupation, did not hesitate to embrace the idea of mass resistance and the implementation of guerrilla warfare. Beyond the desire to fight the occupation forces for its own sake, the new communist leadership sought the creation of a resistance movement as a means to control and ultimately dominate the social, economic, and political future of Greece. Unlike the extreme right wing and a large percentage of the traditional ruling elite, most communists believed in Allied victory because the alternative—the success of the Axis—meant perpetual imprisonment or extermination.

Despite such sentiments in the early months of the occupation, the KKE was still in disarray.[46] The Metaxas regime had incarcerated 2,000 communists, including most of the KKE's senior leaders, in special prisons and had confined others to internal exile on several remote islands.[47] In May 1941, 190 communists escaped from the small islands of Folegandros and Kimolos, along with three members of the original central committee of the KKE (Petros Rousos, Chrysa Hadzivasiliou, and Karagkitsis-Simo), and arrived in Athens on 20 May 1941.[48] Another ten reached Crete just before the German assault on the island, accompanied by two other members of the central committee: Stergios Anastasiadis and Miltiadis Porphyrogenis.[49] By the fall, 300 out of the 2,000 imprisoned communists had managed to escape and could thus take part in the reorganization of the KKE.[50]

After the Axis occupied Greece and assumed control over all prisons, some important KKE members claimed Bulgarian nationality and, with assistance from the Bulgarian embassy, managed to secure their release.[51] The Bulgarians believed that freeing communists, especially those of Slavo-Macedonian origin, would enable them to use these individuals as propagandists for the "Bulgarization" of eastern Macedonia and Thrace.[52] However, the communists knew how precarious their newly found freedom was, and once released they quickly disappeared into the underground. When the Greek security services realized what was taking place, they protested to the occupation authorities that they were freeing dangerous communists, but by the time the Germans reversed their decision it was too late.

Once free, these central committee members were able to regenerate the KKE by the end of the summer. An important factor in the reorganization of the party was that the central committee and politburo now included men and women who, by virtue of their incarceration, had remained uncontaminated by the machinations of Maniadakis, the head of Metaxas' security apparatus. Furthermore, they had no connection with the prewar police-infested central committees.[53]

According to Thanasis Hadzis, who took part in the reorganization of the Communist Party, the KKE leadership ignored the existence of armed bands that were forming in the mountains. Hadzis explains that although the central committee was aware that the resistance would have to take on a military character and ultimately this would be the decisive factor, the KKE lacked experience in guerrilla war; it had to progress from general strikes and small struggles to armed resistance.[54] First and foremost, the KKE had to create a strong political base and achieve legitimacy as a national organization by coopting as many political organizations as possible in the proposed national front. However, attempts to enlist the cooperation of the Republican and Populist Parties met with failure.[55] Ultimately, the KKE had to rely on the smaller parties on the fringes of the Greek political world in order to form a national coalition.

The KKE, in conjunction with the marginal Greek Socialist and Agrarian Parties, established the National Liberation Front (EAM) on 27 September 1941 and invited other interested groups to join the new organization and fight the enemy.[56] The traditional political parties had declined to join EAM, for different reasons.[57] The Populists refused because the KKE controlled EAM. The Liberals declined for the same reason and also argued that organized resistance was premature and would lead to reprisals. Instead, the Liberals proposed the creation of a common front with the aim of preventing the return of the monarchy and the dictatorship after liberation.[58] Despite the refusal of the traditional parties, EAM developed rapidly and attracted an impressive following. Joining EAM did not require any particular sacrifice; one only had to accept the organization as the common resistance front. Under these terms, EAM acquired thousands and ultimately hundreds of thousands of members, who by the simple act of becoming members could believe themselves to be fighting the occupation authorities.

In February 1942, the KKE leadership sent agents into the mountains to instigate armed resistance, and on 10 April, the central committee of EAM together with the KKE officially approved the formation of the guerrilla bands.[59] As a result, a month later (22 May 1942), Aris Velouchiotis established the first unit of what later became the National Popular Liberation Army (ELAS).[60] Although Velouchiotis started with fifteen men and his actions were originally limited to central Greece, by 1943 ELAS had grown into a major guerrilla force. Every effort was made to associate the guerrilla force with the revolutionary bands and heroes that had fought the Ottomans during the Greek War of Independence. Even the acronym *ELAS,* when pronounced, means "Greece," which gave that organization a powerful propaganda tool. Throughout the occupation, EAM and ELAS confined their propaganda to patriotic and simple slogans that aimed to equate their organizations with national pride and Greek history.

Almost concurrently with the creation of EAM (on 9 September 1941), a group of Venizelist officers inaugurated a republican resistance organization that they named EDES (National Democratic Greek League); they, too, could not secure the participation of the established political parties.[61] Indeed, their own Liberal Party refused any kind of cooperation or support.[62] The founding members and most recruits came from the ranks of the discharged officers of the 1930s. In contrast to EAM, EDES had specific political and social aims that included the provision that the organization would prevent, by any means, the return of the monarchy and also outlined a detailed program of economic and political reforms.[63] These reforms included purging royalists from the civil service, the armed forces, and the professional organizations, as well as creating programs to alleviate hunger and establish social justice.

Komninos Pyromaglou, who became the general secretary of EDES, related that EDES intended to fill the gap on the Greek political spectrum between the position of the Greek communists and the traditional political parties. In the end, it failed to accomplish this aim, because the organization did not gain the support of the republican movement. On the contrary, the republican leadership attempted to destroy the organization, some because they assumed an Axis victory, others because they feared reprisals on the country. As a result, EDES was unable to establish even modest political bases in the cities or, for that matter, in most parts of Greece, with the exception of Epirus.[64]

The nominal head of EDES was General Nikolaos Plastiras, an old republican officer who had helped to topple the government in 1922 and a principal conspirator in the abortive 1935 coup. Plastiras, however, had found political asylum in France, where he remained until the end of the occupation. The actual driving force and initiative for the creation of EDES came from Napoleon Zervas and a handful of republican officers. However, Zervas, unlike Plastiras, lacked credibility in republican circles and needed Plastiras' name to legitimize EDES. Zervas had a reputation as a gambler and womanizer, and his role in the numerous coups from 1916 until his expulsion from the Greek army in 1935 labeled him a professional conspirator rather than a committed republican.

It is still not clear why Plastiras allowed his name to become associated with EDES and with the disreputable Zervas.[65] According to one theory, Plastiras' reputation remained high as long as he abstained from active politics; he was after all the defender of the republican cause. The moment he became associated with EDES, immediately labeled as a political organization, Plastiras ceased to be a nonpartisan statesman and was viewed as a political opponent. Many of his supporters refused to join and either actively worked against EDES or created their own resistance groups.[66] These organizations, with their alphabet soup acronyms (EKKA, AAA, YVE), however, were doomed from the start and only served to fragment the republican forces. Over the next two years, ELAS disbanded, absorbed, or destroyed all of these organizations—the remnants found their way to EDES and in some instances joined the Greek Security Battalions raised by the Germans in the spring of 1943.

After the establishment of EAM and EDES, and later of ELAS, the SOE, through its radio contact with Prometheus II, the clandestine republican group in Athens, became aware of the different resistance organizations and groups that were forming in 1942. On 3 March 1942, SOE Cairo instructed Prometheus to provide protection for agents who would shortly be arriving in Greece by parachute as well as to find safe places for the weapons and explosives that would be dropped by airplane. In addition, Cairo ordered Prometheus II to begin the process of recruiting individuals and their families and start preparations for partisan warfare.[67]

In April, the SOE's agent, Odysseus, arrived in Athens from the Middle East with considerable funds and equipment to assist the budding resistance groups with espionage, sabotage subversion, and guerrilla warfare operations. Alexander Levidis, a Greek officer and head of an escape network for MI9 and SOE, arranged a meeting between Odysseus and several senior Greek officers who represented various republican groups in Athens as well as with a representative from EAM. The meeting achieved little except to expose the cleavages within the republican-Venizelist movement and their divergent views about organizing resistance.

Alekos Seferiadis, an associate of Prometheus II, appealed to those present to encourage republican officers to lead the guerrilla bands and do so within EAM.[68] However, all disagreed and insisted that they would terminate all contact with the Cairo SOE if they had to cooperate with EAM.[69] Levidis attempted in vain to make them understand that because the KKE controlled EAM, it was in everyone's interest that republican officers direct the future armed forces of the left-wing organization. He argued that by refusing, they would not hinder EAM from establishing guerrilla bands, but if republican officers led these units, they would minimize the influence of the Communist Party.[70] A few days later, Levidis set up another meeting for Odysseus. This time he also included Zervas, Komninos Pyromaglou, and Charalambos Coutsoyiannopoulos, the head of the Prometheus II network. They agreed to instigate guerrilla activity in the mountains and even outlined areas of responsibility for each organization. Zervas undertook to concentrate his actions in Epirus and western Greece, Psarros received jurisdiction over central Greece, and Stefanos Sarafis agreed to concentrate on Thessaly.[71]

Finally, they directed Odysseus to report these arrangements to the SOE and to request that the 2,000 gold sovereigns he had brought from Cairo be divided among those who had agreed to set up guerrilla bands. Ten days later Levidis met again with Odysseus, but the latter informed him that the SOE had instructed him to divide the funds between EAM and EDES; there was to be no support for any other organization.[72] Because of this decision, the attempt by Odysseus, Coutsoyiannopoulos, and Levidis to establish a large republican resistance organization in Athens as well as field several guerrilla bands in the mountains collapsed. Shortly thereafter, MI9 ordered Levidis not to involve himself with guerrilla activities and instead concentrate on the evacuation of British soldiers to the Middle East; Odysseus gravitated closer to the KKE and Coutsoyiannopoulos had to rely on EDES.[73]

It was not coincidental that it was during this period that Velouchiotis received formal permission from the KKE to establish the first ELAS band in central Greece. Although the SOE had instructed Odysseus to turn over his supply of gold sovereigns to EDES and EAM, Zervas was unhappy with his share and felt cheated, since he assumed that the British now only favored EAM. Odysseus, fearing that Zervas might exact revenge, sought refuge with the KKE; according to postwar accounts, his reports to Cairo began to downplay Zervas' role in the resistance and to advocate more support for EAM-ELAS.[74] He remained with the KKE for four months and supplied it with money as well as a wireless set, enabling it to establish direct contact with Cairo and acquire arms and supplies for ELAS.[75]

Subsequently, the SOE in Cairo decided that Zervas was no longer trustworthy and ordered Prometheus II to end all contact. Coutsoyiannopoulos, however, decided that after all the effort and preparations to organize EDES as a partisan force, it would have been counterproductive to cut off Zervas and leave the field to ELAS. Instead, he threatened to denounce Zervas as a traitor and swindler on the BBC Greek Service, unless he proceeded to organize guerrilla bands. Zervas reluctantly left Athens on 23 July 1942 for the mountains of northwestern Greece to take on his role as the leader of EDES.[76]

In the summer of 1942, both ELAS and EDES, although numerically small and with few antiquated arms, initiated sporadic attacks against the Italians. The Cairo SOE was fully aware of the chaotic political situation in Greece and its effect on the resistance. Through Prometheus II, they were in contact with EDES and EAM-ELAS as well as with other groups that were forming in the winter of 1942, and thanks to the transmitter left behind by Odysseus, they also had a direct link with the KKE.

Before the battles of El Alamein and Stalingrad, "Set Europe ablaze" was the catchword in Whitehall and the raison d'être of the SOE. Any organization, whatever its political outlook, was a welcome addition to Britain's arsenal of secret armies that would rise against the Axis in Europe at the appropriate moment. Until the Gorgopotamos operation, however, the partisan war was a paper tiger. The SOE had mounted several small acts of sabotage, but these were few and of limited effect, which paled to insignificance before the crippling losses inflicted against the British by the Germans in Europe and by the Japanese in Asia.

The SOE was an organization in search of a mission and one that could dramatically illustrate the potential of guerrilla operations in the war effort. All that changed in September 1942 when General Harold Alexander, the commander-in-chief of the Middle Eastern Theater of Operations, asked if the SOE could disrupt the supply lines of the German army that ran from central Europe, through Greece, to North Africa. The SOE could hardly refuse; on the contrary, this request presented an opportunity for the organization to validate its credentials as a fighting service. On the basis of these factors, SOE Cairo decided to send a British team—the Harling Mission—to undertake the first major sabotage action in Greece and to do it in conjunction with the republican guerrilla band of Zervas.

The objective of the Harling Mission was to destroy one of the main bridges in southern Thessaly and disrupt the Thessaloniki-Athens rail link. The operation was to coincide with a major British offensive at El Alamein (Egypt) and block the supplies reaching the German Africa Corps through Piraeus. The SOE persuaded Colonel Edmund Myers, an officer with little experience in clandestine operations but the only available engineer in the Middle East Theater of Operations, to lead the mission and destroy the viaduct. Following the sabotage, a submarine was to evacuate the entire team, with the exception of Christopher Woodhouse and Themis Marinos, who were to remain behind and liaison between SOE Cairo and EDES. What exactly Woodhouse was to accomplish in Greece, in addition to this liaison work, is not clear. According to his

own account, he was planning to transfer to the SAS (Special Air Service), and instead, when he went to Cairo to negotiate his release from
the SOE, someone asked him whether he wished to be dropped by parachute into occupied Greece.[77] There were several delays and abortive attempts, but on 30 September 1942, three groups of four men each
boarded their aircraft. Two of the groups parachuted over Greece, but the
third airplane could not identify the prearranged signal from the ground
and had to turn back.

After he landed in Greece, it took Woodhouse over five weeks to locate Zervas, and along the way, he heard about ELAS, which had given
refuge to the third SOE team that had arrived in Greece on 30 October.
On 10 November, Woodhouse finally reached Zervas' headquarters, and
shortly afterward they set out to join Myers to accomplish the destruction of the Gorgopotamos viaduct.[78] On the return journey, they came
across Velouchiotis' ELAS band, which also agreed to join in the operation even though, according to Woodhouse, EAM did not permit ELAS
to engage in any full-scale confrontations with the enemy.[79]

Eight days later, and after almost two months of delays, the Harling
team with the assistance of EDES and ELAS destroyed the bridge on the
evening of 25 November 1942. Unfortunately, the last act of the Battle of
El Alamein had begun a month earlier on the evening of 23–24 October.
By 7 November, the Africa Corps was in full retreat, and on 9 November,
the Allies successfully invaded French North Africa. In just over ten days,
the Eighth Army pushed the Germans almost 600 miles west, and on 23
November, General Bernard Montgomery, the victor of El Alamein,
halted the advance of the Eighth Army in order to regroup his forces.
The Gorgopotamos operation, consequently, had little impact upon the
war in North Africa. Weeks before the Harling team destroyed the
viaduct Erwin Rommel's supplies had been arriving in Africa from Italy
and Sicily and not Greece.[80]

The destruction of the Gorgopotamos viaduct, however, provided excellent propaganda material for the Allies, who used the success of this
operation to demonstrate that the resistance was fighting back in occupied Europe. It also elevated the status of the SOE in Cairo and with it
the future possibilities of guerrilla warfare in Greece.[81] Toward this end,

SOE Cairo decided not to evacuate the Harling Mission and with the stroke of a pen transformed it into the British Military Mission (BMM) in the Greek mountains. Over the next eight months, the BMM expanded rapidly; SOE teams mushroomed throughout the mountain regions of Greece, enabling the SOE to lay claim to the much-promised guerrilla war envisioned by its planners.

Woodhouse writes that his new orders from SOE Cairo were to establish himself in Athens as a permanent liaison with the BMM and the resistance groups, which the SOE assumed would come under the control of the Six Colonels. To Woodhouse, "This belonged to a world of fantasy," but he agreed to undertake an exploratory visit to Athens, although he was convinced that to remain in the city permanently would be suicidal.[82] At the very least, it would have challenged the most adept expertise in disguises to camouflage the redheaded, six-foot-five-inch-tall Woodhouse to pass as a Greek in Athens. For any SOE agent, let alone one with distinctly Anglo-Saxon features, Athens was a city rife with double agents, collaborators, and traitors who either had infiltrated or had knowledge of the major underground groups and the individuals associated with them.

Despite the obstacles Woodhouse stayed in Athens for several days and afterward reported that the Six Colonels were preparing to form the guerrillas into an army after the collapse of Italy. He dismissed their usefulness as far as the resistance was concerned but stated that they would prove valuable after the occupation. In the same report, Woodhouse recorded that the guerrilla forces would be more "easily directed from the field. . . . The EAM remote control is sure but slow. Luckily Ares [Velouchiotis], their outstanding commander, pays only lip service to their system and acts as he decides."[83] In addition to making a strong case for the future prospects of guerrilla warfare, he implied that it was much easier to control the partisan bands from the mountains than by any central authority in Athens.

Colonel Edmund Myers, the head of the British Military Mission in the Greek mountains, in his first reports on the Greek guerrillas played up the importance of ELAS and indicated that although EAM was communist-controlled, most of its members were not aware of this. As he put it, "The Thessaly guerrillas [ELAS bands] are the largest and best organized of all. Athens attaches importance to them owing to their position astride the main North-South road." He went on to describe EAM "as a genuine body organized to free Greece. It has many Royalist members including a general. After the war ? [*sic*] they desire a plebiscite to decide the government and to be controlled by the Allies, followed by a General Election. The EAM would then dissolve."[84] Woodhouse, on the other hand, highlighted the communist links of EAM and stressed, "The EAM literature has a pro-Russian tinge and abuses the King, Tsouderos and Kanellopoulos. I believe the Communists control EAM unknown to most members."[85]

Myers further advocated the creation of a single command headquarters in the mountains for all the resistance groups. Neither Myers nor Woodhouse could have known that Lord Glenconnor, the head of the Cairo SOE, had proposed something similar and that the Foreign Office was in the process of agreeing that the direction of the Greek resistance, as long it was strictly military in nature, should pass to the SOE representatives in Greece.

Myers also suggested that the British ensure a plebiscite after liberation to determine the fate of the Greek monarchy.[86] This suggestion proved to be too much for the Foreign Office, which "severely chastised" Myers and the SOE for meddling in politics.[87] It was one thing for the SOE to direct the military activities of the Greek resistance, but something entirely different when it attempted to implement a political agenda. After this contretemps, Foreign Office officials in London and Cairo initiated a campaign to curtail the activities of the SOE in Greece. The Foreign Office now claimed that the SOE supported groups hostile to the Greek monarchy and those whose objectives were contrary to British policy. It did not succeed and had to be content with the instructions given to members of the BMM to state "that while they don't mix in politics, they know that His Majesty's Government supports the King and his Government."[88] On 9 March 1943, on the advice of Woodhouse, Zervas proclaimed his loyalty to the Greek king,[89] which helped to ease tensions between the Foreign Office and the SOE, but it was only a temporary truce.[90] Zervas' about-face on the issue of the monarchy, however, altered the political dynamic of the republican movement and set in motion the process that in less than one year would drive the resistance organizations into full-scale civil war.

In the period following the destruction of the Gorgopotamos viaduct, both EDES and ELAS had begun to expand their forces and to increase their operations against the Axis. Although during this time several new organizations took the field, from 1943 to 1944 ELAS and EDES dominated the guerrilla war in the mountains. The smaller bands usually confined their activities to the regions from which they recruited their personnel, but they soon came under considerable pressure from ELAS to join that organization or to disband. By the end of February, according to Myers' estimates, ELAS included approximately 2,000 men and women, while EDES reached 2,420; the combined force of all the other bands did not exceed 550.[91] Myers reported confidently that ELAS, with only 2,000 men and women, ultimately had to accept the direction of a common headquarters guided by the BMM.[92]

Despite these optimistic assessments of the numerical superiority of the EDES forces, ELAS continued to expand at a greater rate. In March 1943, ELAS began to disband the smaller groups near its territory, and by the summer, it had succeeded in establishing control over central and northern Greece as well as parts of the Peloponnesus. By the end of the summer of 1943, ELAS had increased its forces to almost 12,000, with an additional force of 24,000 reserves. EDES, on the other hand, did not fare so well; during the same period (January–May 1943) it only increased its forces to 4,000.[93] One SOE report, however, argued that qualitatively EDES possessed better-trained partisans and a greater proportion of former professional officers.[94]

The relationship of these numbers to the relative strength of ELAS and EDES was, however, deceptive. Unlike EDES, ELAS could rely on the popular support for EAM that had been developed a year earlier in most cities and towns. In addition to a steady stream of recruits and supplies, EAM was able to provide for ELAS a network of support services based in villages and hamlets in the Greek mountains not under the control of EDES.[95] In the summer of 1943, ELAS also started to recruit considerable numbers of Greek officers, many of whom were attracted to that organization because of its recent successes and because they were influenced by other senior officers associated with ELAS.[96]

Originally, the guerrilla bands had been unsuccessful in attracting professional officers. Most senior officers were averse to the idea of resistance because they were in awe of the German military machine or discouraged by the Greek government-in-exile. Many of the cashiered republican officers, however, saw the resistance as an opportunity for reinstatement in a postliberation Greek army. At first, they provided a steady stream of recruits for EDES, but as the resistance expanded in 1943, they were also drawn to republican organizations such as EKKA (National and Social Liberation). These new organizations diverted potential recruits from Zervas, and when ELAS or the Germans dispersed them, very few of their members went over to EDES.[97] In addition, when Zervas made his peace with the monarchy, it drove many of EDES' republican supporters away from resistance activity or into the arms of ELAS. This sharpened the difference between the two major guerrilla bands, as more and more, EDES became associated with the monarchy.[98]

In the meantime, the BMM became more involved in political matters and less able to control the growth or direction of the Greek resistance movement. By the late spring of 1943, there were indications that relations among the guerrilla groups were heading toward a crisis. The BMM, although mandated to guide the guerrilla movement, was quickly losing control. Myers now began to send reports to Cairo indicating that EAM-ELAS was planning to dominate the resistance, but SOE was reluctant to break with EAM-ELAS and there was still some suspicion in Cairo of Zervas.[99] The BMM, on the other hand, did manage to establish almost complete influence over EDES. According to D. J. Wallace, who had arrived in Greece at the end of June 1943 to act as Myers' political adviser, "Zervas is a British creation in the sense that we are responsible for his continued existence today and for all the consequences that may follow there from."[100]

In July 1943, after lengthy and difficult negotiations, Myers convinced the EAM-ELAS leadership to accept coordination with the BMM and the other guerrilla bands. EAM-ELAS agreed, but on the condition that a joint headquarters be set up in its territory and the role of the BMM relegated to liaison. In addition, Myers had to convince the SOE that ELAS should be recognized as a sovereign Allied force and that although it intended to accept general directions from the commander-in-chief in the Middle East, it should retain its freedom of action. In exchange, Myers was able to extract two major concessions from ELAS. The first permitted the BMM to raise new guerrilla bands in areas under the control of ELAS, and the second allowed Myers to coordinate a series of guerrilla operations that were part of a major Allied deception plan.[101] The SOE considered the National Bands Agreement, the name of this arrangement, a major achievement in the development of the guerrilla war, and it even brought Myers the appreciation of the Foreign Office.[102] For the British the advantage of a temporary pause in the clashes between ELAS and the other groups offset the recognition of ELAS as an Allied force, which gave that organization status and legitimacy.[103] In this context, the events that unfolded between August and September 1943 represent a critical stage of the Greek resistance and directly contributed to the outbreak of civil war in October 1943.

As the war swung in favor of the Allies, the leadership of EAM-ELAS was anticipating the liberation of Greece and the possibility that the Red Army would accomplish this. On 18 July 1943, the Greek communist newspaper, *Rizospastis,* announced the Soviet victory at the Battle of Kursk and two days later proclaimed that the Russians would soon reach the Balkans. A short while later the Allies invaded Sicily. Consequently, there was every indication that the liberation of Greece would take place in the very near future. These notions gathered additional momentum with the execution of Operation Animals, designed to deceive the Germans into believing that the Allies were to invade Greece (whereas in reality they intended to land in Sicily).[104] Part of the British strategy was to instigate considerable guerrilla activity in the respective regions of the Greek resistance groups, giving the impression of an imminent Allied invasion.[105]

Operation Animals led to the immediate transfer of three German armored divisions to Greece and contributed to a speedy Allied victory in Sicily and the invasion of southern Italy.[106] In September, Mussolini was deposed, and Italy surrendered unconditionally. The effect of these events upon the Greek resistance was not only to create the perception of an Allied landing in Greece but, for EAM-ELAS and the republicans, also to raise the prospect of the return of the Greek government-in-exile and King George II. The failure of the British and the Greek governments to come to terms with EAM-ELAS in August exacerbated further the climate of mutual suspicion. In August 1943, Myers had arranged for the transportation of a delegation from the main resistance organizations to Cairo.[107] The aim of the mission, at least as understood by Myers, was to facilitate better coordination and organization among the guerrilla bands, the Greek general staff, and the Greek government-in-exile.[108]

Upon their arrival in Cairo the delegation focused exclusively on political issues.[109] They demanded that the king remain outside Greece after liberation until the Greek people decided the fate of the monarchy by plebiscite and that the Greek government-in-exile include three representatives from the resistance organizations.[110] After consulting with both Churchill and Roosevelt, George II rejected all the demands of the resistance, and the Foreign Office instructed its officials in Cairo to terminate all discussions with the delegation concerning the Greek monarchy and the government-in-exile.

In mid-September, the delegation "returned to Greece disgruntled at their treatment and in a most disappointed frame of mind."[111] The only change that they had managed to effect was the acquisition of two American officers, which turned the British Military Mission (BMM) into the Allied Military Mission (AMM).[112] Furthermore, the left-wing and republican leaders were now convinced that the British were bent upon imposing on Greece the Greek king and the prewar political structure that had led to a dictatorship between 1936 and 1941. For the KKE-led EAM, the only means of preventing this outcome as well as achieving control of the postwar environment in Greece was to dominate the resistance. Civil war was now a necessity in order for ELAS to destroy all other resistance organizations and rival guerrilla bands.

In Cairo, the failure by the British and the Greek government-in-exile to address the demands of the resistance delegation brought to the forefront the contradictory policies of the SOE and the Foreign Office toward Greece, which thus far had been cloaked in ambiguity. It was equally relevant that the Cairo crisis forced the British to choose between recognizing the resistance groups politically or continuing their unconditional support of the Greek monarch. In the final analysis, the choice had already been made by Churchill's conviction that after the defeat of the Axis, Europe had to return to the prewar political status quo. The presence of the delegation simply forced the British in Cairo to come to terms with that policy as far as the Greeks were concerned.

Fighting between ELAS and the other guerrilla forces broke out in Greece on 9 October 1943 and within one week had spread to the areas of eastern Epirus under the control of EDES. By the end of November, Zervas had withdrawn his forces from the east side of the Arachtos River to defensive positions from Ioannina to Arta. On 21 December, EDES units attacked the ELAS forces in the region of Amfilochia and Pramanda, approximately twenty-five miles from Arta, and pushed them back across the Arachtos. In January, Zervas began an offensive that forced ELAS to withdraw across the Akhelos. On 23 January, the EAM central committee authorized ELAS to discuss a truce, which lasted only until the 26th, when units of ELAS commanded by Velouchiotis launched a major counterattack that forced EDES back across the Akhelos. By 1 February, Zervas' situation was becoming desperate as ELAS forces were concentrating in the area of Flamburion, approximately twenty miles from Ioannina, EDES' base of operations. German intervention saved Zervas at the last moment. The Germans, fearing that the destruction of EDES would mean that eastern Epirus, along with the essential Ioannina-Arta road, would come under the control of ELAS, on 2 February 1944 attacked the northern flank of ELAS along the east bank of the Arachtos.[113] Although the Germans failed to destroy the ELAS forces in this region, they forced them out of Epirus and saved Zervas. The Germans expected Zervas to take the offensive, but Zervas, having suffered considerable casualties, kept his forces west of the Arachtos; as long as he remained in this region, he no longer needed to fear ELAS, since the presence of strong Wehrmacht units guaranteed his safety.[114] Because of these maneuvers, the still-young civil war now stalemated, and both rival guerrilla organizations accepted the mediation of the AMM to end hostilities.[115] In addition, the civil war demonstrated that the Germans were slowly losing control of the mountain regions of Greece and did not have the resources and military forces to destroy the guerrilla bands.

The civil war also renewed the conflict between the Foreign Office and the SOE, only this time it was the Middle East command that was responsible for the SOE. As mentioned earlier, the military was convinced that the Greek resistance was necessary to tie down as many German divisions as possible in the Balkans to support the Allied effort in Europe. The military thus disagreed with the Foreign Office policy of supporting George II, which it viewed as an obstacle in continuing the expansion of the Greek guerrilla forces, particularly those of EAM-ELAS.[116] General Maitland Wilson, the commander of the Middle Eastern Theater of Operations, as well as the chiefs-of-staff still believed that it was possible to wean ELAS from the communist influence of EAM and reintroduced an earlier SOE proposal to bring Plastiras from France to the Greek mountains and create a regency council headed by Archbishop Damaskinos.[117] The Foreign Office, although skeptical of the military value of ELAS, was prepared to accept the use of such a council, providing that the military break with EAM-ELAS. The latter provision was the price Leeper, the British ambassador, demanded for accepting the Plastiras-Damaskinos compromise.[118] The War Cabinet dealt with the matter on 22 November and authorized Churchill and Eden to deal with the issue in cooperation with the Middle East command. They further recommended that all supplies to ELAS cease, and that the Greek army incorporate EDES as well as ELAS. To ensure this settlement, the king had to agree to accept a regency council and not return to Greece until the Greek people had decided on the future of the monarchy by plebiscite.[119] Churchill and Eden advised George II to accept this proposal, but the king, after consulting with Roosevelt, declined.[120] The most that George II was prepared to do was to declare that he would reconsider the timing of his return to Greece at liberation, in consultation with his government. Once again, the failure to resolve the constitutional issue remained the major stumbling block to either reaching an accommodation with the left or countering the influence of EAM-ELAS with those who opposed the monarchy.

Although ELAS achieved considerable tactical success against Zervas' forces, it failed to destroy EDES. ELAS was also beginning to lose popularity because of the hardships endured by the mountain villages. Aris Velouchiotis, in particular, exacted terrible vengeances upon any villager suspected of aiding the enemies of ELAS. Often, he even forced members of the AMM to watch helplessly as he tortured a simple peasant for some minor offense. In the village of Mavrolithary, ELAS arrested fourteen men simply because they belonged to a rival band. The punishments designed to set an example for all the local inhabitants usually took place in the village square and set the pattern of death and degradation that continued until 1949. On this occasion, Aris' henchmen grabbed the first prisoner and stripped him of his clothes. Then, in front of the villagers, they tied the man to a table, spread-eagled. The victim quickly realized what was in store and vainly pleaded for mercy. In a few minutes, his shrill cries reverberated in the village square as the executioner, splattered with blood, slowly proceeded to hack away at the man's body, pausing long enough for each blow to take effect and prolong the process for as long as possible. The savagery went on until a British officer present at the butchery pulled out his revolver and terminated the man's agony. Aris, shaking with anger, had to be restrained from killing the officer.[121]

Regardless of their fear of the left, the British had come to terms with the Greek civil war and ELAS. The decision of the Allies to implement Operation Overlord, taken at the Teheran Conference, meant support for Tito and the Greek resistance in order to keep the "Balkan pot boiling" for the Germans.[122] Because of this situation, the Foreign Office was prepared not to break with EAM-ELAS but attempted to limit its strength and diminish its influence. To this end, it proposed "to restrain the more ruthless members of ELAS and to build an anti-KKE coalition around Damaskinos and the exiled government which was to be revived and strengthened by including fresh political moderates from Greece."[123] Furthermore, the Foreign Office, despite Churchill's objections, was prepared to accept EAM-ELAS representation in a new

Greek coalition government.[124] In January 1944, consequently, the Foreign Office proposed to initiate talks with EAM-ELAS with the purpose of ending the civil war, and although Tsouderos agreed, he insisted that any negotiations be limited to military matters. In turn, Tsouderos appealed to Archbishop Damaskinos to attempt reconciliation between the leaders of the traditional political parties and the Greek government-in-exile. In addition, if EAM-ELAS accepted an armistice, Damaskinos was to select a committee to negotiate the formation of a coalition government that would include representatives from the left. Tsouderos authorized Woodhouse to represent the Greek premier in the talks with EAM-ELAS, and after fourteen meetings, the civil war ended with the conclusion of the Plaka Agreement on 29 February 1944.[125] The signatories agreed to continue the armistice, to maintain the territorial status quo in their respective regions, and to cooperate in the future. A secret clause was also included that the guerrilla organizations would participate closely in Operation Noah's Ark, designed to harass the German retreat from Greece.[126]

The Plaka Agreement was only a limited success since it essentially established a military truce but did not address any of the outstanding political issues. The absence of a political compromise now acted as a catalyst for EAM-ELAS to begin the process of forming its own government. Although most Greek politicians had rebuffed EAM's efforts to participate in the creation of a Greek government in the mountains, several liberals and republicans decided to work with EAM in order to moderate the KKE's influence and work toward achieving self-determination for postwar Greece. On 10 March 1944, EAM formally established the Political Committee of National Liberation (PEEA). The committee included not only members of EAM but also Alexander Svolos, one of Greece's preeminent constitutional experts; Angelos Angelopoulos, another academic; Emmanouil Mandakas, the only senior Greek officer to lead a coup against the Metaxas regime (in 1938); and Euripides Bakirdzis, who abandoned EKKA and joined PEEA.[127]

The formation of PEEA triggered a political crisis for the British and the Greek government-in-exile because it "presented . . . a real if not legal rival."[128] Many of the officers and men of the Greek armed forces in the Middle East viewed PEEA as the legitimate representative of the Greek people and resented the refusal of Tsouderos and the king to come to terms with PEEA's request for the establishment of a new Greek government.[129] On 26 March, the day after the celebration of Greece's Independence Day, PEEA made another appeal for a government of national unity, and this time it sparked a mutiny in the Greek armed forces in the Middle East. Tsouderos refused to deal with the demands of the mutineers to recognize PEEA as well as broaden the government. The British and particularly Churchill, who blamed the mutiny on extremists and communists, supported the decision of the Greek premier. Meanwhile the liberals and Venizelist politicians in and out of the Greek government-in-exile tried to convince Tsouderos to resign in favor of Sophocles Venizelos, the son of the great prime minister, who, they argued, was in a better position to deal with the rebellious Greek forces. Tsouderos at first resisted but on 13 April gave up his post, and Venizelos took his place as premier.[130] The latter was equally unsuccessful in quelling the mutiny and after thirteen days also resigned. The British then took matters into their own hands and forced the appointment of Admiral Petros Voulgaris as commander-in-chief of the Greek navy to put down the rebels. After a short skirmish, Voulgaris with the help of British military forces restored order by the end of April.[131]

The end of the first civil war in February 1944 and the mutiny of the Greek armed forces in the Middle East left the Greek government-in-exile in tatters and with little credibility in occupied Greece. EAM-ELAS, on the other hand, emerged as a much stronger organization, increasing the prospect of conflict with the British—liberation would not come in the form of an Allied invasion of Greece but follow in the wake of a German retreat, thus leaving most of the country under the control of EAM-ELAS. In the interim period between the spring of 1944 and the German evacuation in October, the British had to plan for two possibilities. The first was to bring about the liberation of Greece with the cooperation of EAM-ELAS, at least long enough for the Greek government-in-exile to reassert its authority over the country. The second was to cooperate with the anticommunist elements linked to the puppet government and use them to maintain control of Greece until the British could bring sufficient forces to secure the country.

Both possibilities required at least a partial reform of the Greek government-in-exile, which had to include representatives from the resistance as well as deal with the question of the monarchy. Although these factors had come into play and had been rejected summarily when the resistance delegation visited Cairo in August 1943, the new realities created by the civil war and the fact that no Allied army would liberate Greece required an accommodation with the left, at least on British terms. Part of the means of addressing this problem required, at the very least, the semblance of a Greek coalition government and a premier who represented the liberal establishment and had credibility in occupied Greece.

The man who had these qualities was George Papandreou. A follower of Venizelos, he had held three cabinet portfolios and had a reputation of supporting progressive legislation. In March 1942, he had signed the petition calling upon George II to remain outside Greece until a plebiscite had determined the fate of the monarchy. During the occupation, Papandreou kept in touch with members of the resistance but declined to join EAM-ELAS and later sent a series of dispatches to Cairo denouncing the left-wing organization, as well as warning the Greek government-in-exile and the British of the growing influence of the KKE. These communications had greatly impressed the Foreign Office—particularly Papandreou's analysis of the international political order, which he divided into Pan-Slavist communism, which threatened to swallow Greece and Europe, and Anglo-Saxon liberalism, the only force able to oppose it.[132] Accordingly, the British and George II decided to bring Papandreou out of Greece, and with Churchill's approval, he became acting premier on 26 April 1944.

Papandreou's first task was to chair an all-party conference in Lebanon on 17 May 1944, the purpose of which was to form a government of national unity that would also include representatives of the resistance organizations.[133] Papandreou skillfully isolated the EAM-ELAS delegates by accusing them of causing the civil war as well as the April mutiny.[134] Next, he sidestepped the constitutional problem by using a letter from George II (8 November), which declared that the king would reconsider his return to Greece in consultation with his government, as the guiding principle of the role of the monarchy in the immediate postliberation period.[135] The conference ended three days later on 20 May with the conclusion of the Lebanon Charter, whose eight points were accepted by all the participants, including the EAM-ELAS and PEEA delegates.[136] Papandreou reported the results of the conference to the king and submitted his resignation. The king, in turn, accepted the Lebanon Charter and asked Papandreou to form a new government based on the principles agreed to at the conference.[137]

Papandreou's main objective was to form a government of national unity that would include representation from the resistance organizations and thus force EAM-ELAS to act in concert with the new government and abandon PEEA. EAM-ELAS, however, upon receiving the terms of the Lebanon Charter, refused to endorse it or to join a government of national unity.[138] For the next several months, Papandreou and the British waged an overt and covert campaign to force EAM-ELAS into a coalition. Papandreou, for his part, interpreted the king's letter of 8 November 1943 to mean that the Greek government-in-exile accepted that George II would not return to Greece until a plebiscite addressed the future of the monarchy, thus removing the most serious objection barring EAM-ELAS from joining the government.[139] The British, on the other hand, had been attempting even before the Lebanon agreement to contain the growing power of EAM-ELAS and search for new coalitions to form an antileft front. Ironically, the Germans at this time were pursuing a similar policy.

After the outbreak of civil war in October 1943, it had become obvious to the British that the Venizelists and liberals were no match for the KKE. The republican forces, which the SOE had so carefully cultivated as the lesser of two evils, had lost their cohesion as a political organization. However, they still represented a considerable force and a potential ally for the Germans, who in the fall of 1943 began to approach counterinsurgency from a political perspective, focusing on anticommunism. From the beginning of the occupation, the Germans had concentrated on occupying and protecting key strategic positions straddling their lines of communication, effectively abandoning the countryside to the guerrillas except for limited and infrequent operations.[140] Until 1943, the Italians had had the responsibility for securing most of Greece as well as conducting antiguerrilla operations, the Germans only taking action in cases of specific sabotage in their zones of occupation.[141]

In the spring of 1943, Ioannis Rallis, a professional politician, agreed to head the third occupation government, with the proviso that his regime could establish a Greek security force. The German authorities agreed in principle, and on 7 April 1943, the Rallis government decreed the mobilization of four Evzone battalions.[142] At first, and in order to allay the fears of their Italian ally, the Germans only armed the newly created battalions with rifles and machine guns.[143] This policy changed with the surrender of Italy, and by October 1943, the first of the battalions came into service in Athens, followed by two more by the end of December.

Despite a persistent and aggressive recruitment campaign, the Rallis forces only attracted a handful of volunteers. The success of EAM-ELAS in the early stages of the civil war subsequently drove many conservative officers to the Security Battalions. During the course of the civil war, some members of guerrilla bands dispersed by ELAS also sought refuge and/or revenge by enlisting in the battalions.[144] Since a large proportion of these men were republicans, they were attracted to the battalions, which were advertised as anticommunist as well as anti-royalist forces. Moreover, after Zervas' reconciliation with the monarchy, EDES had ceased to represent the republican cause.

For the Germans the battalions provided new forces to replace the Italian units stationed in Greece. Early in 1944, the Rallis government seized the opportunity offered by the willingness of the German authorities to increase the battalions and began an intensive campaign to attract new volunteers. In order to maintain a steady flow of recruits, the Rallis regime dismissed hundreds of men from local police forces without any pay or rations. To make recruitment to the battalions more palatable, the puppet regime spread rumors that the British and American governments secretly supported Rallis. In addition, on 19 March 1944, the puppet government enacted legislation that permitted all officers dismissed from the armed forces after 1927 to reenlist at their former rank provided they served in the Security Battalions.[145] This move, coupled with the propaganda that these battalions were to be used to combat communism, offered many cashiered republican officers the possibility of reinstatement in a postwar Greek army.[146]

Ironically, officers loyal to the king faced a similar dilemma. In the spring of 1943, the monarchist faction of the officer corps had attempted to create an organization to represent and maintain the unity of the royalist officers. General Alexander Papagos, the commander-in-chief of the Greek army during the Albanian war, with five other generals, established a resistance group, the Military Hierarchy. Very quickly, the new organization extended its influence among the professional officers in Athens and, through them, to those who resided in the military districts of the Greek army divisions before the war.[147] The aims of the Military Hierarchy were to support the organizations fighting the occupation forces by providing leadership and to maintain the established social and political order by gaining control of Athens after a German withdrawal.[148] Despite the prestige of Papagos, the generals were unable to solicit any interest from the British or from any of the guerrilla bands, and soon the German authorities arrested the six generals and sent them to a concentration camp. Although the Germans incarcerated the leadership of the Military Hierarchy, the organization survived, although it remained dormant until liberation. Then, many of its adherents resurfaced and were able to take advantage of the antileft policies of the British and Greek governments and, once again, to assume control of the armed forces and the security services.

The ambivalent attitude of the British toward these and other collaborationist forces carrying the label *anticommunist* contributed to the development and growth of the Security Battalions. Even prior to the outbreak of the civil war, officers of the British intelligence services had come into indirect contact with the representatives of the Rallis government and with individuals associated with the Security Battalions. In September 1943, Frank Macaskie, the *Telegraph* correspondent in Athens before the occupation and an officer in the SIS afterward, had attempted, with the collaboration of Angelos Evert (the head of the Athens police force) and Archbishop Damaskinos, to form an anticommunist front as a counter to EAM-ELAS.[149] This anticommunist coalition was to include not only several conservative republicans but also certain members of the Athens EDES who were already working for the Germans or had been instrumental in organizing the Security Battalions.[150] EAM-ELAS was aware of efforts by British agents, whether authorized or not, to build a counterorganization to the left-wing resistance, which confirmed their suspicions of the British.[151]

The British and the Greek government-in-exile initially avoided any outright denunciation of the Security Battalions but confined their comments to mild reprimands through the BBC broadcasts to Greece.[152] For example, one directive of 2 June 1944 stipulated that all those who joined the Battalions were assisting the Germans but should not be denounced as traitors. Twenty days later, a second directive suspended all direct attacks against the Rallis forces until July 1944.[153] The Greek government-in-exile finally denounced these units publicly in September 1944.[154]

By the summer of 1944, the Greek political spectrum had altered significantly, as the struggle between the left and the right overshadowed the old royalist-republican schism. Within this framework the Battalions assumed the position of intermediaries between the postwar "political revolution" represented by EAM-ELAS and the reestablishment of the old order identified with EDES and backed by the British. Inasmuch as the civil war spawned the Security Battalions, it also marginalized the role of EDES and with it the republican cause, not only within the resistance movement but also as a potential player in postwar Greece.

On the other hand, between the fall of 1943 and the summer of 1944, EAM-ELAS clearly emerged as a major political and military force that controlled most of the Greek countryside and had an established infrastructure within the major cities and towns. The collapse of Italy provided EAM-ELAS with an added bonus: One Italian division that managed to avoid internment by the Germans in Greece surrendered to the AMM, but in ELAS-held territory. Despite British efforts to keep the Italian force intact, logistical problems forced the British to disperse the Italians, and in the process, they had to abandon their weapons.[155] Most of these ended up in the hands of ELAS, giving that organization a considerable number of artillery and heavy machine guns and hence decreasing its dependence on British supplies.

Thus, with the exception of Zervas' numerically inferior EDES bands and the limited number of guerrillas controlled by right-wing groups, the only force capable of containing ELAS was the Security Battalions. These circumstances forced Papandreou to consider incorporating the Security Battalions into the postwar Greek army.[156] Although this plan fell through, during the summer of 1944 the absence of any strong and outright denunciation of these forces served as indirect pressure for EAM-ELAS to join the Greek government-in-exile.[157]

After many mutual denunciations between EAM-ELAS and the Greek government-in-exile, on 29 July EAM-ELAS informed Cairo that it was prepared to join the government providing Papandreou stepped down as premier. Both Churchill and Eden, however, denounced EAM-ELAS' call for Papandreou's resignation. On 18 August George Siantos, the acting secretary of the KKE and a member of the central committee of EAM, dropped all previous demands and accepted the admission of five EAM-ELAS representatives to the Greek government.[158] In the meantime, the British had decided to send a small force to Greece, in part to facilitate the transition from occupation to liberation, but primarily to prevent EAM-ELAS from seizing power.[159] In early September, the Greek government-in-exile moved to Caserta, Italy, and on 26 September, in conjunction with the British and the representatives of the resistance, it concluded an agreement (the Caserta Agreement) to deal with the immediate problems of security after liberation. The main concern of the British and the Papandreou government, however, was the demobilization of the guerrilla bands and the transfer of the Government of National Unity (the name of the government-in-exile after May 1944) to Greece.

The agreement was signed by Maitland Wilson, as the Supreme Allied Commander, Mediterranean Theater; Papandreou, on behalf of the Greek government-in-exile; Harold Macmillan, representing the British government; and Zervas and Sarafis for EDES and ELAS, respectively. Remarkably, EAM-ELAS accepted these conditions, which after liberation effectively gave the British and the Greek governments control of key areas, thus enabling them to offset some of the strategic advantage held by ELAS. On 18 September 1944, almost a week before the Caserta Agreement, Harold Macmillan, the resident minister of state, confided in his diary that Greece was "in grave danger of EAM seizing power whenever the Germans are leaving."[160] Nonetheless, despite the concessions given by EAM-ELAS, the British assumed that the communists would use the resistance to gain control of Greece. For the next several months, this underlying principle guided British policy toward the Greek resistance and inevitably contributed to the outbreak of the December Uprising.

On 12 October 1944, the Germans pulled their forces out of Athens and began their withdrawal from Greece. Six days later the Greek government-in-exile, along with a small British force, arrived in the capital.[161] Despite the Herculean tasks facing this government, the most pressing issue was the establishment of a new national army to replace the guerrilla bands and to participate in the defeat of Nazi Germany. With the exception of the Greek navy and a small air force, the Greek government had under its control only the Third Mountain Brigade and the Sacred Squadron, the latter made up of officers. These forces were all that remained of the Greek units in the Middle East after the mutinies and the subsequent purges. Their composition, following the dismissal and court-martial of liberals and republicans who had participated in the mutinies, was conservative and included many republicans such as Constantine Vendiris, a senior Greek officer, now transformed to devout royalists. This made them unacceptable to EAM-ELAS, which feared that any new army led by such officers would simply restore the prewar political establishment. For the time being, the Third Mountain Brigade was in Italy, and its future disposition, at least officially, remained in question.

In the fall of 1944, consequently, the Greek government was dependent upon a small British force made up of logistical personnel, the goodwill of EAM-ELAS, and the Security Battalions. It seems clear from the events that unfolded in November and December that the Papandreou government had decided, in cooperation with the British, to reinstate, quietly, at least the officers who had served in the Battalions.

At the same time, it had become British policy to dissolve EAM and dismantle ELAS while using collaborators to support the Greek government. One SOE report of 8 September 1944 recommended that "a combination of secret and overt means [be used] to persuade the moderate majority to desert EAM-ELAS at an opportune moment and join the supporters of the legal government. Details must vary slightly according to local conditions but the two essential principles are that secrecy must be maintained and that HMG must not appear to be connected with this scheme." The same report also outlined British policy toward other groups, including collaborators: "By contrast with EAM, the fragmentation of right wing groups Quisling and non-political formations has less importance. Leaders and rank and file could easily be made to support the legal Government of Greece when the time comes."[162]

After liberation, the British incarcerated the majority of the Security Battalions in the Goudi barracks outside Athens and in other locations in Attica. In the middle of November, the British started releasing Security Battalion officers from Averoff prison, and soon some of them were freely walking in the streets of Athens wearing new uniforms. The British and the Greek general staff assisted others to leave Greece for Egypt and placed those released in early November in regular army units.[163] On 23 November, the Ministry of Defense published a list of 250 officers designated to command the new National Guard units; of these, 8 had served with the Security Battalions.[164] EAM-ELAS and the press were so outraged that the government had to revise the list and drop those associated with the battalions. They also had to replace the undersecretary of defense with an ELAS officer, General Ptolemaios Sarigiannis.[165]

The British army continued to provide protection and to assist in the gradual rehabilitation of the former quisling units in the Greek army and the police forces. They were guided in this policy, even before liberation, by the almost absolute conviction that EAM-ELAS and, through them, the KKE were determined to seize power.[166] On 9 August 1944, Anthony Eden, the British foreign secretary, outlined Britain's strategic interest in postwar Greece to the War Cabinet and stressed that it was imperative to prevent a communist coup in that country. Eden warned, "Were the Greek Communist forces, who were strongly armed, to seize power a massacre might follow. This would be very injurious to our prestige, and might even add Greece to the post-war Balkan Slav block which now showed signs of forming under Russian influence, and from which we were anxious to keep Greece detached."[167] The daily marches and protests by EAM-ELAS bolstered these fears, and ultimately fear created the conditions for a confrontation between the British and ELAS.

3

BLOODY DECEMBER:
THE SECOND ROUND
OF THE CIVIL WAR

Democracy is no harlot to be picked up in the street by a man with a tommy gun.[1]

✺ WINSTON CHURCHILL

USUALLY DECEMBER IS A MERCURIAL MONTH IN GREECE. THE weather ranges from the soft warmth of the winter sunlight in the middle of the day to brisk evenings and damp cold mornings. On that tragic Sunday, 3 December 1944, Athens was a city on the verge of chaos. It had rained the previous day and the chill and dampness drove most Athenians indoors. At dawn, the rays of the sun pierced the darkness, and the light blended with the morning dew, making the city sparkle and gleam. People slowly began their daily ritual of scrounging for scarce supplies and bits of wood so they could keep warm during the frosty night.

Severe shortages of food and heating fuel made December even colder and took the bloom off liberation, which had occurred only a short two months earlier. During those heady days, parades of soldiers and resistance fighters, along with the frivolity of round-the-clock celebrations, shattered the gloom of occupation, but by December, Athens had once again descended into darkness. Recriminations and charges of collaboration or treason replaced the sudden exhilaration of freedom. Accusation, in fact, became the national discourse. Indeed, fear stalked every corner of Athens, grinding down the little trust that remained and diminishing any hope for the future.

On that historic sunny morning of Sunday, 3 December 1944, several processions of Greek communists, socialists, republicans, and antimonarchists were advancing to Constitution Square, the center of Athens and the heart of Greek political life. All were members of the wartime National Liberation Front (EAM), a coalition of communist, socialist, and agrarian parties that developed into a mass resistance organization during the occupation. A disproportionate number of young women, followed by teenagers, old men, and even children, filled the ranks of the demonstrators. Some came as unwilling participants, since the day before, bands of young men had gone through most of the streets of the city and, armed with paper megaphones, issued orders to all citizens to come and show their support for EAM by participating in the demonstration.

During the eight weeks of liberation, Athenians had grown accustomed to the daily cacophony of slogans and rants that paraded the grievances of the left. This time, however, it was different. Anyone who stayed away, the young men with the megaphones warned, would be considered an enemy of the people and would be dealt with accordingly.[2] Most had little reason to doubt the urgency of the exhortations or the veracity of the threats, and the next day they made their way to the center of Athens. Threats aside, EAM enjoyed a mass following that had greater faith in the wartime resistance than in the provisional government. Many had walked from the outskirts of Athens, others from the suburbs and nearby villages; a hastily established EAM transportation system, composed of a motley collection of dilapidated trucks and automobiles, had brought a lucky few to the capital.

The demonstrators were descending on Athens to protest the decision of the Greek government to demobilize the resistance bands that had fought the Axis and to replace them with a new army. During the three and a half years of brutal occupation, the Allies had hailed the resistance fighters as the torchbearers of freedom in Nazi-dominated Europe. Yet, by December 1944, the resistance had become the unwanted creation of war, a threat to the Greek government and an embarrassment to its British patrons. The realities of peace could not fulfill the promises made during the occupation, and the demonstrators believed that their grievances had to be addressed before Greece could truly be liberated. They suspected that a new Greek army would simply force the return of the unpopular King George II and enable the provisional Greek government to reinstate the prewar political status quo.

As far as the Greek left was concerned, the resistance bands had to remain intact in order to ensure an equitable balance of power—the communist leadership, however, had other ambitions as well as fears. Even though the membership of EAM reached close to 750,000, the KKE did not have faith that this mass support would remain constant. Certainly, they could not rely on a broad-based endorsement of a communist platform in a future election; thus the KKE continued to operate behind front organizations such as EAM. The best chance the communists had of exerting influence in postwar Greece and nursing any hope of achieving control over the country was by preserving the military options provided by ELAS. The decision of the provisional government to order the demobilization of the guerrilla forces meant that the KKE would lose its only practical and direct means of imposing its will on events.

However, the fate of the resistance bands and the issue of a new army were symptoms of much deeper divisions that had circumvented any hope of political progress in liberated Greece. Fundamentally, two visions of the country's future always lingered: a radical Greece ruled by the "will of the people," the so-called popular democracy, promised by the rhetoric of EAM-ELAS; and the reestablishment of prewar society, represented by the traditional political establishment and the crown. Both political concepts had antecedents whose roots reached back to the Greek War of Independence, but by December 1944 they were on a collision course. Supporters of each side suspected the other of hidden agendas and duplicity. The right believed that behind the promise of a liberal, socialist, and democratic Greece loomed the KKE and the prospect of a Soviet-style state, while the left was convinced that references to stability and order implied the specter of monarchy and authoritarianism.

Despite the suspicions of the left, the resurrection of a political system dominated by military and reactionary cliques was not necessarily a fait accompli—at least in the immediate postliberation period. The power and influence of the traditional elites and political factions had become dissipated by war and occupation, as well as challenged by a mass-based resistance. Tragically, the hasty and precipitous actions of the left practically guaranteed the return of the stifling rule of the prewar traditional elites, who would impose a new authoritarianism with a vengeance. On that morning in December, those thousands of demonstrators were marching to regain the political initiative that war and occupation had created for the left, which supporters now believed was being hijacked by the provisional government.

Police cordons blocked off all streets leading to the center of Athens, but one group of approximately 100 demonstrators broke through from Sygrou Street and advanced toward the police station located on the edge of Constitution Square near the Grande Bretagne Hotel. As the columns of demonstrators snaked around the streets, converging on the center of the city, the men with the megaphones egged them on, and every so often the crowd stopped and chanted, "Down with Papandreou!" "Down with intervention!" "Try the collaborators!" "Down with George Glucksberg (the king of Greece)!" or "Death to traitors!" The police had set up barricades to block off the streets leading to the square, but the sheer weight of numbers overwhelmed them. Angry young women, in particular, caught up in the excitement of the moment, screeched at the police; some even left the columns, ran out into the street, and shook their fists at the muzzles of the rifles.[3]

At approximately 10:00 A.M., a large group of demonstrators made its way to the apartment building of George Papandreou, the premier of the provisional government. A torrent of threats accompanied the chants of "Down with Papandreou!" Trapped inside his apartment, Papandreou watched anxiously as his police guard struggled to hold back the protestors. Suddenly, someone threw two grenades, killing one passerby and severely wounding another bystander.[4] The sight of blood further enraged the demonstrators, and they attempted to force their way into the lobby of the apartment building. Fortunately, Papandreou's guards (with the aid of automatic weapons) succeeded in dispersing the angry crowd.[5]

According to Panagiotis Kanellopoulos, a minister in the provisional government, Sunday's crisis almost unhinged Papandreou. Earlier in the morning, when Kanellopoulos first went to see the premier to discuss the pending demonstration, he was told that Papandreou was sleeping and could not be disturbed. A little later, Kanellopoulos tried once again to see the premier and reached his fifth-floor apartment just a few minutes after the police had beaten back the demonstrators. Once inside, he saw five or six ministers huddled in a corner; despite the circumstances, they remained unfrazzled, but the premier had withdrawn alone into his bedroom. Half an hour later, Papandreou finally emerged from his isolation, recalls Kanellopoulos, but "he appeared confused, nervous and incapable of making decisions."[6]

The crisis that followed liberation had taken its toll on the Greek premier and his family. Papandreou's daughter, Miranda, was a communist who took part in the EAM parades and demonstrations, and the premier's son, Andreas, was serving in the United States navy. Staring from his window, Papandreou may have mused that one face in that crowd could easily be that of his own daughter screaming for his blood. Later on, during the thirty-three days of the December crisis, Miranda went completely over to the other side and gave stage performances for ELAS. She further tried to raise the morale of the insurgents by drawing sketches that lampooned her parents. In the meantime, while the premier was trying to grapple with a country on the brink of civil war (as well as with the future of his own family), Sunday's events were acquiring their own relentless momentum.

By approximately 10:45 A.M., one column of demonstrators was spilling into Constitution Square. They quickly formed into ranks of eight to ten abreast, while every fourth person carried either a British, a

Greek, an American, or a Soviet flag. Others waved banners with slogans engraved in red print.[7] W. Byford-Jones, who witnessed the event, writes:

> The ages of those who were taking part ranged from ten to twelve years of age to sixty and more. A few of the children were without shoes, most of the people without overcoats, but there were many who were well dressed. As before, there were a predominant number of girls between eighteen and thirty years of age. There was nothing sullen or menacing about the procession. Some of the men shouted fanatically towards the police station and the hotel, but there was a good deal of humorous banter, and many jokes were exchanged between demonstrators and those who watched from the kerbs.[8]

Between the demonstrators and the police station were approximately twenty terrified police, who had taken position between the palace and the corner of the Grande Bretagne Hotel that faced the square. Armed with little more than Italian carbines that were loaded with blank ammunition, the police had no illusions as to their fate if the crowd got out of control.

The police had every reason to fear for their lives, since having served under the jurisdiction of the occupation authorities, they had, rightly or wrongly, been labeled collaborators by the majority of Athenians. Although many Greek police officials had covertly assisted the resistance and the Allies, not enough time had passed since liberation to permit a clear distinction between the absolute traitor and the sunshine patriot. Indeed, some had had to wear the mask of the former in order to assist the latter.

Making matters worse, the provisional Greek government had failed to purge the security establishments and civil service of collaborators, whose continued presence now tainted every state apparatus. The government had argued that time was required to conduct a meticulous and judicious purge, but such reasoning was lost on the crowds advancing toward the center of the city on the morning of 3 December 1944. To the half-starved population of Greece, what truly mattered were symbols, and the gray uniforms of the police invoked the fear and agony of the occupation.

The handful of police positioned a few yards beyond their station were aware of this reality, and for the past several hours they had witnessed dozens of wounded fellow officers being carried off on stretchers into the station following clashes with groups of demonstrators. As the crowd got closer and closer, the fears of the police turned to panic, and some began to replace their blank rounds with live ammunition.

When the crowd advanced to within less than 100 yards of the police cordon, suddenly a man in military uniform ran out of the station and shouted, "Shoot the bastards!" He then dropped to one knee and began firing his gun.[9] A few seconds later the panic-stricken police followed suit. They did not fire in unison like a disciplined unit but discharged their weapons sporadically. A few of the officers hesitated for a few seconds; some remained transfixed by the spectacle before them, but one after another, each began to fire. The first ranks of the crowd cascaded onto the ground; the fortunate ones found protection behind trees or nearby walls, but most simply lay flat on the ground.

The shooting continued for approximately half an hour, and when it was over twenty-two of the demonstrators remained still, twelve of them dead.[10] A couple of brave souls gingerly darted out onto the square to drag back the bodies of their comrades, while others attempted to cover the wounded with their bodies. Once the firing ceased, rage instantly replaced the fear of the police and anguish over the casualties. The metamorphosis from a disciplined crowd into a frenzied mob took place suddenly, triggered by the sudden release of paralyzing fear and accelerated by anger. Almost straight away, hatred replaced terror, and according to Byford-Jones, "the demonstrators went mad. Thousands of people roared their threats and defiance at the police. It was the ugliest scene I had ever witnessed. . . . The demonstrators stood screaming and shouting, tearing open their shirts and crying, 'Shoot me, you cowards, you Papandreou hirelings.'"[11]

By noon, a second crowd of demonstrators had broken through the police cordons and thousands more soon joined them, until the square was jammed with almost 60,000 people.[12] The police retreated within the walls of their station and locked themselves in. Over the next thirty minutes, the remaining police barricades disintegrated, and most of the officers discreetly left the scene and sought refuge in nearby private homes or managed to reach the safety of the police headquarters. A few police stragglers near the square, however, were not as fortunate. They were seized by dozens of hands, punched, kicked, and spat upon. A torrent of verbal abuse drowned out their protestations of innocence. The lucky ones were dragged off to the nearest lamppost and lynched; some, however, could not be pried away from the clutches of the mob, which, intoxicated by raw animal savagery, tore the men literally limb to limb.[13]

The crowd in the square continued to shout slogans and to wave banners as well as Greek, American, British, and Russian flags. Regardless of the chaos and commotion, every effort was made to display EAM's affection for the United States and its president. The masses repeatedly shouted, "Roosevelt, Roosevelt," and carried numerous large flags of the Stars and Stripes. A group of boys pounced on an American officer passing by, raised him on their shoulders, and carried him over forty blocks until the man managed to kick himself free.[14]

In the midst of this angry mass of humanity, an old woman dressed in widow's black stood outside the police station and, like the furies of ancient myth, hurled threats and curses at the men inside the building. For some time she stubbornly stood leaning on her stick, her presence the incarnation of hatred, fear, and helplessness that had become a metaphor for Greece.

After several hours, the crowd quietly dispersed, and a squadron of British paratroopers advancing single file easily pushed the remaining demonstrators across the square. Despite the bitter fighting that would take place later, most firsthand accounts agree that initially there was no perceptible hostility toward the British. For the time being, and as far as most of the demonstrators were concerned, the killings were blamed on the police and the provisional government. After the last groups of participants and spectators abandoned Constitution Square, a strange silence engulfed the place, interrupted briefly by a crisp wind that playfully chased the odd bits of paper and brownish leaves across the pavement. Shortly, the skies darkened, and a heavy downpour lashed the bare streets of Athens, driving indoors the handful of lingering protestors and onlookers.

The police continued to remain within the confines of their station, while the man who had initiated the shooting in the square had disappeared. His identity remains a mystery and yet another strand in the folklore that eventually framed the story of the December Uprising. The questions still linger: Was he an agent provocateur of the left or of the right? Over the years no one has ever come forward to take credit or provide evidence concerning the identity of this man. The identity of the man who almost single-handedly provided the fuse for a sequence of events that catapulted Athens into the brutality of the December Uprising remains an enigma.[15]

The next day, Monday, 4 December, a sea of demonstrators held Athens hostage and this time took to the streets to protest the killings. In the morning, thousands of EAM supporters joined a long funeral procession led by several trucks carrying twenty-four makeshift coffins. Reactions to the funeral delineated the left and right wing cleavages of Athenian society, which also had permeated all of Greece. Although some Athenians mourned the death of Sunday's victims, others seized on the occasion to denounce the tactics of EAM. According to EAM's detractors, the display of twenty-four coffins was exaggerated and intentionally provocative; they also claimed that stones filled several of the coffins and that not all the corpses were those of the victims of Sunday.

At the cemetery, leading members of the KKE and EAM eulogized the dead and condemned the Greek government for Sunday's murders.[16] The demonstrators then headed back to the center of the city. Three young women at the head of the procession carried a long banner proclaiming, "When the people are in danger from tyranny they choose either chains or arms." The rest of the demonstrators chanted slogans, which were also inscribed on placards and carried along with Allied flags and blood-stained pieces of cloth as testimony of Sunday's casualties. Once again a disproportionate number of young women were at the forefront of the columns and, rendered almost hysterical with rage, spat curses and threats.[17]

The path for Monday's procession was carefully chosen to challenge the authority of the Papandreou government and, failing that, to provoke a reaction. The possibility of casualties was of little consideration to EAM or to the government—fresh killings would simply generate new martyrs for either side. Around noon, the demonstrators headed to Omonia Square, but before they could advance any further they came under fire from the police and members of the right-wing EDES and pro-monarchist X (pronounced "chi") organizations, who were positioned on the rooftops and in the outlying rooms of several hotels that faced the main streets.

This time, the demonstrators were flanked by armed ELAS cadres, who began firing back.[18] In a few minutes pandemonium broke out as most of the demonstrators started to run away from the shooting and scrambled for protection in the nearest doorways, store entrances, and any other possible sanctuary to shelter them from the gunfire. The main confrontation took place around the Metropolis Hotel, and by the afternoon, when British troops managed to restore order, forty more people had lost their lives and seventy were seriously wounded.[19]

These new shootings and killings had almost coincided with the gunfire of the reserve ELAS units opening the preliminary round of the battle of Athens. Remarkably, despite the threats and claims by the left of a mass uprising against the Papandreou regime, the initial crisis was a slow burn rather than a sudden eruption or even part of a carefully calculated strategy. The first choice of targets was the police, which the left identified with the provisional government and the last vestiges of the occupation. Over the next several hours the reserve ELAS units sparked dozens of small sieges against the police stations in Athens and Piraeus. By 3:00 P.M., ELAS had captured twenty-one of the twenty-four police stations in metropolitan Athens and had unraveled the tenuous compromises that had held the peace since liberation.

These attacks followed a familiar pattern, in which dozens of small, heart-wrenching dramas were played out. After a police station was captured, those not killed during the fighting were accused of collaboration and other crimes against the people. The police would plead innocence, but their entreaties fell on deaf ears. This exchange seldom lasted for more than a few minutes, and afterward the unfortunate officers were

THE GERMAN VICTORY PARADE IN ATHENS ON 7 MAY 1941. (Credit: *"Documents of occupation of the German propaganda"* From the files of journalist Takis Psarakis. Kastaniotis Publications, Athens 1980 page 27, Courtesy of Kastaniotis Publishers.)

"THE PEOPLE OF CRETE WANT THE GERMANS." A German propaganda photo of a demonstration in Crete on 2 August 1944. The German caption claims that the people of Crete have faith in the German occupation forces and proclaim a common struggle against the handful of murderers, bums, and rustlers roaming in the mountains and claiming to be fighting for Greek liberty. (Credit: *"Documents of occupation of the German propaganda"* From the files of journalist Takis Psarakis. Kastaniotis Publications, Athens 1980 page 131, Courtesy of Kastaniotis Publishers.)

THE NOTORIOUS POULOS BATTALION. Colonel Poulos was a senior Greek officer who during the occupation re-defined himself as a fierce anticommunist and agreed to fight for the Germans. His volunteers came from the dregs of Greek society. Poulos and his men killed, raped, and pillaged with little regard for anything except profit. After liberation he was tried in absentia and condemned to death. However, as was the case with most of the collaborators, he only served a few years in prison and was set free. (**Credit:** *"Documents of occupation of the German propaganda"* From the files of journalist Takis Psarakis. Kastaniotis Publications, Athens 1980 page 139, Courtesy of Kastaniotis Publishers.)

GERMAN STUKAS DIVE BOMB BRITISH POSITIONS ON THE ISLAND OF LEROS (NOVEMBER 1943). In the late summer of 1943, the British attempted to capture some of the Aegean Islands. Although the attempt failed, initially the British succeeded in liberating some of the Aegean Island. The operation, however, along with the invasion of Sicily and Italy, convinced the Greek resistance that liberation by the allies was imminent. (**Credit:** *"Documents of occupation of the German propaganda"* From the files of journalist Takis Psarakis. Kastaniotis Publications, Athens 1980 page 145, Courtesy of Kastaniotis Publishers.)

MILITARY OPERATIONS AGAINST THE BANDITS IN DECEMBER 1943. A photo of a German counterinsurgency operation at foothills of Mount Olympus. The Germans often referred to the Greek resistance fighters as bandits, terrorists, or gangsters. (**Credit:** *"Documents of occupation of the German propaganda"* From the files of journalist Takis Psarakis. Kastaniotis Publications, Athens 1980 page 155, Courtesy of Kastaniotis Publishers.)

THE WAR AGAINST THE BANDITS (DECEMBER 1943). A German unit is observing a Greek village suspected of harboring resistance fighters. Later the village was burned down in retaliation. (**Credit:** *"Documents of occupation of the German propaganda"* From the files of journalist Takis Psarakis. Kastaniotis Publications, Athens 1980 page 157, Courtesy of Kastaniotis Publishers.)

CAPTURED RUSSIANS EMPLOYED BY THE GERMANS. (**Credit:** Courtesy of Kostas Kouvaras, *"O.S.S., with the Central Committee of EAM: The American Secret Mission Perikles in Occupied Greece"* Athens: Exantas Publishers 1976 page 120.)

ARIS VELOUCHIOTIS. Velouchiotis was a communist and instrumental in organizing ELAS, the military wing of EAM. Velouchiotis was a harsh disciplinarian, feared by friend and foe alike. (**Credit:** Courtesy of Kostas Kouvaras, *"O.S.S., with the Central Committee of EAM: The American Secret Mission Perikles in Occupied Greece"* Athens: Exantas Publishers 1976 page 113.)

A WELL-ARMED AND WELL-DRESSED MEMBER OF ELAS. Usually, ELAS troops carried a variety of weapons (German, Italian, and British) and wore anything handy. Later, some units were dressed in military uniforms. (**Credit:** Courtesy of Kostas Kouvaras, *"O.S.S., with the Central Committee of EAM: The American Secret Mission Perikles in Occupied Greece"* Athens: Exantas Publishers 1976 page 117.)

MENI PAPAILIOU, ONE OF THE FIRST WOMEN TO JOIN THE RESISTANCE IN CENTRAL GREECE. (**Credit:** Courtesy of Kostas Kouvaras, *"O.S.S., with the Central Committee of EAM: The American Secret Mission Perikles in Occupied Greece"* Athens: Exantas Publishers 1976 page 121.)

WOMEN IN THE GREEK RESISTANCE. Although women played a prominent role in the resistance movement, only in ELAS women served and fought in the field as guerrilla troops. (**Credit:** Courtesy of the Public Record Office, Kew, Surrey, U.K.)

GERMAN PRISONERS LINING UP FOR THEIR MEAL AT THE ELAS POW CAMP IN AG-GRAPHA. During the occupation the Greek guerrilla bands captured more than 20,000 Germans. (**Credit:** Courtesy of Kostas Kouvaras, *"O.S.S., with the Central Committee of EAM: The American Secret Mission Perikles in Occupied Greece"* Athens: Exantas Publishers 1976 page 123.)

UNSUNG HEROES. Thousands of village women, using donkeys and mules, supplied the guerrilla bands. To avoid German patrols they used remote passes and steep mountain trails. (**Credit:** Courtesy of Kostas Kouvaras, *"O.S.S., with the Central Committee of EAM: The American Secret Mission Perikles in Occupied Greece"* Athens: Exantas Publishers 1976 page 121.)

KOSTAS KOUVARAS WAS ONE OF THE MANY YOUNG GREEK AMERICANS WHO JOINED THE OSS, AMERICA'S WARTIME INTELLIGENCE SERVICE. Unlike the British SOE, the Americans were inclined to sympathize with EAM-ELAS. (**Credit:** Courtesy of Kostas Kouvaras, *"O.S.S., with the Central Committee of EAM: The American Secret Mission Perikles in Occupied Greece"* Athens: Exantas Publishers 1976 page 114.)

THE FIRST GUERRILLA FORCES ENCOUNTERED BY THE OSS MISSION. In the background is the small boat that brought the Americans from Izmir, Turkey. (**Credit:** Courtesy of Kostas Kouvaras, *"O.S.S., with the Central Committee of EAM: The American Secret Mission Perikles in Occupied Greece"* Athens: Exantas Publishers 1976 page 119.)

KOSTAS KOUVARAS (CENTER) AND HIS RADIO OPERATOR, ALONG WITH OTHER MEMBERS OF THE OSS PERICLES MISSION. (**Credit:** Courtesy of Kostas Kouvaras, *"O.S.S., with the Central Committee of EAM: The American Secret Mission Perikles in Occupied Greece"* Athens: Exantas Publishers 1976 page 122.)

TWO ITALIAN PRISONERS. THE ITAL-
IANS FOUND EMPLOYMENT WITH THE
AMERICAN OSS MISSION IN THE
GREEK MOUNTAINS. After the first sup-
ply drop, the Americans were able to pro-
vide the Italians with shoes and clothes.
(**Credit:** Courtesy of Kostas Kouvaras,
*"O.S.S., with the Central Committee of
EAM: The American Secret Mission Perik-
les in Occupied Greece"* Athens: Exantas
Publishers 1976 page 118.)

SECOND FROM LEFT: Ioannis Siantos, leader of the Greek Communist Party with a senior
member of the Agrarian Party, was transported to Athens by sea just after liberation in October.
(**Credit:** Courtesy of Kostas Kouvaras, *"O.S.S., with the Central Committee of EAM: The American Secret Mission Perikles in Occupied Greece"* Athens: Exantas Publishers 1976 page 123.)

COLONEL GREGORY POPOV, THE HEAD OF THE SOVIET MISSION IN GREECE, AND GENERAL MANDAKAS, A SENIOR GREEK OFFICER WHO JOINED ELAS. (**Credit:** Courtesy of Kostas Kouvaras, *"O.S.S., with the Central Committee of EAM: The American Secret Mission Perikles in Occupied Greece"* Athens: Exantas Publishers 1976 page 123.)

YIANNIS IOANNIDIS, THE SECOND MOST POWERFUL MAN IN THE KKE, HIS WIFE DOMNA, AND YIANNIS ZEVGOS, ANOTHER INFLUENTIAL COMMUNIST LEADER, AT A PICNIC IN THE SUMMER OF 1944. Ioannides, an obscure barber before the occupation, helped to organize the dreaded OPLA units that are held responsible for many of the executions during the December Uprising. (**Credit:** Courtesy of Kostas Kouvaras, *"O.S.S., with the Central Committee of EAM: The American Secret Mission Perikles in Occupied Greece"* Athens: Exantas Publishers 1976 page 122.)

ONE OF THE MASS RALLIES ORGANIZED BY EAM AFTER LIBERATION. This one took place at the end of October. (**Credit:** Courtesy of Kostas Kouvaras, *"O.S.S., with the Central Committee of EAM: The American Secret Mission Perikles in Occupied Greece"* Athens: Exantas Publishers 1976 page 124.)

ONE OF THE MANY DEMONSTRATIONS FOLLOWING LIBERATION. Hundreds of actors and performers joined the Left-wing EAM as well as the Greek Communist Party. The large banner with the hammer and sickle carries the label: "The KKE Theater Organization." Another banner demands the arrest of collaborators (bottom right); the others proclaim "long live the KKE." (**Credit:** Poluvios Marsan, *Eleni Papadaki: A bright theatrical march with unexpected ending,* Third Edition, Kastaniotis Publications 2001, Athens, Greece page 336, Courtesy of Kastaniotis Publishers.)

GREEK ACTORS DEMONSTRATE ON BEHALF OF EAM. During the occupation, some actors became enthusiastic collaborators. Kaiti Economou (center) married a notorious traitor who betrayed dozens of Greeks hiding British soldiers. After liberation, Economou joined EAM and took part in the frenzy of denunciations against performers suspected of having ties with the Germans or the Greek puppet regimes. **Credit**: Poluvios Marsan, *Eleni Papadaki: A bright theatrical march with unexpected ending,* Third Edition, Kastaniotis Publications 2001, Athens, Greece page 327, Courtesy of Kastaniotis Publishers.)

ELENI PAPADAKI. Considered one of the best actresses in the Greek theater, she was executed by the KKE towards the end of the December Uprising. Her crime was her relationship to Ioannis Rallis, the last puppet premier of Greece. (**Credit**: Poluvios Marsan, *Eleni Papadaki: A bright theatrical march with unexpected ending,* Third Edition, Kastaniotis Publications 2001, Athens, Greece, page 14, Courtesy of Kastaniotis Publishers.)

BLOODSTAINS ON THE PAVEMENT AND SOME BANNERS FROM THE DEMONSTRATION OF 3 DECEMBER THAT LED TO THE OUTBREAK OF THE SECOND ROUND OF CIVIL WAR IN GREECE. (**Credit:** Courtesy of Kostas Kouvaras, *"O.S.S., with the Central Committee of EAM: The American Secret Mission Perikles in Occupied Greece"* Athens: Exantas Publishers 1976 page 124.)

MANY HOMES WERE DESTROYED IN ATHENS DURING THE DECEMBER UPRISING EITHER BY ELAS DYNAMITING HOUSES TO CREATE DEFENSIVE POSITIONS OR BY STRAFING FROM BRITISH AIRCRAFT. (**Credit:** Courtesy of Kostas Kouvaras, *"O.S.S., with the Central Committee of EAM: The American Secret Mission Perikles in Occupied Greece"* Athens: Exantas Publishers 1976 page 125.)

Μᾶς περνᾶνε γιὰ βλάκες

ANTI-COMMUNIST CARTOON, FROM A PAMPHLET, REPRESENTING A
COMMUNIST MAKING HIS APPEAL TO "FREE WORKERS." The caption at
the top reads "They think we're fools." (**Credit:** From "The Communist
Lie and the Truth," supplemental publication of *Ethniki Amyna* magazine;
courtesy of Mr. Konstantinos Antonakopoulos.)

ANTI-COMMUNIST CARTOON, FROM THE SAME PAMPHLET. The caption at the top reads "What happens to countries occupied by the Soviet." (**Credit**: From "The Communist Lie and the Truth," supplemental publication of *Ethniki Amyna* magazine; courtesy of Mr. Konstantinos Antonakopoulos.)

AN ELAS UNIT. (**Credit:** Courtesy of Kostas Kouvaras, *"O.S.S., with the Central Committee of EAM: The American Secret Mission Perikles in Occupied Greece"* Athens: Exantas Publishers 1976 page 119.)

A LARGE NUMBER OF PROFESSIONAL OFFICERS JOINED ELAS. After the war, most were excluded from the new Greek armed forces and often persecuted by the Right. The man in the middle with the pseudonym of Captain Loggos had been a major in the Greek army. (**Credit:** Courtesy of Kostas Kouvaras, *"O.S.S., with the Central Committee of EAM: The American Secret Mission Perikles in Occupied Greece"* Athens: Exantas Publishers 1976 page 120.)

shot outright or dragged to the nearest lamppost, tree, or telephone pole and hanged. In some instances British troops, still encountering little or no opposition from ELAS, managed to rescue the condemned. In others, the presence of British soldiers served to encourage the extreme elements to descend into greater human depravity.

In the port city of Piraeus, a British unit attempted to interpose itself between a police station and ELAS but faced overwhelming opposition. After a tense verbal exchange, the guerrillas dragged out several of their prisoners and in front of the British soldiers proceeded to gouge out the eyes of these hapless prisoners. The British soldiers gawked, transfixed by the horror unfolding before their eyes, and felt disgusted by their impotency to interfere. The screams of the police reverberated along the empty streets and shortly were reduced to low guttural moans, but the ordeal was far from over. For a few minutes, the ELAS executioners just grinned while savoring the spectacle of torment and the vulnerability of the British. Then, they took out butcher's cleavers and began to hack off the forearms of the blinded police and continued slashing until the bodies resembled heaps of human pulp. The agony, for victims and spectators, ended when the police were put out of their misery by bullets to their brains.[20] The tormentors exploited such sadistic brutality on several levels—as an exercise of their total superiority over their victims and, by forcing the British to observe the atrocity, a creation of de facto British participation.

Yet collectively or individually, other members of ELAS were also capable of remarkable demonstrations of human dignity and courage. During the early days of the fighting and before Ronald Scobie, the commander of all Greek and British forces in Greece, fully committed his forces to battle, a British squadron supported by one tank moved against the EAM-ELAS headquarters in Athens located on Constitution Square, across from the Grande Bretagne Hotel. After the unit captured the building and took a few prisoners, a lone ELAS guerrilla approached them and, ripping off his shirt, stood bare-chested in front of the tank, challenging the British tank to pass over him. In that brief moment, the conflict was no longer anonymous, and for the British tank crew the enemy had a face, commitment, and determination. The intimacy of the moment proved too much, and the embarrassed crew turned the tank around and abandoned the street to the ELAS soldier.[21]

Civil war, with few exceptions, quickly degenerates into brutal slaughter because the violence and killing are localized and personal. Athens in 1944 was a small city in which life revolved around equally small neighborhoods, where everyone knew just about everyone else. The killing, execution, or torture of one individual seldom remained isolated but rippled across many lives. Under these conditions, the emotional involvement of the participants was supercharged, and, as exemplified by the man standing in front of the tank, in Athens it was absolute. Fanaticism and revulsion to it dominated Athenian society during the December Uprising and continued throughout the next stage of the civil war from 1946 to 1949. In this jungle of extreme emotions, atrocities were common and not exclusive to one side or the other.

Another immediate target during the early days of the battle was the extreme right-wing X organization. ELAS units in the early afternoon of 4 December advanced on the X headquarters near the Temple of Theseus, close to the Acropolis, and laid siege to several buildings. X had approximately 1,000 members and was led by Colonel George Grivas, a fierce anticommunist and committed royalist. The organization had come into existence primarily in Athens during the last year of the occupation to counter the overwhelming influence of EAM and ELAS. The left had almost immediately denounced all members of X as reactionaries and collaborators, lumping them with the notorious German-led Security Battalions.

In a short time a fierce firefight ensued, and neither side expected nor was inclined to give quarter. The battle raged all day, and after several failed attempts to capture the X headquarters, ELAS began to bombard the building with mortars. Some structures caught fire, and by late afternoon flames from the burning buildings darted upward, licking the low-hanging clouds. In the evening the glow from the fires rested like a red crown over a dark and dreary Athens.

In another part of the city, a smaller contingent of X came under fire from ELAS and, in the ensuing fight, trapped innocent bystanders and local residents. On the afternoon of 4 December, Alexander Zaousis opened the door of his apartment on 85 Solonos Street, near the University of Athens. Before he could step outside, a crescendo of gunfire and the thud of grenades forced the young Athenian back inside. The shooting went on for hours, as thirty-five young members of X were trapped in the building at 108 Solonos Street by a superior ELAS force. The ELAS fighters attempted to penetrate the building from the roof but failed to break through. For the next twenty-four hours, the two sides exchanged sniper fire, using the nearby building as cover. The local residents were caught in between and had no choice but to wait out the battle.

The situation seemed to turn worse for Alexander and his family. One group of X snipers had positioned themselves on the roof of his apartment building, and by late night he heard angry voices outside calling on the X members to surrender; otherwise ELAS would use mortars. Fortunately for Alexander, the bombardment did not take place, but his ordeal was not over. Over the next several hours, the night was punctured by the short bursts of automatic weapons, the loud pop of rifle fire, and the frantic shouts of neighbors yelling, "We are unarmed," as X or ELAS gunmen kicked down doors or came crashing through windows in a deadly game of hide-and-seek.

The next day British troops, accompanied by armored cars, arrived on the scene and were able to rescue the X survivors, but not those who had been taken prisoner and were now held as trophies by ELAS. They were able to hear their colleagues being led to safety on British army trucks, but they had no doubt about what was to be their fate. When the last truck left, clanking along the empty streets of Athens, each one of the prisoners was made to kneel down. Some crossed themselves, others simply stared blankly, and then a man stood over each one and in sequence dispatched him with a single bullet to the back of the head.

Over the next several days the fighting in Athens was sporadic and ranged from intensive firefights between armed combatants to scenes of gut-wrenching individual trauma. Rigas Rigopoulos was a remarkable young man in his early twenties who witnessed one of several spectacles of violence and death. During the occupation, he and a group of close friends had established one of the most effective espionage cells in Athens and Piraeus. For two years, he had led the double life of a spy and lived in constant terror of arrest, torture, and execution at the hands of the Axis. By the summer of 1943, the Gestapo was closing in, and Rigas had barely managed to escape to the Middle East.

In December 1944, Rigas was back home, but before he could take up his life again, Sunday's crisis hijacked the promises of liberation. On the fourth day of the Uprising, he was walking along narrow Omiros Street, which led to the much broader Panepistimiou Boulevard, when he heard the characteristic gurgling sound of a mortar shell. "Incoming missiles," he yelled and took refuge beside an iron fence. A few seconds later two mortar shells exploded in the middle of Panepistimiou Boulevard in front of the National Bank of Greece.

Almost six decades later, sitting in the comfortable living room of his Kolonaki apartment, Rigas, with some difficulty, summons back the painful recollections of the first days of the crisis. He remembers that approximately ten people were hit: "Two British soldiers lay side-by-side, face down on the tramlines. Their brains were scattered all around. I tried to lift up a woman dressed in black. She did not appear to be wounded, but she was moaning slowly. She turned her head and died in my arms. From her open purse, a pension book fell out with pictures of her and her two small children." Rigas closed her eyes, and turning away he saw that "a young girl, dragging herself across the asphalt with her hands, was crying loudly and calling me by name. It was an acquaintance of mine from Mytilini Island. 'I can't stand up,' she was screaming. 'I can't breathe, I am going to die.' Her back was full of blood. Two other men helped me, and we carried her to the municipal hospital. She had a fragment in her spinal cord but did not die immediately. She lived for quite some time, paralyzed and in horrible pain."

Despite the passage of so many years, Rigas cannot easily excuse the actions of ELAS: "The Germans and Italians had never hit Athens. They respected the city and its historic monuments that shed light on humanity. This was not the case with ELAS. During the course of the Uprising, machine gun fire chirped from the windows and street corners. Snipers fired from behind shutters. Shells embroidered most of the facades of the houses. Every so often you heard explosions as ELAS was blowing up houses, collapsing them to block the streets."[22]

On 5 December, General Ronald Scobie, the commander-in-chief of all Allied and Greek forces in Greece, received orders from Churchill to commit British forces and prevent the left from gaining control of Athens. Scobie issued orders to ELAS to withdraw all its units from Athens within seventy-two hours and cease attacking police stations. The KKE and EAM ignored this demand, but beyond that, they were not certain how to proceed. It may be that George Siantos, the acting head of the KKE and an influential member of EAM's central committee, was expecting that the provisional government would collapse and Papandreou would resign, opening the door to negotiations and the establishment of a new regime that would include a large number of EAM and KKE ministers. More important, the ELAS forces would then not be demobilized until a new army was established, which would be free from the influence of the right.

Papandreou did submit his resignation, but Churchill would not hear of it. He ordered Rex Leeper, the British ambassador to Greece, to "force Papandreou to stand to his duty, and assure him he will be supported by all our forces if he does so. . . . Should he resign, he should be locked up till he comes to his senses."[23] According to Nigel Clive, at the time working for the SIS in Athens, Churchill used even stronger language and commanded Leeper to keep Papandreou as prime minister even if it meant "tying him to a chair and placing him under arrest until he changed his mind."[24]

However, Leeper was able to persuade Papandreou to change his mind without resorting to any drastic measures. This unexpected turn of events left the KKE and its partners in EAM in a quandary. The hard-liners were adamant to continue the battle, even if this meant fighting the British. The socialist members of EAM were not convinced and argued for compromise. After hours of uncertainty and heated arguments, both sides agreed to continue the war against the provisional government but not to engage British forces. How they believed they could achieve this is not clear.

Vasilis Bartziotas, the head of the Communist Party organization in Athens, claimed after the civil war that ELAS could have taken on the British as well as the Greek government forces: "Again we had all the people of Athens with us and we would have fought in the capital for the lives of our children and for our homes." Bartziotas argued, "This was the most ideal moment . . . to strike immediately against the forces for the reaction and the British and seize power. . . . We had then for the third time—after 12 and 15 October 1944—the forces to seize power."[25]

However, Thanasis Hadzis, one of the leaders of the KKE during this period, was less sanguine about the prospects of a quick victory. He writes that the KKE faced two serious problems with respect to an armed confrontation. First, there were the reactions of EAM's followers to Sunday's bloody confrontation; although EAM supporters had been reassured by the widespread outrage against the police and the Papandreou regime, the majority of EAM's supporters still considered the British allies and friends. After the shooting was over on Sunday, thousands of demonstrators continued to wave Allied flags and shout, "Long live Churchill," "Long live Roosevelt," and "Long live Stalin." This open enthusiasm for the leaders of the major Allies, according to Hadzis, indicated that Athenians only held the police responsible for the killings. Hadzis also states, "The other disappointing factor was the paralysis that took hold of the masses once British troops arrived on the scene and saved the murderers, which prevented any further action against the provocateurs and the police who were shooting at the demonstrators from the hotels in Omonia Plateia."[26]

Hadzis believed that the ELAS reserve units in Athens were not ready, and it would have taken some time to prepare them for war against the "mighty British Empire." Hadzis also realized, he later wrote, "On 4 December the popular movement and its political and military leadership were not ready for a general armed revolt. It was imperative to allow for some time to pass and to acquire tangible evidence . . . in order to convince the masses, that it was necessary to fight the allies when they [the Allies] violate their national independence."[27] The bravado of communists such as Bartsiotas and the tempered analysis provided by Hadzis are conveniently reflected in their memoirs, which were written years later, to explain or absolve them of their part in the ultimate failure of the Uprising. Nevertheless, Hadzis' account, in particular, does offer some insight into the reluctance of the KKE leadership to rely on the support of the Greek population for a civil war. More than anything else, this lack of confidence that EAM's followers would participate in an uprising that also included fighting the British retarded the KKE's ability to launch an all-out offensive in the first weeks of December.

For a short while, this peculiar situation placed the British troops in the awkward position of being simultaneously bystanders and participants. They were seldom fired upon, at least in the first days of the crisis, but had to confront ELAS units daily. In some instances they tried to disarm ELAS members; in others it was a matter of persuading them to hand over prisoners or abandon captured buildings. Frequently British officers were obliged to take part in long-winded discussions with representatives of ELAS or the neighborhood EAM and KKE bosses. Most of these men, especially junior officers or those recently arrived in Athens, often found themselves in a bizarre and surreal environment.

Richard O'Brien had studied law at Cambridge and in 1940 joined the army. For three years he fought in North Africa and Italy, and in early December he and his company were transferred to Athens. After the hard fighting in Italy, O'Brien was not quite certain why his unit might be forced to fight ELAS, an organization that ostensibly had been an ally only a few days earlier. In his unpublished, and partially completed memoirs, O'Brien captures some of the frustration, confusion, and strain that these soldiers underwent during their stay in Athens and Greece. A few days before ELAS escalated the battle to include the British, O'Brien was ordered, despite his protests, to disarm an ELAS unit in the Piraeus area. He arrived at the ELAS headquarters, located in a small house near the sea, with only an interpreter. According to his account:

We began by negotiating. Nothing is more of a strain when it is not certain whether the other side is going to shoot you or talk to you. . . . My interpreter and I were ushered into a small room and given seats around a table. The door was kept closed throughout, but during the meeting, it was regularly opened by a guard outside, who would pass in dirty pieces of paper, and mutter furtively to persons inside the room. This comic, if rather sinister, sideshow provided light relief throughout our somewhat tense and protracted discussion. The argument was not important. It

followed the obvious lines and went round in circles. I said we did not
wish to fight, the Greek people were our allies, not our enemies, for were
we not both fighting the Germans? They admitted this; but said that
they must keep their arms to defend themselves against their own fascists. They maintained that Britain had no right to interfere in Greek affairs. To begin with, I more than held my own. In the room were three or
four elderly amiable civilians, who were ready to agree with me, and had
not wished to fight us. There was one soldier, a smartly dressed officer in
a blue turn-out, who obviously took no interest in politics but only enjoyed parading around in his uniform; he was ready to do what anyone
told him. My defeat was caused by a civilian who came in later, a small-
ish mean-looking man with a sallow complexion and spectacles. He was
a true Communist—narrow, fanatical, embittered; and he swayed over
to his side many who before were in two minds. He made no attempt to
argue but monopolized all attention by a stream of impassionate ha-
rangues, during which he banged on the table, glared feverishly about
him, and uttered the usual fatuous clichés "death to the fascists", "freedom to the people", "liberty for the masses". He was so effective in turning everyone against me that I began to feel like a secret agent in a
Hitchcock film who suddenly realizes he is about to be found out. I lay
back in my chair trying to appear cool but wondering if I was going to
get out of the place alive. In the end, we concluded amiably enough, but
they refused to hand over their arms, and so my efforts had failed.[28]

To many Athenians, the outbreak of hostilities was almost a relief
from the atmosphere of gloom and tension that had gripped the capital
for the previous two weeks. A great deal had taken place in Greece during the last three years, and feelings across the political spectrum had
run very high. The Greeks had suffered occupation, famine, reprisals,
and even a small genocide. These cataclysms had brutalized and desensitized Greek society—people became harder, almost pitiless, and too easily tolerant of killings and torture.

The infighting between the left-wing EAM-ELAS and the other resistance as well as with various paramilitary organizations, including the anticommunist quisling formations, had spawned bitter hatred and even a

degree of sadism. The early rhetoric of the resistance claiming liberation, popular rule, and appeals to patriotism had, over the course of the occupation, been dipped in blood, and the outrages committed by the left and right could not easily be forgotten or forgiven. These sentiments promised that the December Uprising would raise the threshold of cruelty in the upcoming battle.

The events that led to the second round of civil war not only epitomized the mistrust and fear that permeated relations between the left-wing resistance and the Greek government-in-exile but fundamentally reflected a manifestation of the collapse of civil society. The occupation had robbed Greece of the institutions that ameliorated political differences in place of vigilantism, leaving the raw power of the gun as the arbitrator for legitimate authority.

In this environment, particularly in the countryside, what passed for justice seeped out of the politics of the resistance. Security was hostage to political affiliation, on the indulgence of one or another of the guerrilla bands, and at the mercy of the occupation forces. Neutrality was tantamount to collaboration. The anarchy of violence ruled the shambles of Greek society. There was little time in the six weeks following liberation to rebuild the political and economic infrastructure of the country and, more important, to start healing the trauma of hate and division inflicted by the occupation.

Amid the ruins of postwar Greece people expected relief from hunger and a modicum of justice, especially punishment for the collaborators. When the provisional government failed to address these critical priorities, there were few avenues to challenge the decisions of the ramshackle state or to seek redress for past wrongs. The followers of the left-wing resistance and the KKE found recourse for their grievances in the street, and when that was denied to them, they accepted the application of violence as a viable alternative.

The provisional government, for its part, daunted by almost insurmountable problems, could only rely on British troops to uphold it as a legitimate authority. In so doing, Papandreou contributed to the transformation of the British troops from liberators into an occupation army. Churchill's directive to General Scobie—"Do not however hesitate to act as if you were in a conquered city where a local rebellion is in progress"—underscored not only the preponderance of Britain's sway over Greek affairs, but the helplessness and ultimately the irrelevance of the provisional government.[29]

A contributing factor to the estrangement between the postliberation government and the rest of society was that the political regime that now represented the state had not shared the experience of occupation. Concurrently, for three and a half years the puppet regimes, foisted on Greece by the Axis, had gutted the credibility of government. Although individual members of the government had lived in Greece during those dark days and later made their way to the Middle East, the government as an institution, and the monarchy, operated in exile and as an institution remained alienated from the Greek world. In addition, during the occupation, contact between the Greek government-in-exile and the resistance was sporadic at best and overshadowed by the British. The SOE maintained almost exclusive control over contact with the resistance groups, further marginalizing the official representatives of the Greek state.

For the most part, the resistance supplanted the role of the state, especially the KKE-dominated EAM, by creating a civil and military infrastructure, wherever possible, and assuming the traditional trappings of governmental institutions. In the mountain communities of central and northern Greece, away from the immediate reach of the Axis, the KKE, through EAM, had established a parastate that still remained entrenched after liberation. As a result, in December 1944, Greece was shared by two societies: the small mountain villages that enjoyed a measure of freedom from the Axis, and the left-wing resistance underground groups in the larger cities. In contrast, large segments of urban dwellers as well as parts of the Peloponnesus remained loyal to traditional authority and hostile to the KKE and its front organizations. These two faces of Greece effectively confronted each other over the next thirty-three days and continued to remain segregated long after the end of the fighting.

Despite these cleavages and mistrust, the question remains: Was the bloodletting of December inevitable? The spark that set off the chain of events that led to Sunday's demonstration and killings was the failure or

inability of the Papandreou government to balance the problems of security and the strategic interests of the British against the suspicions of
the left. The critical issue was control of the Greek army and police
forces. The side that commanded the military and security apparatus
would also dominate the state. The KKE and EAM had proposed that
all armed forces in Greece be demobilized and a new army be created by
conscripting eligible men from the general population. In practical
terms this meant that the ELAS guerrillas, as well as any other resistance
bands, would turn in their arms and return home. At the same time, the
Greek government would order the Third Mountain Brigade and the
Sacred Company to disband.

The Papandreou government, with the exception of the EAM and
KKE ministers, was reluctant to lose the only two loyal military formations at its disposal. The British, for their part, were not prepared to
surrender to the KKE and EAM any military or political advantage.
Churchill and the British Foreign Office were suspicious of all resistance
organizations in Greece and viewed them as radical and revolutionary
groups that would undermine the traditional establishment in the country
as well as threaten British interests in the region. For Churchill, only the
return of the Greek monarchy would guarantee stability and legitimacy.

Although this claim is not substantiated by any documentation, some
historians as well as postwar accounts of these events claim that Papandreou at one point agreed to disband the Third Mountain Brigade and
the Sacred Squadron but was prevented from doing so by the British.
There is no doubt that Churchill was opposed to this disbanding and
had written to the Foreign Office that ". . . the disbandment of the
Greek Brigade would be a disaster of the first order."[30] The Foreign Office, in turn, had transmitted Churchill's view to Leeper, the British ambassador in Athens, who passed it on to the Greek prime minister.
According to several accounts, Papandreou was inclined to accept the
demobilization of all volunteer units but was unable to convince either
the British or the right-wing elements in and out of the government.[31]

On 28 November, the three EAM ministers (Ioannis Zevgos, Alexander Svolos, and Ilias Tsirimokos) in the provisional government, at the
suggestion of Papandreou, proposed another compromise in which the

new army would consist of one brigade of ELAS, another of equal strength to be recruited from the Third Mountain Brigade, the Sacred Squadron, and EDES—all other Greek forces would be disbanded by 10 December. The cabinet accepted the compromise, but twenty-four hours later, on 29 November, Zevgos, one of the EAM ministers, returned to Papandreou's office, accused him of bad faith, and withdrew the offer, demanding once again that all forces be disbanded, including the Third Mountain Brigade and the Sacred Squadron. What caused this about-face is not clear. The explanation provided by the KKE and EAM is that they withdrew their consent because Papandreou was planning to trick them, by excluding the Third Mountain Brigade and the Sacred Squadron from the total strength of the proposed new brigades.[32] Papandreou rejected the KKE's demands outright.

Another explanation for the December Uprising is that it was a show of strength organized by George Siantos, the acting general secretary of the KKE. Siantos gambled that the small number of British forces in Greece, as well as the Third Mountain Brigade and the Sacred Squadron, would not have been sufficient to prevent ELAS from gaining control of and dominating Athens, which effectively meant dominating all of Greece. If that was the case, it is not clear why the KKE leadership decided to handicap its effort by committing only the reserve elements of ELAS in Athens, while the most experienced and best-equipped units were kept away from the capital during the first critical weeks of the fighting. All accounts agree that the December Uprising was triggered by the clash between the demonstrators and the police on that fateful Sunday, but the recourse to a full-scale war, rather than just an attempt at retaliation by the left, is more complicated. It is all the more remarkable because the communists had accepted a compromise that had enabled the British to send forces into Greece after the German withdrawal, as well as the decision of the KKE and EAM to participate in a provisional government led by George Papandreou.

On 26 September 1944 in Caserta, Italy, the Greek Government of National Unity along with all the resistance organizations had concluded an agreement to facilitate the transition from occupation to liberation, which also included that all guerrilla bands and Allied forces in Greece would be placed under Scobie's command for the duration of the war or until a new Greek army was established. With the stroke of a pen, the KKE and the other left-wing organizations had surrendered their military advantage in Greece and handed over control of the country to their opponents.

In the summer of 1944, the KKE-dominated ELAS numbered over 50,000 well-armed men and women and could have easily opposed the landing of British troops in Greece. Under these circumstances, the British would have been obliged either to fight ELAS after the Germans left, creating a public relations nightmare for Churchill as well as for the Allies, or to accept the inevitable and leave the KKE in control of the country.[33] Either option presented serious difficulties, but ultimately the KKE, thanks to Soviet intervention, went along with the Caserta Agreement.

The Soviet contribution to the sticky negotiations between the British and the Greek Government of National Unity with the KKE and the left-wing resistance took place in the Middle East and culminated, according to some sources, with the sudden arrival of a Russian military mission, headed by Colonel Grigori Popov, to occupied Greece on the night of 25 July 1944.[34] For several months following the winter of 1944, the Soviets and the British were working toward developing some type of compromise over their mutual interests in the Balkans, pending the German pullout from the region. The only drawback to a potential Soviet-British understanding was whether the United States would accept the division of the region into spheres of influence.

During the negotiations, the Soviet embassy in Cairo was gingerly trying to send a message to the KKE that the Russians preferred an amicable resolution of the Greek situation. In July 1944, Nikolai Novikov, the Soviet ambassador in Cairo, recommended to Svolos, the head of the PEEA (Political Committee of National Liberation), that EAM should join the Greek Government of National Unity. The same message was conveyed to Petros Rousos, the KKE representative in Cairo, by the Soviet attaché, who was told to make sure that the ambassador's view was transmitted to the left-wing resistance in Greece.

In a recent analysis, Peter Stavrakis states that once the Soviets received direct confirmation of American willingness to accept a British-Soviet agreement over the Balkans, it became essential for Stalin to make sure that the KKE did not disrupt the delicate horse trading between the Allies. Stavrakis suggests, "A plausible hypothesis is that Stalin felt compliance would be guaranteed only by the dispatch of a military mission to the partisan strongholds in the mountains of Greece, to present the KKE with direct instructions to adopt a more conciliatory policy."[35]

At the very least, the Popov mission to the KKE and ELAS underscored the Russian ambivalence toward the Greek communists while its presence in Greece alarmed and surprised the British. Previously, in a gesture of Allied solidarity, the British had invited the Soviets to join the Allied military mission to the Greek resistance, but the Russians declined. Despite earlier indications that the Soviets were prepared to reach an accommodation over the Greek issue, the arrival of the Popov mission came unexpectedly, catching the British unprepared. The Soviets had flown from Yugoslavia to an Anglo-American base in Barri, Italy, and then asked permission from the British authorities to make a test flight over the Adriatic. Instead, once in the air, the Russian plane proceeded to Greece and landed on a makeshift airfield in Neraidia, western Thessaly, near the location of the ELAS headquarters and the headquarters of the KKE. The Greek communists were jubilant, but after the initial celebrations and talks with Popov, they quickly became downcast.

There are several accounts of the Soviet mission, one provided by Nicholas Hammond, the British liaison officer with ELAS, and the other by the Greek communists who were present in Neraida or who participated in the subsequent meetings. According to Hammond, the Soviets were cordial but refused to be drawn into a discussion on the purpose of their mission or on any political subject; the same restrictions applied to Hammond and West, his American counterpart. Both parties were limited to polite chitchat and exchanging pleasantries. On the second day of their arrival Hammond organized a lunch in honor of the Russian visitors, and afterward Popov reciprocated with an invitation to tea. "The tea," recollects Hammond, consisted of a saucer of tomato slices, a bottle of whiskey from Italy, a flask of vodka, another of brandy from Russia, and the reserva, a demijohn of ouzo. Popov explained to me that it was the Russian practice to drink their tea "bottoms up", at one gulp. We sat down and he poured out a small tumbler of whiskey for me first, as I had been longest in the Greek mountains. Then he toasted, "long live Churchill!" We duly gulped it down. As I emerged from the shock, I heard "long live Roosevelt!", reached out to find my tumbler of Vodka, and gulped that down. From very far off I heard the cry, "long live Stalin!", groped blindly for my tumbler, and downed it like the others. I awoke in the grey light of dawn in a strange room. I went next door and there in the room of the tea-party lay the three Russians flat on the floor, fully dressed with their boots on. In another room I discovered West, who was lying fully clad on a bed with his boots off and his socks on. I had some difficulty in rousing him. He opened a bleary eye, remarked "Say bo, we said nothing," and he went to sleep again.[36]

It is evident that the attempt by the Russians, and undoubtedly Hammond and West, to use alcohol to pry information resulted in a draw. However, what transpired between the Soviets and the KKE remains controversial, and no firsthand account so far has been produced. If Popov's mission was to assess the fighting capability of ELAS and the extent of the KKE's sway over Greece, it is apparent from the few comments he did make to the British officers that he did not develop a high opinion of the capability of the left-wing resistance. C. M. Woodhouse, the head of the British Military Mission in Greece, writes that:

ELAS, who had expected the Soviet Mission to bring manna from heaven, found Colonel Popov unable to supply his own party with vodka, let alone ELAS with gold, arms and ammunition. On the other hand, the Soviet Mission, which expected to find an army of at least the same kind, if not in magnitude, as Tito's partisans, found a rabble thinly veiled by an elaborate centralized command.[37]

The unwillingness or inability of the Soviets to replace the British as the arsenal of the left-wing resistance was a severe blow to the Greek communists. The KKE, through its newspaper, *Rizospastis,* had been exalting the success of the Red Army against the Germans and was anticipating that in a matter of time the Russians would liberate the Balkans and Greece. No doubt for many of the KKE leadership the arrival of the Soviet mission was a prelude to a Soviet advance on Greece, but Popov's cool reaction to their enthusiasm dashed any hopes of Soviet liberation.

Most of the KKE accounts, on the other hand, vary about the sequence of events and play down the influence of the Soviets. There are differences on the dates of the Popov Mission, and whether it influenced the KKE's decision to join the Government of National Unity and later to accept the Caserta Agreement remains murky. Yiannis Ioannidis, a key member of the politburo and second in command of the KKE, in a long interview, states that when he broached the subject of ELAS fighting the British with the political representative of the Soviet Mission, Colonel Tschernichev, the Russian made a "face," making it clear that the Soviets would not endorse such a move.[38] Petros Rousos summarized the discussions with Popov more directly:

> What we extracted from exchanging opinions with the Soviets—and from the subsequent course of events—was that, the Greek issue, because of Churchill's position, was a thorn in the alliance against Hitler and that, according to all indications, from a strategic point of perspective we would have a serious problem confronting the imperialism of the British (and American) "allies."[39]

Indeed, all of the published accounts of the Greek communists who wrote about the Popov Mission agree that the Russian delegation discouraged any notions of the KKE's using ELAS to take over the country. Vasos Georgiou, the editor of *Rizospastis,* and a principal assistant to George Siantos, provides recent testimony about these events and, in a roundabout way, conveys the elation and eventual disappointment generated by the arrival of the Soviets:

> We waited for them [the Soviets] with great anticipation and we welcomed them very warmly in the early afternoon, as the real liberators.

. . . We were all strong pro-Soviets because we understood the decisive contribution of the Soviet Union in the struggle to destroy Hitlerism and we linked our liberation to the advancement of the Red Army in the Balkans.

However, the leadership of the resistance, even though it took care to hide this [the nature of the Soviet mission], did not calculate well. Because it became apparent very quickly that the Soviet Mission was not sent to PEEA—with which it would naturally have relations—but accredited to the General Headquarters of ELAS and that it was not independent, but represented an echelon of the greater Soviet Military Mission of the Red Army to Tito's Popular Liberation Army.[40]

Georgiou, as in some of the KKE published accounts, simply cannot bring himself to say that the Soviets made it known that the KKE had to cooperate with the British and the Greek government-in-exile. Instead, he writes that the Soviets were there in a narrow military capacity and therefore the mission was only accredited to ELAS and not PEEA or any other political organization. The fact that the Popov mission didn't include a political role indicated how noncommittal Soviet government was toward the Greek resistance, whereas in the case of Yugoslavia, the Soviets backed Tito comprehensively.[41] However, what is certain is that immediately following the arrival of the Soviets, the KKE and EAM suddenly decided to join the Government of National Unity as well as place ELAS under British command.

Until Soviet documents are released, the exact purpose of the Popov Mission will remain a partial mystery, and an analysis of its impact must be based, to some extent, on speculation.[42] Either Stalin had decided to abandon any hope of including Greece within the Soviet system and sent Popov to discourage the KKE from any adventures that may have led to a clash with the British or conversely, the Russian officer's report persuaded the Soviet dictator that the Greek communists were not in a position to take over and keep control of Greece after the Germans departed. Unknown to both the KKE and the British liaison officers in Greece were the negotiations between Stalin and Churchill over the division of the Balkans into Soviet and British spheres of influence.

These discussions culminated with the so-called Percentages Agreement between Churchill and Stalin in Moscow on 9 October 1944. The minutes of the meeting between the two leaders indicate that after dealing with the problem of Poland, Churchill turned to Stalin and said:

There were two countries in which the British had particular interest. One was Greece. He was not worrying about Rumania. That was very much a Russian affair and the terms which the Soviet Government had proposed were reasonable and showed much statecraft in the interests of general peace in the future. But in Greece it was different. Britain must be the leading Mediterranean Power and he hoped Marshal Stalin would let him have the first say about Greece in the same way as Marshal Stalin about Rumania. Of course, the British Government would keep in touch with the Soviet Government.[43]

According to the minutes, Stalin acknowledged Churchill's position with regard to Greece and said that it was a "serious matter for Britain, when the Mediterranean route was not in her hands." He agreed with the Prime Minister that "Britain should have the first say in Greece."[44] Following this amicable exchange, Churchill writes:

The moment was apt for business, so I said "let us settle about our affairs in the Balkans. Your armies are in Rumania and Bulgaria. We have interests, missions, and agents there. Don't let us get at cross-purposes in small ways. So far as Britain and Russia are concerned, how would it do for you to have ninety per cent predominance in Rumania, for us to have ninety per cent say in Greece, and go fifty-fifty about Yugoslavia?"[45]

While this was being translated, Churchill produced what he called a "naughty document" showing a list of Balkan countries and the proportion of interest in them of the Great Powers.[46] Churchill then pushed this paper across the table to Stalin, who had by then heard the translation. After a brief pause, recalls Churchill,

He took his blue pencil and made a large tick upon it, and passed it back to us. After this there was a long silence. The penciled paper lay in the center of the table. At length I said, "Might it not be thought rather cynical if it seemed we had disposed of these issues, so fateful to millions of people in such an offhand manner? Let us burn the paper." "No you keep it," said Stalin.[47]

The hopes, ambitions, sacrifices, and pain inflicted by the Greek communists on their compatriots were consigned to a scrap of paper in which the British prime minister had sealed the fate of the Balkans until almost the end of the twentieth century.

The fortunes of the Greek communists and the left-wing resistance with respect to the immediate postwar period, insofar as Stalin was concerned, took second place to the security and grand strategy of the Soviet Union. Beyond that, anything was possible after the Allied victory over Nazi Germany and Imperial Japan. In early September 1949, Stalin confided to Nikos Zachariadis that he could not advance the Red Army into Greece in 1944 because he did not wish to clash with the British; besides, the Soviet Union did not have a navy for such an undertaking. It is not known, and unlikely, whether Stalin also told Zachariadis about the Percentages Agreement.[48]

Churchill had informed Roosevelt that the arrangements with Stalin did not amount to a permanent division of the Balkans into spheres of influence but were intended as a temporary war measure to facilitate the Russian and British presence in the region. Regardless of the sop to the Americans, Churchill had no illusions that he and Stalin had now determined the future for the region. At their historic meeting in Moscow, both men were anxious to avoid the appearance of dividing the spoils of war. Churchill suggested to Stalin that "it was better to express these things in diplomatic terms and not to use the phrase 'dividing into spheres,' because the Americans might be shocked." Nevertheless, as long as he and Marshal Stalin understood each other he could explain matters to the U.S. president.[49] This caution did not diminish Churchill's imperial moment, especially as Britain by 1944 was quickly becoming a junior partner in the

Grand Alliance, nor Stalin's pragmatism in reaching an accommodation with an empire that was soon to be eclipsed by the United States.

The KKE learned about the Percentages Agreement in 1952, which raises an intriguing question: Had they known earlier, would they have acted otherwise in December 1944? As devout communists and Stalinists, the KKE leadership had to conform its policies to those of the Soviet Union and accept doing so without knowing all the facts. The needs of the Soviet motherland superseded the immediate ambitions of the Greek communists, and the KKE had little choice but to toe the line blindly, even when the leadership could not even be certain what that line was.

Under the leadership of Nikos Zachariadis, the policies of the KKE were practically dictated by the Soviet Union via the Third Communist International. Zachariadis had been Moscow's choice to head the KKE in the 1930s, and he managed to oversee the Bolshevization of the party during this critical period. After he became general secretary of the central committee in 1934, he succeeded in terminating the internal divisions that had plagued the KKE almost from its inception. After this change, the senior leadership of the Communist Party identified exclusively with Moscow and any deviation resulted in purges.

The occupation, however, altered the dynamic of the KKE and shifted the direction of the party to other men, especially after Zachariadis remained in prison and was subsequently transferred to Dachau concentration camp and thus took no part in the events that followed. George Siantos, one of the senior cadres who had evaded capture, took over the direction of the KKE, and thanks to him the communists established the mass-based EAM, which quickly dominated the resistance.

Siantos, a tobacco worker by profession, unlike Zachariadis and Markos Vaphiadis was a mainland Greek from a small village in Thessaly, central Greece. To those who met him, he appeared less a fanatic communist leading a revolution than a kindly village elder. A self-made man with little formal education beyond the fourth grade, he started working from the age of thirteen as a tobacco worker in Karditsa and at fifteen joined the Tobacco Workers' Union. Within a short time he became an active member and took part in strikes, demonstrations, and riots. From

1911 to 1920 Siantos served in the Greek army and rose to the rank of sergeant. In the early 1920s he joined the KKE, and during this ideologically turbulent period he was a key player in the factionalism and infighting that plagued the party.

He survived the purges, but he was demoted in the party hierarchy and lost the post of general secretary. In 1934 he was downgraded to a substitute member of the politburo, but a year later he was reinstated as a full member. After 1936, he was one of the few KKE leaders to escape arrest and thus, by default, became part of the handful of senior KKE leaders in a position to rebuild the party during the early period of the occupation. Friends and enemies alike described him as a mild-mannered and soft-spoken individual. He was a dedicated workaholic, with simple tastes and few pleasures, who took comfort in chain-smoking an endless supply of cigarettes over strong cups of coffee.[50] C. M. Woodhouse, who spent three years in Greece trying to counter the influence of the KKE in the resistance, describes him: "Ruthless and ambitious though he was, Siantos had a simple bonhomie and good humor. He was a tobacco worker, like many other communists, but he seemed to have no bitterness about his hard life."[51]

To the party faithful he was known as "O Yeros," the old man. According to Vasos Georgiou, who served for a time as Siantos' aide at KKE headquarters in the remote mountains, Siantos was monkish in his habits and endowed with almost limitless patience. In contrast to some of the other, more sophisticated KKE leaders, most of whom had grown up in cities and large towns, he had a better understanding of the Greek villager and an appreciation of the power of nationalist sentiment in Greece. Siantos understood that in order for the party to exploit the opportunities created by the war, it was necessary to drop the narrow and dogmatic communist rhetoric and replace it with moderate and nationalist slogans that appealed to mainstream society. The establishment of EAM as a patriotic and pan-Hellenic organization gave the KKE legitimacy and placed it on a par with the mainstream political parties. Despite EAM's invitation to all to join a common front to fight the Axis, the traditional parties viewed EAM as a front for the KKE and declined to participate—they failed, however, to offer an alternative. This omission enabled the KKE, through EAM, to establish a predominant and powerful influence over the armed resistance and to hijack the intellectual discourse over the future political reorganization of Greece.

The KKE, under the direction of Siantos, saw the possibilities offered by the establishment of guerrilla forces—specifically, that they could be used to impose a political settlement in the aftermath of liberation. In October 1943, ELAS was not only fighting the Axis but also attempting to absorb all other partisan units in the field so that at the moment of liberation the Allies—and the British in particular—would be confronted by a unified resistance movement.

Later in the same year, Ioannidis commissioned a military plan designed to take over Athens once the German army withdrew. Ioannidis claimed that ELAS could have secured Athens and would have been in an advantageous position to oppose the arrival of the British. He had proposed this strategy to Siantos and the other KKE leaders, but at that time they were not interested.[52] Ioannidis' hindsight is obviously self-serving and a means of distancing himself from Siantos and from the KKE policies that ultimately led to failure and defeat. In the post-mortems conducted by the KKE after the December Uprising, responsibilities for the Caserta Agreement, participation in the Government of National Unity, the decision not to oppose the arrival of British troops, and the December Uprising were all consigned to Siantos and his closest associates. Sharing the grave with Siantos is the ghost that the KKE did not consider: the possibility of taking over the country just after liberation. According to Ole Smith, "It is one of the KKE's cherished fairy tales that at the time of the country's liberation from the Germans there were no plans for a military takeover and that the party did not face squarely the question of political power."[53]

After Siantos' mysterious death in 1947, his opponents went so far as to accuse him not only of incompetence, but also of being an agent of the security services, which they argued explained why he went along with the Caserta Agreement and intentionally lost the Battle of Athens. In October 1950, at the Third Party Conference he was denounced by Zachariadis as a "traitor and an agent of the class enemy." In the same year Zachariadis wrote that the strategy of the KKE was:

the strategy of Siantos, that is the strategy of capitulation to the English, the strategy which did not serve or speed up the victory of the peoples revolution in Greece, the strategy which delayed and finally shattered the revolution, the strategy which promoted the plans of the British, the restoration of the bourgeois-feudal power, the return to the regime of foreign dependence.[54]

Vassilis Bartziotas, at the same conference, added his own condemnation of Siantos, as well as invoking the theme of grave errors, betrayal, and treason:

On October 12, 1944 we could easily have seized power with the forces of the First Army Corps of ELAS alone (that is the 20,000 Elasites of Athens and Piraeus). We did not seize power because we did not have a correct line, because we all vacillated, including me. . . . Thus, although we had decided on armed insurrection, beginning in September 1944, instead of going ahead, instead of organizing the struggle for power, instead of seizing power, we capitulated and kept order.[55]

These allegations, of course, are far from the truth and are part and parcel of the ritual demonization of those purged from the KKE. Of course, there was more than one strategy contemplated by different members of the KKE leadership for achieving power.

The KKE, despite its reputation for organization and ideological cohesiveness, could not remain monolithic and survive as an organization during the occupation. The successful decentralization of the party also resulted in a certain degree of fragmentation at the top, which created several centers of decision making. Siantos and Ioannidis informally shared the leadership of the KKE, but neither had the influence nor the authority to impose his will on all aspects of policy. The two men represented different elements and strains within the party and by virtue of this duality attracted separate followings. Ioannidis is often described as the hard-liner and along with Aris Velouchiotis advocated a revolutionary approach in dealing with the period following liberation.

Siantos was equally committed to revolutionary means but, as mentioned above, was more sensitive to Greek nationalism and the peculiarities of the Greek peasant and worker. Most Greeks were small farmers, and those in the industrial sector were too few and too disorganized to be effectively mobilized. Peasants who had land or wanted land were not well disposed to the KKE's plans for collectivization. "In general," writes Woodhouse, "the devotion of the Greek people to their family and their Church made them poor material for ideological recruitment."[56] EAM had been not only a successful political organization but a convenient mask for the KKE, which many Greeks continued to identify with the Soviet Union, atheism, and Slavism. A naked grab for power at the moment of liberation that resulted in a fight with the British would have made it difficult for the KKE to take over the country.

Whether the Soviet intervention prevented this scheme will remain a contested issue among historians, but the military and political realities confronting the KKE and the British in the late summer and fall of 1944, perhaps, played a decisive role in Siantos' plans. It does not seem likely that during the critical period (July–September 1944) Siantos was willing to hand over the country to the Greek government-in-exile just to accommodate the Soviets, nor was he prepared to fight the British on the beaches—at least not without external support. Once the Soviets had declined to get involved in the politics of liberation and made that known to the KKE, an alternative strategy was necessary. What the precise aims of that strategy were went with Siantos to his grave. Unfortunately, the man who directed the KKE and the left-wing resistance during the December Uprising left no record of why he chose a showdown with the provisional government and the British, and having done so, why he decided to confine it only to Athens. Even after his strategy began to unravel and ELAS was hard-pressed to achieve control over all of Athens, Siantos refused to back away from his plan, until it was too late.[57]

A decisive factor that, for better or for worse, contributed to the chain of events that led to the fighting was that the organization still had to function under the conditions created by the occupation, which made travel and communications extremely difficult and dangerous. The polit-

buro and the central committee met occasionally to consider new policies, but it was not always possible to adapt quickly to new situations.
For example, in April 1944 the KKE had sent delegates to a conference
organized in Lebanon to replace the Greek government-in-exile with a
Government of National Unity that would include representatives from
all the resistance organizations. After torturous negotiations, the KKE-
EAM representatives accepted the new government, based on Soviet advice, but when they returned to Greece, the KKE leadership denounced
their actions. Yet a few months later, because of the Popov Mission, the
KKE agreed to join the Government of National Unity under the same
conditions proposed in May.

In the post-liberation period, the communists, like all other parties,
had to overcome problems that resulted from the wretched condition of
the country, which made it difficult to maintain party discipline over
the KKE, EAM, and ELAS as well as all the other left-wing resistance
organizations. This situation continued to play into Siantos' hands, because it left him and Ioannidis, along with a small group of trusted associates, in control of the party's tactics and strategy. Therefore, a great
deal of what took place in December 1944 is partly the by-product of
the fears, ambitions, and prejudices of this old-time communist.

In an ironic twist of fate during the late summer of 1944, both the
British and Siantos were working to avoid a clash and to limit the number
of Allied forces that would enter Greece, the British because they needed
troops for the Italian front and Siantos in order to exploit the enemy's
numerical weakness in a future attempt to take over the country. By early
December, Siantos was in a position to exploit this exact scenario. The
British only had approximately 20,000 troops, mostly administrative and
technical support units, concentrated in Athens, Thessaloniki, and a few
other urban centers, which left the rest of the country under the control
of ELAS. The KKE and EAM were enjoying tremendous popularity,
while the provisional government was losing credibility, culminating with
the botched handling of Sunday's demonstration.

It is clear that Siantos had decided that he would direct the forthcoming battle only against the forces of the provisional government
and avoid striking at the British. There is every indication that Siantos

believed that if ELAS could seize control of Athens quickly, the British would have little choice except to recognize a new government dominated by the KKE. Consequently, to maintain this delicate balance and avoid provoking the British, the battle had to be confined to the capital and waged against government targets. The choice of tactics was also motivated by ideological as well as practical considerations.

Siantos was a committed Marxist who subscribed to the notion that the party could count only on the proletariat. All his adult life he was steeped in the mantra of the workers' revolution and orthodox communist revolutionary tactics. Like most Greek communists, he did not have much faith in the Greek peasant, and since a large percentage of ELAS was recruited from the countryside, he may have had doubts about the commitment of the rank-and-file to a civil war. Siantos was also a pragmatist who understood that an all-out war would not be necessary if the capital was quickly secured. Besides, lacking sufficient transport, it would have taken much more time for the main ELAS units to move on Athens, which would also provoke the British.

Even at the beginning of the armed resistance against the Axis, Siantos was fond of saying, "He who ruled Athens ruled Greece." Siantos also added that "the Athenian workers would be organized into military formations so that at the moment of liberation they could seize the city."[58] However, Soviet intervention had stayed that strategy. The KKE had to change its plans and develop a political approach to power, at least for the time being. A critical element in the KKE's ability to shape events, vital to its future as a power broker on the Greek political scene, was ELAS. The guerrilla army enabled the KKE to control most of the countryside, almost all the towns and villages, while the reserve units in Athens, neither as well trained nor as well equipped as the regular ELAS force, gave the communists a direct means to stare down the provisional government and its British allies. As long as the KKE could fall back on ELAS, it could continue to negotiate from a position of strength.

During the crucial weeks prior to the Uprising, the monarchy, which represented the most incendiary issue, was, at least for the immediate future, held in abeyance. George II had agreed to stay out of Greece un-

til the future of the monarchy had been decided by referendum. The other demands by the left, such as the punishment of the Security Battalions (raised during the occupation by the puppet government of Ioannis Rallis), as well as of all collaborators, were more-or-less compatible with the government's policies. The KKE and EAM had respected the Caserta Agreement and kept ELAS formations outside of Athens. The KKE went so far as to call on its members to join the new National Guard. In a cable to party organizations on 22 November, Siantos instructed that all KKE members "of the 1936 class must be the first to join the temporary National Guard. . . . Communists and Eamites must organize themselves securely with the National Guard."[59]

At the same time, Siantos told the potential volunteers that before enlisting they had to visit the nearest party headquarters and receive orders on the course of action to be adopted once they were in the army.[60] Clearly, Siantos had settled on a policy of infiltration rather than military confrontation on the road to achieving power. Similarly, KKE ministers in the provisional government were attempting to place loyal communists in key positions. Miltiadis Porphyrogenis used his portfolio as minister of labor to consolidate the KKE's base in the trade unions by setting up a provisional committee of the General Confederation of Greek Workers in order to use this as a vote generator for the next elections, which were to take place on 1 December. Since the provisional committee was staffed entirely by members of EAM, which, in turn, was controlled by the KKE, the communists would be able to instigate a general strike at a time of their choosing.[61]

There is no agreement among historians or even the participants in these events on when or what precisely forced the situation in Athens past the point of no return, but when Papandreou refused to resign over the blood-shedding of 3 December the KKE lost any immediate advantage it would have gained from the establishment of a new government. Regardless of the failure to bring about a change in regime at that time, the KKE leadership, particularly Siantos, chose force as a means of achieving the same end—the collapse of the provisional government— while keeping the British from taking sides in a Greek civil war. Siantos, therefore, had to keep control of events and decided to resurrect the

ELAS central committee, rather than operate through EAM or the KKE, in order to limit the battle against Greek government targets and not attack the British. At the same time, he took appropriate measures to ensure that the ELAS committee would bow to his will by ensuring that the only other two members (including himself) were Michaelis Hadjimichaelis and Mandakas, both compliance officers. He was determined that no one would question his authority or decisions and explained to Ioannidis that Hadjimichaelis had no opinions and that Mandakas did what he was told.[62]

Consequently, the general headquarters of ELAS, along with most of the experienced officers and battle-hardened troops, remained in Lamia in central Greece. Although Athens was the focus of the battle, the ELAS headquarters was ordered to launch an attack against the forces of Zervas in Epirus, thus diverting three well-equipped divisions that could have tipped the scales in Athens. Other ELAS units were sent to destroy the guerrilla bands of Anton Tsaous, the leader of an independent right-wing group operating in the Dram district in northern Greece. After fighting had broken out in Athens, Stefanos Sarafis, the military commander of ELAS, asked permission from Siantos to attack all British units throughout Greece, which would have been a relatively easy task, but his request was rejected outright. A little later, Sarafis pressed Siantos to allow him at least to disarm the British garrisons outside of Athens, but instead, the ELAS central committee instructed him to notify the British garrisons that all movement on their part was forbidden. Before any action was taken on the part of ELAS, however, the British were able to withdraw their smaller garrisons into Athens and Thessaloniki.

Siantos' strategy was to confine the fighting to the capital and deploy the reserve ELAS units in Athens. He was subsequently severely criticized by the KKE for not committing the main body of ELAS forces, but had he done so, it would have undoubtedly brought the British immediately into the battle. Siantos, of course, did not know that Churchill had ordered Scobie to intervene in Athens, and no matter how carefully the KKE leader planned to conduct the battle, it is unlikely that the outcome would have been any different.

In other words, Siantos planned not so much for an all-out military assault as for a series of rapid small engagements sufficient to eliminate all vestiges of the provisional government but not enough to provoke the British. ELAS was already in control of most of Greece, and once the capital was in the hands of the KKE, the British would be confronted with a new political reality and one that would oblige them to accept a government dominated by the KKE. If not, then the onus would be on the British to fight a new communist-dominated regime that would represent the Greek state, instead of simply appearing to provide support to an Allied government trying to keep order. Despite the thinnest veneer of sovereignty, Greece in December 1944 was a British protectorate. Yet, for the sake of the Grand Alliance and to pay lip service to the principles of the newly founded United Nations, Churchill's government had at least to pretend to act as an interested bystander. Under these circumstances, it would have been very difficult for the British to fight the left on their own and certainly impossible, if they had been forced to withdraw from Greece, to return in the future.

The issue came down to the force of arms imposing legitimacy. The occupation had swept away the old political establishment and brought to the forefront new leaders and institutions. King George II and his government had spent the occupation years in London and Egypt and were sidelined to irrelevance. As far as most people in Greece were concerned, the monarchy and the government-in-exile were creatures of the British and part of the discredited Metaxas dictatorship. They had few followers in Greece and even fewer in the resistance movement. Indeed, the Greek body politic had been in a revolutionary state since Ioannis Metaxas had, with the connivance of the king, usurped power in August 1936. The constitutional status of the Metaxas regime and the monarchy had not been resolved when Greece fell under the control of the Axis. In fact, the constitutional situation was further made complicated by the quisling regimes, which lasted from April 1941 to October 1944 and served merely as puppets of a foreign power.

Meanwhile, during the war, EAM and its army, ELAS, were recognized and supported as Allied forces by the British, the Americans, and the Soviets. This recognition not only provided the left-wing resistance with moral and material support but created a legal framework for EAM to function as a valid political entity. In the constitutional morass of the time, EAM could claim lawful relevance as much as the Greek government-in-exile. In the fall of 1944, the British had cobbled together a Greek Government of National Unity, which included ministers from EAM and the KKE as well as from all the other major resistance organizations. This arrangement provided political as well as military recognition to EAM, giving it parity with the traditional ruling establishment.

In October, this broad coalition arrived in liberated Greece as a provisional government and attempted to run the country until circumstances permitted a general election. When the EAM and KKE ministers resigned on 1 December, the authority of the Papandreou government was invalidated, and it had to be replaced by a new provisional regime. How this would be accomplished—whether by violent or peaceful means—as far as the left was concerned was a matter for the Greek people. The left had helped to establish the first postwar government and by the same token could now demand to have it replaced. Once such a new government was in place, how could the British intervene and escape the ire of world opinion in addition to that of their allies? Fundamentally, this was the rationale of the left and Siantos' strategy.

For a few hours on 4 December, Papandreou's resignation confirmed the reasoning of the KKE and EAM, but the Greek prime minister, after considerable pressure from the British, changed his mind. Technically, if not morally, the provisional government could remain in power as long as King George II was prepared to acquiesce. As head of state, the king, in the absence of a general election, could lawfully extend the mandate of the provisional government despite the resignation of the EAM and KKE ministers. Suddenly the issue of the discredited monarchy emerged, and until a plebiscite decided to the contrary, George II remained as the constitutional arbiter of the Greek state.

However, this legal sleight of hand was lost on EAM and its multitude of followers and made little impression on world opinion. Matters were made worse for the British as well as the Papandreou government by the fact that just about all foreign correspondents in Athens were living at the Grande Bretagne Hotel located at the corner of Constitution Square and across from the central police station. When the crisis broke out on Sunday, the correspondents were afforded a spectacular view of the pandemonium.

The first report of the crisis came out in *The Times* of London on 4 December; it was dramatic and inaccurate and gave the impression that the demonstrators included mostly children, who were mercilessly gunned down by the police. According to *The Times* special correspondent in Athens:

> The seeds of civil war were well and truly sown by the Athens police this morning when they fired on a demonstration of children and youths. . . . About 10 o'clock crowds began to gather. One section of the demonstrators, mostly girls and boys, with a sprinkling of adults, started to leave the square, presumably en route for the Ministry of Foreign Affairs, where the Prime Minister has his office. Just as the procession was halfway across University Street . . . the police opened fire with rifles and tommy guns. The crowd immediately fell flat to escape the bullets, but the police continued firing. When they stopped, the demonstrators got to their feet and started to pick up the wounded and dead and the police then fired again.[63]

Despite the inaccuracies, the early newspaper articles set the tone for most of the reporting for the duration of the Uprising. The American and British press, in particular, gave considerable credence to the grievances of the left and remained critical of Churchill's and Papandreou's handling of the crisis.

Although on 6 December *The Times* apportioned part of the blame for Sunday's killings to the left by stating that "the action of the EAM and Communist Ministers in perceptibly withdrawing from the Government on an issue which seemed to have been already amicably settled must be held partly responsible for the present crisis," the newspaper placed most of the blame on the Greek prime minister. The influential conservative paper went on to say, "It was a misfortune that M. Papandreou should have failed to use the opportunity of his broadcast on Sunday night to disassociate himself from the senseless and unnecessary display of force by the Athens police." In the same article, *The Times* also cautioned against British intervention in Greece and underlined the right of the resistance to participate in governing the country: "In Greece, as in all other liberated countries, the allied military authorities have a direct and overriding interest in the preservation of order while military operations are in progress. . . . This interest, however, must not be allowed to imply any participation in the politics of Greece." The article went on to say that the resistance organizations had "won the confidence of and loyalty of the people in a measure not easily emulated by patriots who have not shared the experience of enemy rule."[64]

The next day, 7 December 1944, the negative press reports continued, and even before British troops were fully committed in the battle, *The Times* editorial commented, "The disagreeable truth revealed by the news of the past three days from Athens is that British armed forces, originally invoked in the desire to avoid bloodshed, have become involved in a Greek civil war." The same editorial warned the British government away from getting involved in Greek affairs and echoed the sentiments of the Greek left:

> If M. Papandreou is now maintained in power by the ban of a foreign government on any alternative, his moral authority in Greece can hardly survive; and British lives sacrificed, fighting against Greeks on behalf of a Greek Government which exists only in virtue of military force. Neither Greece nor Britain can afford such an issue of this tragic struggle. Grievous errors, some recent, some of longer date, have been committed. For the Greek parties the imperative task is to re-establish a Government fairly representative of both wings under a head acceptable to both, and thus bring about a situation in which desperately needed measures of relief and reconstruction can be undertaken. For the British Government the paramount duty, and the only one consonant with British tradition and British interest, is to seek to bring

about such a reunion, and at all costs to avoid taking sides in a Greek conflict. For the British Army the only conceivable role, in the face of every difficulty and every provocation, is one of strict neutrality and favour to none.[65]

Drew Pearson, the influential *Washington Post* journalist, with close links to the State Department and the White House, in his weekly column lashed out at Churchill's policy, accusing the British of being in league with Nazi collaborators. He claimed that they wanted to secure postwar economic advantages in the region and planned to force the Greeks to cede the island of Crete.[66] The British suspected that the American Office of Strategic Services (OSS), which was often critical of how the British dealt with the Greek left, had inspired Pearson's article.

For almost the duration of the December Uprising, the left continued to enjoy the support of the British and American media, which undermined Churchill and Papandreou but sustained the morale of the ELAS troops and the supporters of EAM and the KKE. Inadvertently and indirectly, the positive press helped to encourage the KKE and EAM to stick to their demands and remain intransigent over a peaceful resolution of the crisis.

Initially, and for the wrong reasons, the slow reaction of the British forces seemed to prove Siantos right. During those crucial few days Scobie's units, except for the rescue of Greek police officers, remained on the defensive. From the perspective of the KKE leadership, and certainly from that of Siantos, it was evident that the British were reluctant to get involved in a Greek imbroglio.

General Ronald Scobie, the British commander of all Greek forces, was the wrong man in the wrong place and at the wrong time. Scobie had limited battlefield experience and was ill equipped to participate in the intricate and convoluted labyrinth of Greek politics in the aftermath of liberation. He failed to understand or appreciate the growing impact that the resistance had had on the Greek psyche, whose popularity and increasing mythology was in inverse proportion to the rapid deterioration of the popularity of the provisional government. At the same time, matters were made worse by the failure of the British and the provisional government to ameliorate the economic crisis that accompanied the liberation.

Mass unemployment, a burgeoning black market that sucked up most relief supplies, and hunger devoured the initial enthusiasm and goodwill generated by liberation. Under these circumstances, the glory of resistance remained the only staple in an otherwise bleak environment. Yet Scobie chose to ignore the resistance and perfunctorily dismissed its leaders. Scobie was the quintessential British officer and had had little contact with, or exposure to, guerrilla warfare and the politics of resistance. The British general believed that, regardless of the contribution of the guerrilla fighters, liberation had come to Greece because of the victories of regular forces over the German army. To conventional officers like Scobie, the achievement of the partisans and of covert operations was merely an adjunct to the real war fought by the Allied armies in the field. Now that the resistance groups had completed their allotted task, it was time for them to go back to their homes and resume their civilian lives.

The assessment of guerrilla warfare as less than secondary in importance to the war effort and the failure to appreciate the impact of the resistance were prevalent among most British officers, who had taken over Greek affairs from the men of the SOE. This was evident from almost the day of liberation up to and including the outbreak of hostilities in December. In the early days of jubilation that followed the withdrawal of the German army from Athens, preparations were made by Scobie's staff for a victory parade. Woodhouse, the head of the Allied Military Mission in the Greek mountains and one of the few SOE officers left in Athens after liberation, was offered a seat in one of the automobiles that would take part in the victory celebrations. When Woodhouse inquired "where the guerrilla leaders were to be placed" Scobie's adjutant remarked, "The guerrilla leaders . . . what has it got to do with them?"[67] The rapid removal of most SOE personnel from the country took away the few people who had a thorough knowledge and understanding of the delicate political situation in Greece. However, even had they remained, the conventional British officers who arrived in Greece were not inclined to listen to them. Woodhouse discovered that "incoming officers had been advised to disregard us, because we had been too long in Greece and our judgment had become untrustworthy."[68]

Disdain for the military capabilities of guerrilla forces in general and those of the Greek left in particular also created a false sense of security, along with an overconfidence that irregular forces were no match for the British army. According to William McNeill, who in 1944 was stationed at the American embassy in Athens, when fighting broke out in early December:

> British military circles seriously underestimated the resistance they had to deal with. Armored cars and tanks were able to move freely throughout the streets, and no systematic resistance was made to British troops. Most Britishers thought that the leftists would yield after a few days, when they had seen British strength and determination.[69]

From early November, Scobie began receiving warnings from Churchill and General Maitland Wilson, the commander-in-chief for the Middle East, that a confrontation with EAM-ELAS was probable. On 8 November, Churchill had telegraphed General Wilson and Rex Leeper, requesting urgent reinforcements to be sent to Greece, and instructed Leeper, "British troops should certainly be used to support law and order, even by shooting if necessary."[70] On 15 November, General Wilson instructed Scobie "to hold all troops already in Greece to concentrate on Athens whose neighborhoods would be declared a military area and he should order ELAS to withdraw from the capital." Scobie was to "disarm or if necessary imprison any ELAS forces that refused to leave Athens." In the event of attack, Scobie had orders to "use British and Greek forces to crush any opposition."[71] In addition to the warnings and in response to the escalating agitation by EAM and the KKE, the Middle East command increased British forces in Greece to 22,600 along with five squadrons of aircraft by the end of October.[72] Increasing the number of British troops further contributed to the climate of suspicion, recriminations, and mutual hostility that had infected relations between the Greek left and the British and the provisional government.

Matters almost reached the breaking point with the arrival in Athens of the Third Mountain Brigade and the Sacred Squadron on 9 November, and relations collapsed after Sunday's violence.

Remarkably, and despite the deterioration of the political situation, Scobie was ill prepared for a confrontation with ELAS. Throughout October and to mid-November, British forces were concentrated in Athens, Thessaloniki, Patras, and a few other cities. Little effort was made to maintain secure communications with Piraeus and the airfield outside Athens. To make matters worse, a great many of Scobie's troops were spread thin in the capital, guarding government buildings and important installations. The rest of the country (with the exception of Epirus, the Drama district, and a few islands), including the region around Athens, was under the control of ELAS. Because of this deployment, the British, even before the outbreak of hostilities, were virtually besieged.

ELAS, meanwhile, enjoyed the strategic advantage of controlling most of mainland Greece along with active supporters in almost every corner of the country. By the end of November, the ELAS order of battle was based on approximately 49,000 men and women in eleven divisions, a regiment of cavalry, and a makeshift navy. ELAS also maintained a reserve of 45,000, of which 22,000–23,000 were based in Athens. In late November, the Athens reserve was designated as the First ELAS Army Corps. Most of the rank-and-file of these reserve forces were of uneven quality and limited fighting experience and were poorly equipped, but at least 6,000 were armed with rifles, and another 3,000 carried revolvers and pistols.[73] A few of the men and women had attained considerable experience in urban warfare during the last year of the occupation, but a large proportion had little or no combat experience, and many had not ever fired their weapons. Despite the initial advantages enjoyed by ELAS, the insurgents were hampered by serious difficulties and liabilities. As mentioned earlier, Siantos had decided to wage the battle through the ELAS central committee and essentially try to control the battle by himself. Bypassing the experienced ELAS general headquarters staff meant that Siantos had to fight a campaign without a proper command structure, a system of communication, logistical organization, and a transportation plan to enable him to shift units quickly from one part of the battle to the other. Siantos himself had practically no command or military experience and had taken no part in the ELAS campaigns during the occupation. He had fulfilled military service as a noncommissioned officer in the Greek army, but that experience was hardly adequate, and Theodoros Makridis, a former Greek officer and a senior commander in ELAS, often referred to Siantos as the "general of sergeants."74

As ELAS was a guerrilla army of uneven quality, armaments, and discipline, the ELAS reserve was a pale reflection and woefully inadequate as a military force. Siantos made matters worse by a combination of indecisiveness and naïveté. In addition to dividing his forces by sending three ELAS divisions to destroy EDES in Epirus, he also hampered the political conduct of events by splitting KKE headquarters between Athens and a small village, Hashia, in northern Attica. The senior KKE cadres, who were critical in securing supplies, maintaining communications, providing intelligence, and conducting a host of other critical duties, wasted valuable time moving back and forth between the two locations, while the situation in Athens slowly spun out of control.

The British had kept a watchful eye on the movements of the regular ELAS units outside of the capital practically from the first day of liberation. The increasing agitation of EAM in the streets of Athens throughout October and November was seen as a barometer of leftist sentiment, but hardly as a military threat. The British assumed that if, or rather when, hostilities broke out, ELAS would attack Athens from the outside, with help from KKE and EAM supporters in the city acting as a fifth column and not the primary force. As late as 6 December, Scobie's staff were still concerned about ELAS proper and reckoned that ELAS had concentrated approximately 20,000 troops in Attica and that a full-scale attack seemed imminent.75

The mistaken notion that an attack against the capital would come from outside partially explains why Scobie refrained from committing his troops and forcing a battle with ELAS in the streets of Athens until his army was besieged. In other words, each side misread and misunderstood the other's intentions. Scobie was husbanding his strength to meet the expected assault, and until the arrival of reinforcements, it was not prudent to provoke any street battles. Siantos, on his part, must have assumed that Scobie's restraint was an indication that the British were not yet committed to participating in a Greek civil war. Consequently, ELAS was thrown against Greek government forces and targets, while making a determined effort not to provoke the British.[76]

This strategy was evident from the beginning of formal hostilities on 6 December, when Scobie's ultimatum concerning the withdrawal of all ELAS forces from Athens expired. In the early dawn, hundreds of grim ELAS men dressed in civilian clothes and armed with only rifles briskly advanced through the Royal Gardens and headed toward the side that led to Kifissias Boulevard. An iron fence surrounded the gardens and the drab-looking ELAS men bunched up, as they had to climb over the railing to reach the street. Kifissias is a broad avenue along which were located the ministries of Foreign Affairs, War, and other key government agencies. The object of the attack was for ELAS to seize the physical symbols of the state and quickly supplant the Papandreou government with its own creature. As the ELAS men approached the government buildings, the early light of day revealed that British sentries guarded the front entrances. The attackers paused—they had no instructions to fight the British but orders to capture the buildings. Some of the more aggressive officers urged their men on, while others held back and some even began retreating. The assault, consequently, proceeded unevenly, was quickly stalled, and was easily repulsed by the police detachments assigned to protect the buildings.[77]

After a week, the fighting escalated but, for the most part, remained confined to Athens, and not until after 14 December did ELAS launch any intentional attacks against British units.[78] On 12 December, Siantos met with Scobie to discuss a negotiated settlement, but Scobie insisted on full compliance with his original demands—evacuation of Athens and the disarmament of ELAS. Siantos refused to accede to this and discussions broke off.[79]

Despite the limited battlefield, ELAS was not able to overwhelm completely the few government forces, nor could the government forces, along with the available British units, contain ELAS, let alone drive the guerrillas from the city. As a result, the British government was forced to transfer to Greece thousands of troops from the Italian front during the final phase of the Second World War. These troops were committed to destroy the very forces that their own government had so desperately tried to create three years earlier in order to fight the Axis. It was a cycle of violence that had already caused the death of many Greeks by the hands of other Greeks and would continue to claim thousands more.

4

THE POGROM OF
THE LEFT: THE PRELUDE
TO WHITE TERROR

A revolutionary movement is first betrayed by its means, second, by
its people, and third by its purpose.[1]

             THEOPHILOS FRANGOPOULOS,
                         "Betrayals"

"YOU ARE LUCKY TO BE GOING TO GREECE" RAN THE OPENING
sentence of the pamphlet issued to each member of the Eleventh Battalion of the King's Royal Rifle Corps. They were embarking for Greece after a protracted period of inactivity in Egypt. Ron McAdam, one of the battalion's young recruits, leapt with joy at the news that the unit was finally on the move: Any action was preferable to enforced idleness. Like most of the men in his battalion McAdam could no longer stand the tedium and vast emptiness of the desert, where each day bled into the next without form or variation.

McAdam had volunteered to join the British army from his home in Rhodesia to defend a country he hardly knew in a war that had engulfed the entire world.[2] For over fifty years, he has not thought about his experiences in Greece, nor has he had occasion to visit the country, but six decades ago this young man from Rhodesia found himself in the vortex of a battle far removed from the simplicity and monotony of the desert, and even farther yet from the vast expanse and lush countryside of southern Africa.

On 12 October 1944, McAdam, along with most of the men of the Eleventh Battalion, embarked on the Royal Navy cruiser, the *Black Prince*, in Alexandria, Egypt, and steamed north toward Piraeus. For the voyage, the young lieutenant had decided to deploy his platoon on the deck near the bow, to avoid the stifling interior of the ship. The autumn day was sunny, but on the cool side, and McAdam reflected:

The sea was clear and we could see the German mines bobbing in the water. We amused ourselves watching the ship's machine guns firing at the mines and the great showers of water cascading when one them exploded. . . . As we were nearing Piraeus, it became obvious that we were in the midst of a very large minefield and we had lost ships. The person in charge of the flottila wisely turned it about and another set of minesweepers moved in and we eventually docked on 15 October 1944.[3]

According to the Eleventh Battalion war diary, a German noncommissioned officer, for fifty gold sovereigns, had given the British directions to a gap in the minefield covering Piraeus harbor. Unfortunately, the information proved false, and the flotilla lost five ships. By 16 October the troops had disembarked and were proceeding to their objectives, passing through a dilapidated landscape stripped bare by the retreating Germans. The population greeted the British with applause and pelted them with flowers. After such a welcome, very few had any notion that they had traded a war in which the enemy was easily identifiable for one where death lurked behind doorways, in sewers, and on balconies and rooftops. A smiling face was no guarantee of welcome; at times it was rather a mask to lure the unsuspecting soldier into a trap. McAdam remembers that "On arrival in Athens we were welcomed by the civilians, some of who obviously remembered the 9th Battalion that had been there in 1941. We spent most of the 16th to the 29th of October reorganizing the city. I was impressed, as we moved into Piraeus, that first day with the lack of any animals and that there were not enough men around."[4]

McAdam's impression of the Greek interior was even grimmer:

On the 21 November our company was ordered to Lamia; this was a small provincial town which actually when we got there, we found out was the headquarters of ELAS. Our job was to take supplies to the countryside as they were very short of food and short of transport; the villages had been badly damaged by the Germans who as they left destroyed bridges and in fact had burnt down many houses. People were short of clothes; they had malaria and were without any drugs; they also had typhoid, and it was a very difficult job to get the food out to them.[5]

Like most British forces in Greece, the Eleventh Battalion was spread out over a large area, each of its six companies trying to distribute relief supplies over a large area. Reports from the company commanders mirrored McAdam's observations. An extract from one patrol typifies the conditions the British encountered in the Greek interior and the obstacles they had to overcome in order to provide some assistance to the local population:

Visited Karpenisi—population approximately 2,100. Only fourteen houses left standing out of an original 204. Remainder burnt by Germans. Supply center for 25,000 people in the surrounding villages. These can only be reached on foot—many three days' journey—and mules are short. . . . Food situation very bad—beans being the main diet. Last distribution of food early last October. This consisted of rice, milk powder and macaroni. Clothes urgently needed. No single person possesses anything but what he stands up in. Children looked miserably cold. Clothes were sent up recently by Red Cross, but unfortunately had not been inspected. They turned out to be light summer frocks and useless articles such as handbags. Eighty percent of the population have malaria. No quinine or atebrine. Twenty-five people have typhoid. More serum needed. There is no doctor in the whole area, the only medical officers being two Greek Red Cross Sisters.[6]

The difficult conditions that prevailed in Karpenisi, with few exceptions, reflected the plight of the population in the rest of Greece. Lamentably, little would change for large segments of the country over the next five years. Greece seamlessly passed from the harsh grip of the Axis occupation to the agony of a civil war that dragged on until the summer of 1949. Even afterward, parts of the countryside continued to suffer deprivations for another two or more decades.

On 1 December, McAdam, as well as the other men in the company, became aware that ELAS troops were heading south toward the Athens area, and a day or two later they spotted large numbers of civilians streaming out of Athens to the north and northwest of Greece. Unsurprisingly, on the first day of the December Uprising (4 December) the relationship between the British and the local EAM-ELAS in Lamia started to unravel and got progressively worse as the violence in Athens escalated. On 9 December, the Eleventh Battalion received orders to decamp for Athens and by the evening was fighting its way to the center of the capital. The diary of the battalion describes a city desolate and shrouded in darkness:

> At Athens things were very different from what we had expected. There were no lights and not a sign of anyone about. Broken tram wires festooned the deserted streets, and these nearly accounted for more than one rifleman perched on the cab of each vehicle. Automatic fire and sniper's bullets whipped across practically every crossroads. There was nothing for it but to put the foot and the head down at the same time and run for it. Somehow we arrived without casualty. Firing and heavy explosions were going on all over the city, but in the immediate neighborhood of Constitution Square all was fairly quiet.[7]

During the battalion's first night in Athens, ELAS had dynamited the front door of the house occupied by one of the battalion's platoons and in two separate attacks penetrated as far as the hall before the British unit drove them back with heavy casualties. Similar assaults erupted throughout the night, engaging elements of units of the Eleventh Battalion in a series of firefights, but at different times enabling the British to defeat the ELAS forces piecemeal. In the morning most of the houses around the battalion's positions were burning, but the British took one hundred and fifty prisoners, including some women, looking "quite respectable until a grenade fell . . . from one [of] the ladies' handbag[s]."[8]

From 8 to 12 December, the scale of the ELAS offensive intensified as ELAS regulars gradually reinforced the reserve units and joined in the fighting. The ELAS also deployed mines on the principal streets as well as artillery and heavy machine guns. ELAS demolition teams, using sewers, rooftops, and back alleys, easily moved about the city blowing up houses and police stations. In a desperate attempt to break through the lines, ELAS squads also packed dynamite into tramcars and hurled them against British defense positions.

In the face of these reinforcements and firepower, General Ronald Scobie, the commander of all British and Greek forces in the country, withdrew most of the isolated British units into the center of Athens but inevitably had to abandon several supply dumps, which provided additional food and ammunition for ELAS. However, the Greek Third Mountain Brigade, located on the outskirts of Athens (before the outbreak of fighting), remained exposed and was forced to hold its ground for the duration of the hostilities. ELAS surrounded the brigade and subjected it to mortar bombardment and a steady stream of small arms fire for almost a month. The British could supply the brigade with food and ammunition, but only at night and with convoys of armored cars.

Initially, the battle swung in favor of ELAS; the British forces were quickly forced back into three small pockets. The first included a small group of soldiers who had managed to retreat to the tip of the peninsula in Piraeus, but they were immediately isolated from the main British force in the center of Athens, although they managed to keep contact with the Royal Navy flotilla anchored in the harbor. A second British unit defended the main airfield at Hassani and a sliver of the shore leading to Phaliron Bay. Remarkably, ELAS did not make any serious efforts to capture the airport and paid for this blunder when a little later the

British air-lifted an entire army division from Italy to Athens, which turned the tide of battle. The third, and the largest, concentration of British forces was in the center of Athens. Within this narrow perimeter, the British and the few Greek government units were compressed into an area just two miles long and five or six blocks wide, which included Constitution Square, the main government buildings, part of the business quarter, the district of Kolonaki, and the Grande Bretagne Hotel. The rest of the capital, as well as most of Greece, fell under the sway of the KKE-ELAS-EAM.

After 12 December, both sides settled into a deadly pattern. The British, under siege, had to repel daily and nightly attacks as well as contend with sniper fire and ambushes in the unfamiliar streets of the capital. ELAS, with much superior numbers, sustained almost a constant offensive, with waves of infantry shifting from one part of the British position to the other, while maintaining round-the-clock sniping and ambushes. In some respects, the Battle of Athens was a mix of conventional firefights, but with streets and buildings as the primary targets, accompanied by the uglier side of urban warfare that blurred the line between civilian and soldier. A good number of the ELAS troops did not wear an identifiable uniform. Snipers, in particular, dressed in civilian clothes and operated from rooftops and balconies. They could fire at the British and quickly retreat within a house or apartment building, hide their rifles, and thus make detection almost impossible.

Very often, ELAS did not hesitate to overstep even these bounds in order to gain an advantage over the British. This is not surprising considering the fact that just two months earlier, the ELAS reserve units in Athens and, to a lesser degree, the regular ELAS in the mountains had been fighting the Germans in a conflict in which the rules of war did not apply and did not allow quarter for guerrillas or civilians. The occupation forces did not hesitate to employ torture, killing of hostages, burning of villages, and other reprehensible reprisal tactics against the resistance groups.

Under the conditions of the time, consequently, the mixed units of ELAS reserves and regulars could hardly fall within the strict definition of a conventional military force. At the same time, the British had condoned and applauded the use of guile and subterfuge by the guerrillas against the Axis. Indeed, the British, during the course of the Second World War, pioneered the use of deception tactics and strategy, some of which took place in Greece.[9] The ELAS-EAM had learned quickly from the British liaison officers attached to the various guerrilla bands. In addition to picking up British techniques, they could fall back on a long history and tradition of covert skills honed by Greek partisans in the struggle for independence against the Ottoman Empire. Although this may explain the use of deception tactics, it does not dampen the odious impression caused by the ELAS "dirty tricks" campaign.

For example, ELAS troops occupied hospitals and while disguising themselves as patients (going so far as to wear mock bandages) attacked unsuspecting British patrols while lying in bed with their rifles concealed. On 10 December, a British patrol of armored cars in the southwest area of the Likavitos district came under fire from an ELAS hospital, from where nurses in Red Cross uniforms threw hand grenades from the windows at the passing British unit. The patrol responded with heavy machine gun fire, and after a while the ELAS troops inside the hospital raised a white flag. Even so, when a British officer approached, he was gunned down by a sniper firing from the same window from which the white flag was hanging. In frustration, the commander of the unit forced two of the ELAS nurses from the hospital to stand on top of one of the armored cars to ensure the safe withdrawal of his men. Later, the same unit secured the perimeter of their position with booby-trapped barbed wire, which shortly killed three ELAS troops, two of them women, trying to cut the wire.[10]

The British deplored the ELAS tactic of using women and, occasionally, children to lure their soldiers into a trap. In a typical ambush, a young woman would call soldiers from a balcony, and when one approached (for what he assumed would be a chat with a pretty girl), a sniper, hiding behind the girl's skirts, would open fire. In one incident, an armored car passing through a street came across the same girl five times, who, like the sirens of old, beckoned to the occupants, and each time a machine gun around the corner opened fire with deadly consequences. The sixth time, the British were forced to shoot the girl.[11] On other occasions, a little boy would stand on a balcony waving a Union Jack, while a sniper fired between his legs. Often battle-hardened British troops refused to fire at women and children, until circumstances forced them to reconsider. According to the war diary of the Eleventh Battalion, "Lieutenant B. E. D. Collier ordered a rifleman to fire at a young woman approaching his house with a tray of food and wine. The rifleman obeyed, and then begged not to be given such an order again. He quickly changed his view when the German stick grenade in her right hand was pointed out to him."[12]

Nevertheless, shooting at women and children was demoralizing for British soldiers, who, over and over again, had to keep coming to terms with this new twist in the inhumanity of war. Regrettably, the exploitation of women and children did not end with the Battle of Athens; it assumed an even greater role in the next round of the Greek civil war, eventually becoming a feature in all the dirty little wars of the twentieth century and beyond.

"I did not fear the frontal ELAS attacks, but the sniping was another matter," McAdam reflects on his time in Athens. "Snipers were used a fair bit by ELAS and they were very effective. They caused an awful lot of fear in the troops because we never knew when we might expect them to be active." Another disconcerting factor for British soldiers was the inability to separate friend from foe, in addition to the language barrier. A few days before Christmas, McAdam received instructions for his platoon to guard a bridge on Sygrou Boulevard straddling the road between the capital and Piraeus and over which Winston Churchill was to reach Athens from the airport. Churchill was coming to Greece to negotiate an end to the civil war with EAM-ELAS, and McAdam's job was to make sure that no one booby-trapped the bridge. The young officer had his doubts about securing the position and even more when local Greeks warned him that he would be eradicated during the night. "I will never know if these people had my welfare in mind or the warning was simply a trick to chase me away," McAdam continues to speculate over half a century after the event.

"In this environment of subterfuge and deadly games of hide and seek between snipers," McAdam reminisces:

We devised a simple technique for conducting patrols. We moved along a district and after securing one street, we fired a flare so that machine gunners and mortar bombers, behind us, could set their sights to cover us to the next block. On some patrols we had the assistance of a tank. The infantry would travel along either side of the tank. Each soldier carried a rifle with tracer bullets to indicate the direction of a shot and its target. The gunner on the tank would then be able to locate the spot which the enemy was firing from and would then remove the side of the house with an eighty-millimeter shell.[13]

During the December Uprising, the Greek government was practically a bystander and watched helplessly as the British and EAM-ELAS fought for control of the streets of Athens. The prime minister and the other members of the government, accompanied by their wives and children as well as most of the foreign notables, withdrew to the Grande Bretagne Hotel. The hotel, one of the largest and most luxurious buildings in southeastern Europe, was constructed in the early nineteenth century under the supervision of Othon I, the first king of Greece. It was one of the few structures in Athens that offered modern conveniences such as electric door locks (operated from above the headboards), light signals, house and city telephones in every room, and individual safes.[14] However, for the besieged government ministers, the hotel's most important feature was its thick exterior stone walls.

For the duration of the battle, the Grande Bretagne accommodated well over 1,000 people, with rooms set apart for cabinet meetings; offices for the prime minister, as well as for the other ministers, former Greek generals, and well-known writers; space for war correspondents; and rooms for the United Nations Relief and Rehabilitation Agency (UNRRA) and for senior British officers. When the city center was cut off, the hotel bar transformed into a hospital for civilian and military casualties, whose awful groans filtered throughout the main floor. A makeshift bar was created from one of the small rooms, although refreshments were limited to Samos wine, retzina (a Greek resin wine), and ouzo.[15]

In addition to Scobie and his staff, the six members of the former Soviet mission had—tellingly—decided to take their chances in the hotel rather than trust the hospitality of the KKE. Colonel Grigori Popov, the former head of the Soviet mission, spent his time sitting at a table in one of the main rooms of the hotel, saying very little except to lament the quality of British rations. Culinary disappointments, on the other hand, did not deter the Russian colonel from insisting that General Scobie provide him with a British armed guard.[16]

In the early days of the siege, everyone had to accept minor inconveniences and adjustments. Because of the scarcity of servants (some had joined ELAS, many more were just too frightened to ignore EAM's call for a general strike), all the guests, regardless of rank or status, had to line up outside the kitchen for their meal of bully beef with biscuits, a second course of cheese, and a cup of tea. All the guests had to make their own beds and clean their rooms with the communal brooms (leaving the garbage in the corridors). In some instances, ingenuity overcame adversity with unexpected results. For example, old military maps from the Italian campaign replaced the stained and dirty tablecloths in the dining room. However, as one British historian has written, "This had its consolations. Many officers were able during meal-times to discuss their battle experiences, to point out which particular valley or mountain had been the scene of their feats of daring."[17]

As the fighting crept closer, conditions in the hotel degenerated. When ELAS cut off the water supply for central Athens, the ration was strictly limited to half a gallon per person each day for drinking and washing. This did not dampen the spirits of the guests, who had to join yet another line in order to collect their half gallon in empty gin, brandy, or whiskey bottles. Despite the deprivations, Byford-Jones' account of the December events offers a nostalgic description of the Grande Bretagne, including images of the hotel's two pianos being played daily and often well into the night, accompanied by the din of battle raging in the streets. The bonding experience was further enhanced by the sure knowledge that the hotel (as well as its occupants), or the "Royal Kingdom of Greece," as it was called by the KKE and EAM, was one of the primary targets of ELAS.

For the men and women trying to storm the British defenses outside the walls of the Grande Bretagne, the battle held a different legacy. Despite

notions to the contrary, ELAS-EAM did not represent homogeneous organizations. The degree of commitment, loyalty, fighting ability, and even
fanaticism of the ranks was uneven and varied within each unit. The
ELAS formations included recruits from the countryside and mountain
villages, from the working districts as well as the upper and middle classes
of the cities and towns. Some of the volunteers were naive young men and
women who had rarely left their villages and could hardly differentiate
between Marxism and monarchy—they fought because they trusted the
leadership of EAM-ELAS in their communities. Village priests often accompanied units raised in their parishes, thus lending another layer of
credibility.

Others, especially recruits from the urban centers, discovered the appeal of EAM and ELAS in the first stages of occupation and flocked to
its banner because they had come of age when the influence of the left,
for the first time in Greece, dominated most of the country. Even for
the sons and daughters of the largely right-wing upper- and middle-
class Athenian families, membership in EAM-ELAS became fashionable. During the harsh winter of 1942, when most Greeks were trying to
survive the famine, some of the fashionable homes in Kolonaki hosted
parties for the newly established EAM. The parties, explains Petros
Makris-Staikos in a recent study of the period, provide a curious link
between the mass-based EAM with the privileged classes in Athens. At
one such event:

> The mistress of the house, one of the daughters of the Papastratou (the
> owner of a major tobacco company), was open and "sympathetic" to
> every ideological current that appeared progressive. This particular party
> attracted the "reactionaries"—the children of the major Right-Wing
> families of Athens, who did not go hungry and the occupation had not
> interfered with their preoccupations. Now, however, that they saw that
> their class offered approval, the road to EAM was open. For many it was
> a way out of their tedious and stifling environment or a means of escap-
> ing the suffocating grip of their parents. In a short while, accordingly,
> EAM became a fad. Kolonaki, Psychiko as well as other wealthy districts
> were filled with male and female EAM members.[18]

With the assistance of these new recruits, EAM succeeded in seizing control over most of the relief work in Athens and permeated all the professional guilds and student organizations. Invariably, for many of the sons and daughters of the Athenian establishment EAM served as a transition step to the KKE. EAM also attracted a large number of professionals, particularly among the ranks of university professors, who used their influence with the student body to secure the election of EAM candidates in the various university societies.[19]

The fad quickly turned into a mass movement and spawned the revolution that exploded into the streets of Athens after liberation. The leaders of the KKE may have planned to use the December Uprising as a means of increasing their representatives in the Government of National Unity, or of influencing the formation of a new army, or even as part of a strategy of getting control of the Greek state in stages, but after the fighting erupted, they progressively lost control of events. In effect, the movement created through EAM and its subsidiary organizations became larger than the sum of its parts as individuals and groups exploited the fighting to pursue their own ends.

Between 1943 and 1944, EAM and the antileft groups at the University of Athens and the Polytechnic School fought bitterly over control of the student societies in the Greek institutions of higher learning. These battles took place in the streets, in coffeehouses, and in back allies. The various antileft forces could count on the indirect support of the German authorities and the puppet government, and some did not hesitate to collaborate with the occupation security services in their common struggle against communism. Occasionally, the Athens Security Battalions raided the university, arresting dozens of students; some of the unfortunate young men and women underwent extensive interrogation and torture in the dungeons of the Greek Special Security Service, while a lucky few escaped, but only after their parents used bribes to secure their release.

At other times, the battles between left- and right-wing organizations revolved around a cycle of killing, revenge, and counterrevenge. For example, in 1944, a few months before liberation, the KKE assassinated a member of the far-right-wing X organization just as he was about to board a bus. In retaliation, X dispatched six teams of five men each to terrorize EAM-ELAS and KKE groups. At 10:00 P.M. the teams broke into the usual haunts of the left shouting, "Hands high in the air." They proceeded to search all those present and severely beat anyone caught with weapons. In one place they found a couple of groups with red paint in their possession for writing slogans on walls. The X team forced them to drink the red paint and then proceeded to dynamite two KKE offices in the neighborhood. Afterward they dragged ten of the communists to the square, forced them against a wall, and went through the motions of a mock execution.[20]

In response to the arrest of its followers and those of EAM, the KKE broadened the mission of OPLA (Organization for the Protection of the People's Struggle), originally established as an intelligence unit in the winter of 1942–1943, to carry out assassinations. The scope of OPLA was further expanded after liberation to include torture and executions of the KKE's Marxist rivals, collaborators, and reactionaries. In the countryside and some neighborhoods of Athens, OPLA members also served as officers in the KKE's National Civil Guard (Ethniki Politophilaki). Although former police and gendarmes filled the ranks of OPLA, the communists also preferred to employ local cadres from the neighborhood of a designated assassination. This had the advantage of making identification of the prospective victim easier as well as binding the newer members of the KKE closer to the party by implicating them in the killing. As the day of liberation approached and the grip of the German occupiers weakened, Athens was quickly transforming into a battleground.

In this context, the KKE pursued narrow goals dictated by Stalinist principles such as purging of collaborators, rivals, potential rivals, and particularly members guilty of apostasy—even at the expense of the party's broader interests. One example is that of the ill-fated Kitsos Maltezos, a young Athenian poet, a representative of the intellectual and cultural elite, and also the last living relative of Ioannis Makriyiannis, one of the heroes of the Greek War of Independence. Although Maltezos fell victim to the KKE's assassination units in the last months of the occupation, the manner of his murder was used against others during the December Uprising and provides a rare insight into the tactics of the communists.

When Maltezos joined the youth wing of the KKE, he was more than just a trophy convert, as his connection to the legendary Makriyiannis gave the KKE another avenue for associating the EAM movement with the Greek War of Independence. Consequently, when Maltezos decided to leave the Young Communists in 1943, it constituted not only betrayal of the movement but a dangerous precedent. Making matters worse, Maltezos openly condemned the communists and went over to the anti-KKE forces that had sprung up in reaction to EAM-ELAS.

In early 1943, the KKE held a secret trial of Maltezos in absentia and condemned him to death; the execution was to take place at the first opportunity. On 1 February 1944 at 9:30 A.M., Maltezos left his apartment and was making his way to Panepistimiou Street to the nearest tram stop. As he walked across Sygrou Boulevard to Amalias, four men came behind him and followed discreetly. When he passed the statue of Lord Byron and was about to board the tram, two of the men pulled out their guns and yelled, "Now." One of the assassins then called out his name, "Kitsos," and when Maltezos turned, the first bullet struck him on the right temple, followed by several more in the chest.[21] In the midst of so much killing, the demise of Maltezos, albeit tragic, hardly seemed unusual in a city fraught with death.

Yet this talented young man became a tragic symbol of his generation and a metaphor for the fratricide that had infected Athens and in a short time would consume Greek society. Although the KKE ordered his execution, it had done so with the cognizance and at the urging of young men, classmates, and even friends of Maltezos, who had grown up in the neighborhood and until the occupation had shared the same values. Adonis Kyrou, the son of the publisher of *Estia* (one of the oldest conservative Greek newspapers) and the scion of a powerful Athenian family, was a member of the KKE. In 1943, Kyrou was instrumental in the KKE's decision to condemn Maltezos to death. The primary executioner, Mikes Kouroniotis, had been Maltezos' close friend in university and a classmate of Andreas Papandreou (Greek prime minister in the 1980s) when they both attended the American College before the war. Like Kyrou, Kouroniotis came from a well-established and prosperous family and had joined the KKE in university during the occupation.

In the eyes of his family, Kouroniotis had abandoned and betrayed his class, and they were anxious to avoid a scandal. The old establishment quickly sprang into action to protect one of their own. The Greek Special Security Service, which had apprehended Kouroniotis and conducted extensive interrogations that had revealed the names of others connected to the crime, received orders to hand the young man over to the Germans. Kouroniotis' family preferred that he be executed by the Germans for carrying a weapon (an offense punishable by death) to his going through the motions of a trial that would have revealed his membership in the KKE and, of course, implicate other sons and daughters of prominent Athenian families.

Despite the assassination of a high-profile member of Greek letters, the censored press did not report the killing until two days later and omitted to name the assassin or any of his accomplices. On 21 March 1944, Kouroniotis, along with eleven others, was executed by firing squad. He died in obscurity, which suited everyone concerned. His family was spared further scandal, and the occupation regime was spared the embarrassment of appearing helpless in failing to protect so prominent an Athenian. The KKE and OPLA were also relieved by the quick elimination of Kouroniotis rather than having their secrets exposed during the course of a public trial.

Certainly, not all the men and women from the Athenian elite succumbed to murder and assassination. The father of the current prime minister of Greece, Kostas Simitis, at the time a popular professor in the business school, was one of those who persevered to get EAM students elected to the boards of student societies at the universities. Later he joined PEEA, established by EAM in the Greek mountains as a rival to the Greek government-in-exile in London and Cairo, and struggled against George Papandreou, the premier in 1944 and the father of Andreas Papandreou, who led the Greek Socialist Party (which claims EAM's ideological mantle) to victory in 1981.

However, for most Athenians, the terror of the December Uprising was not of ideology but of fear exacerbated by the misery of a general strike that for the next thirty-three days paralyzed the city. The KKE and EAM organized the strike as a means of placing additional pressure on the Papandreou government over the issue of the new army. Electricity, water, and gas supplies ceased, and for the duration of the fighting only a few telephones remained in operation. Once all workers went on strike, theaters, stores, hotels, and restaurants closed. Transportation came to a halt, as did the work on the docks, which prevented, for the duration of the fighting, the unloading of ships that carried foodstuffs, medicines, and other critical supplies needed by a desperate and hungry population. The strike spread to Attica and Thessaloniki, thwarting the first attempts to revive the economy.[22] During the occupation daily hardship as well as violence had unfolded in a constant and predictable pattern, but people had learned to adapt to the new realities and adjusted their lives accordingly. Now, though, the random nature and intensity characteristic of urban warfare compounded the chaos and street-to-street gun battles of December. Suddenly firefights erupted, and then, just as quickly, the streets came under long periods of sniping, forcing people to remain indoors. The enforced confinement created an atmosphere of claustrophobia, along with the hunger and fear Athenians suffered.

Like many Athenians, Dione Dodis was trapped by the outbreak of hostilities. In December 1944, she was a resident of the fashionable Kolonaki district, and although at the time she was only fifteen, the deprivations caused by the national strike are still etched in her memory. After almost sixty years, she recalls, "We suffered during the occupation and had little food, but during the Uprising we got to know real hunger. On some days it was impossible to go out, but regardless of the danger it was necessary to dispose of the garbage and waste in nearby makeshift dumps."[23] Dodis adds, "During the curfew, which started by allowing us out for only two hours (12 to 2 P.M. and later until 6 P.M.), our main concern was to get water from the nearest wells. Another great concern was how to cook our limited amount of stored food without electricity or gas. We resorted to chopping down and burning our kitchen chairs."[24]

Sadly, during the occupation, the small trees that lined the streets of Kolonaki as well as those of other Athenian districts had vanished along with the nearby forests. As in all the areas within the British zone, an influx of people from other parts of the city displaced by the fighting streamed into the upscale district. This situation added a new burden to the besieged residents, whose spare rooms were liable to be temporarily requisitioned by the government to accommodate the refugees. Local residents knew only too well that once rooms were commandeered, they would become protected quarters long after the end of the crisis. If the Kolonaki residents had to play host to anyone, British officers and soldiers were preferable to the uncertainty of visitors imposed by the government. The British could be counted on to pay a small but regular rent, and they would eventually leave; at the same time their presence would forestall any imposed guest.[25]

The Athenians endured the December Uprising, isolated in their homes, hungry, cold, and in the dark. For most people, the Battle of Athens was not a terrible spectacle of war but short vignettes of bitter street fighting and long hours of sniper fire. Many were also fully cognizant that a knock on the door could come from the police searching for communists or a visit by the KKE security forces hunting down suspected collaborators. In either case, the issue of guilt and innocence was hostage to the whims of the grim visitors. Mostly accusation was tantamount to condemnation, and nondescript men anxious to take vengeance in the name of ideology, nationalism, God, king, country—or simply to settle old scores—often delivered justice in a seedy basement or back alley. For weeks following liberation some Athenians indulged in an exorcism of guilt by placing blame on each other. It became common practice to denounce individuals for collaboration, and those singled out were then summoned by the authorities to give an account of their activities. At best it was a long process, often leading to arrest and long periods of detention. Michael Ward, an SOE officer who took part in vetting people accused of collaboration, relates:

> All these accusations had to be investigated, which in the nature of things involved long delays, and until a victim had at length cleared himself he became a file number in the records of the Greek and British security services, forbidden to leave the country and unable to find work in a wide range of jobs. Denunciation, therefore, became the ideal means of settling many irrelevant private grudges and vendettas.[26]

The poison tongue of the informer was aimed at followers of the right and the left, with less regard for political susceptibilities than for private motives. During the course of the December Uprising the consequences for those denounced were often lethal. OPLA, the KKE secret police, and the Communist National Civil Guard generated lists of names of current and potential enemies as well as of those accused of collaboration with the Germans or, for that matter, with the British. On the whole, OPLA agents were less concerned about accuracy than about simply purging large numbers of suspects. Similar conditions applied in the Greek and British security services, but they had more flexibility, and as Ward states, "While the civil war in Athens was raging . . . it was decided to ship away all detainees, as and when they were arrested, to Tobruk where they could be interrogated at leisure and out of the way."[27]

On both sides, self-serving individuals exploited the chaos to satisfy greed or ambition or to cover up their own crimes. Kaiti Economou fell into this category. Economou was a young actress in the Greek National Theater and during the occupation had lost little time coming to terms with the new order. In the fall of 1941, she married Kostas Petrotsopoulos, a notorious traitor and agent of the German secret police. Petrotsopoulos served his German masters by posing as an enthusiastic anglophile, anxious to render assistance to the Allies, but in reality he was working to betray Athenians hiding British soldiers. Occasionally, Economou also played the role of informant for the Axis at the expense of her compatriots, all the while pretending she was a patriot. In time, Athenians saw through the charade spun by the couple and used every opportunity to heap scorn and abuse during Economou's performances. Theater audiences often assailed her with verbal abuse and obscene gestures and by sending her threats.[28]

At the end of the occupation in October 1944, Petrotsopoulos left with the Germans, but Economou remained in Athens and, to squelch the stigma of collaboration, became an enthusiastic supporter of EAM. She took part in demonstrations against the monarchy and the Papandreou government and styled herself a leftist liberal as well as anti-British. It was not enough, however, to dispel completely the aura of traitor and, like others of her ilk, Economou chose to mask her past by denouncing Eleni Papadaki, another actress, as a collaborator. Papadaki had emerged in the 1930s and particularly during the occupation was one of the best actresses in Greece; she is an example of the tragic convergence of fear, greed, and professional jealousy exacerbated by the occupation and resistance.

In the charged atmosphere following the liberation of Athens, the National Theater mirrored the divisions of Greek society, and some of the actors carelessly flung accusations of treachery and betrayal at each other with little regard for the consequences. The actors, the managers, and even the stagehands had to distance themselves from the potential charge of entertaining the enemy during the occupation. Indeed, the maxim that "the show must go on" regardless of circumstances was often lost on a population coping with hunger, disease, and reprisals. Although few could criticize those in essential services, such as sanitation, medical, fire, and ordinary police work, performers, especially high-profile entertainers (in occupied Europe), were vulnerable to charges of collaboration since quite often their audiences included German and Italian officers as well as officials of the local puppet regime.

After the war, many flocked to radical and antiestablishment organizations, partly because all of the puppet governments had sprung from the right-wing spectrum of society, and partly to retroactively acquire bona fide resistance credentials. Most chose the mass-based EAM.

On 20 October, Economou joined the other EAM members of the National Theater Actors Guild in purging from the organization a number of actors, including Papadaki, suspected of collaboration and treason during the occupation. However, the actors were hardly in a position to differentiate between traitor and patriot—they did not conduct even a cursory investigation, and some exploited the chaos and cacophony of accusations to eliminate rivals. Katina Paxinou, Papadaki's older rival, allegedly played a key role in the arrest and subsequent execution of the younger actress. Paxinou, according to this claim, had been the leading actress in the theater until Papadaki surpassed her during the occupation, and thus she took advantage of the December Uprising to get rid of her rival.[29]

Papadaki's crime was twofold: She had had a relationship with Ioannis Rallis, the last puppet premier, and she had quickly emerged as the most popular and successful actress in the theater, peaking during the occupation. Furthermore, she was an easy target. As a high-profile actress, she was easily identified when in the company of German officers, but it was her links to Rallis and his obsession with her that dogged Papadaki until her death.

During the last year of the occupation, Rallis showered her with gifts as well as provided protection and patronage. The puppet premier was smitten despite the twenty-five years in age difference. Kenneth Matthews, a friend and an admirer of Papadaki, in his personal memoir of the Greek civil war, reflected on this unusual relationship:

> Of the fatal friendship with Rallis, I heard a little and shut my ears. There was no need to think it love. Prime minister and young actress complemented each other; he with his powers could offer advancement, she with her glamour, flattery. I knew Rallis too. Born into a ruling family, he had the patrician's values and manners: with a monocle at his eye and a gardenia in his buttonhole, he could have strayed out of the courts or council chambers of the nineteenth century. He was fond of women: by a strange accident, I came into the possession of a letter he wrote in French, which portrayed him as a wooer, at great pains to charm and to please. Vanity, perhaps, destroyed him—vanity, fogged principles, faulty judgment in that he did not foresee who was going to win.[30]

Years later, Rallis' son, George, declared that Rallis was convinced of an Axis victory, but during the first years of the occupation he did little else but express this point of view. In 1941, the Axis had first offered Rallis the opportunity to form a government and only turned to General Tsolakoglou when he refused. Ironically, Ioannis Rallis slid into the vortex of occupational politics and collaboration in the spring of 1943, when it had become obvious even to the most obtuse sympathizers with the Third Reich that the Germans were facing defeat. Yet, according to his son, Rallis believed he could save Greece from the clutches of the left and ensure that the country would pass from Axis rule to liberation with little upheaval.[31]

Nevertheless, the relationship between the naïve actress and the love-struck premier caused a sensation in Athens and drew considerable fire from the left-wing underground press.[32] On 15 October 1943, the newspaper *Ellinikon Ema* ("Greek Blood") condemned Rallis and with considerable sarcasm:

> The puppet government of Athens does not take any measures to . . . protect the people but is focused on the amorous fixation of its president, Ioannis Rallis, towards the well-known actress (Papadaki). It should be noted that Rallis has given the object of his attention a platinum belt, worth hundreds of millions. Meanwhile, the premier plays the potent lover while the nation is dying of hunger.[33]

Two months later, the paper reported that Rallis was in the process of proclaiming a new law to facilitate his third divorce in order to marry Papadaki.[34] The rumor of an impending wedding was baseless, but the speculation persisted, and after liberation some people even believed that Rallis and Papadaki had married secretly; most took it for granted that the two had carried on a love affair.

After the outbreak of hostilities in December, despite her close association with Rallis and the label of collaborator, Papadaki refused to leave her home in Patisia, then a relatively upscale Athenian neighborhood, for the safety of the British zone in Kolonaki. In the early afternoon of 21 December, Kostas Bilirakis, a medical student, and two other men from the EAM chapter of Patisia came to pick her up for questioning from the apartment of a friend. According to witnesses, Papadaki remained unconcerned even when her interrogators pressed her to confess her marriage to Rallis and slapped her across the face when she repeatedly denied the accusation.[35]

The next morning, two men transported the unfortunate actress in a black Ford taxi to Galatsi, a modest settlement nestled on the outskirts of Athens that served as one of the KKE's slaughter centers. According to the few survivors, an oil refinery scarred this otherwise bucolic setting of pine trees and rolling hills, and the acerbic odor of stale petroleum immediately assaulted the senses, creating the impression that the place reeked of death.

Fresh victims came almost every hour and at all times of the day and night. The communist leadership served makeshift justice from a cluster of ramshackle houses, unfettered by legal procedure or rules of evidence. A typical trial consisted of a brief interrogation, usually taking less than a quarter of an hour, and those found guilty of an ever-growing list of crimes were sent to the grounds of the oil refinery less than 100 yards from the "court." There hundreds of luckless people, including a large number of police and gendarme officers, were executed after being tortured.

The standard means of execution was the axe. Each victim had to undress and kneel with the head resting on a large stone. The executioner could decapitate the condemned man or woman (occasionally even a child), slice his or her throat, or hack away with the axe, reducing the individual to a heap of flesh and bone. Gendarmes and police officers usually suffered ghastly and extensive torture just prior to execution, but exceptions were made for well-known members of the right or collaborators.

Upon arrival in Galatsi, Papadaki was taken to one of the houses expropriated by the KKE that served as a holding area for the accused. The commander of the unit, Captain Orestes, was a twenty-two-year-old sadistic killer who was less interested in Papadaki's guilt or innocence than in her fur coat, or at least this is how he was later portrayed by the KKE. The "trial" of Papadaki along with that of seven officers of the gendarmerie was quick and decisive. Captain Orestes, followed by two of his henchmen, approached the accused and brusquely, in the name of the people, collected all their valuables: jewelry, watches, and money.

At first, he decreed that Papadaki be held as a hostage and then moved on to the next batch of prisoners. A little later, he remembered Papadaki and, turning to one of his colleagues, inquired, "What did she say her name was?" and "Isn't she the one denounced by the actors' union?" After these queries, Orestes changed his mind and condemned Papadaki to death, specifying the use of the axe for the execution.[36]

Once again, she was hustled into the same black Ford taxi and in a few minutes covered the 100 yards to the oil refinery. Vases Makaronis, a former grocer and the one charged with killing the actress, recalled at his trial a few months later, "She arrived in a car squeezed between two members of the Civil Guard. She was clutching her fur coat to ward off a devil of a cold day." Orestes arrived in another car and ordered her to hand over the fur coat; she meekly complied, but when he demanded all her clothes, Papadaki finally realized that the end was near, broke down, and started to scream.

The guards then seized the poor woman and dragged her a few yards to the side of an open pit. There, they tore off the rest of her garments and for a few minutes left Papadaki, shivering and whimpering, waiting for the inevitable blows from the axe. At his trial, Makaronis testified that he felt sorry for the actress and decided not to use the axe. Instead, he sat her down at the edge of the open grave and fired one bullet into her right temple. Seconds after the shot rang out, Papadaki's body slid effortlessly into the improvised tomb.[37]

Whether this version of Papadaki's end is true or just the killer playing on the court's sympathy is not certain, just as it is not completely certain which person or persons were in fact ultimately responsible for her death. However, it is plausible that the individuals who caused her arrest were the EAM theater actors who had denounced her as a collaborator and expelled her from the actors' guild.

More than a month later, on 26 January, Papadaki's remains were uncovered in one of a series of shallow graves, not too far from the place of execution. Papadaki's body was found buried with those of four other victims in the garden of a small villa. All her clothes were gone except for a silk slip that was raised to her chest and a garter belt still fastened about her waist, suggesting sexual assault. According to the autopsy report, in addition to extensive trauma, large parts of her skin had been ripped off before or after decapitation.[38] News of the discovery and the dreadful condition of Papadaki's body spread rapidly. Dozens of students from the School of Drama rushed to the grave site and attempted to guard her modesty by covering what was left of Papadaki with branches from nearby cypress trees.[39]

They were not alone. North of Athens in the suburb of Peristeraki clusters of people hung about the edge of a mass burial site that stretched across an empty field along a rocky hillside. A desperate few strayed onto the field to pick through the decomposing human fragments in a valiant effort to identify fathers, mothers, brothers, sisters, husbands, wives, and children and at least spare them the indignity of a common grave. Approximately 1,500 victims of the KKE's pogrom were discovered there. The victims, according to witnesses, had been executed mostly with axes and knives. Some of the women and girls had been sexually violated, and most had been mutilated. The bodies had been dumped in trenches 200 yards long, and during the course of the exhumations the coroners and their workers came across an extraordinary sight: a bucket filled with gouged-out human eyes.[40]

Many of the dead were military and police officers, but the Peristeraki mass burial site also included a good cross section of Athenian society and members of the intelligentsia.[41] "If there ever was a scene straight from hell, this was it," wrote Kenneth Matthews, the BBC correspondent in Athens:

> The bodies were being exhumed from a series of parallel trenches in which the diggers were still working. As each was uncovered, it was laid out on the lip of the trench, naked or half naked, just as it had been buried. Scattered in small groups on the hillside, the women folk of the victims kept up a low wailing which rose from time to time to a blood-chilling shriek of lamentation. Over all a charnel smell making the air sick, and the bright January sunlight, which picked out every detail in dreadful clarity.[42]

Evidence of further atrocities materialized when the British, joined by newly recruited Greek national guard forces, drove ELAS away from the parts of Athens they had controlled. Each new discovery of executions and mass burial sites underscored the random and indiscriminate nature of the killings. Many of the KKE's victims were ordinary people who had, at one time or another, made disparaging comments about EAM or with whom a neighbor had simply exploited the circumstances to settle a vendetta. In many such instances, the accused were apprehended late at night and dispatched with machine guns, and their bodies thrown down the nearest well. Hundreds of wells and cisterns had provided water to Athens and the surrounding districts for millennia, but after the construction of the Marathon Dam they had fallen into disuse. In the course of the fighting, the wells became makeshift burial sites and a convenient place for corpses of murdered and executed Athenians.

One such victim was a twenty-seven-year-old gardener, Charilaos Karlis, who remarkably survived execution and entombment in a well. The knock on the door for Karlis came at 3:00 A.M. on 25 December 1944, and when he answered a group of men burst into his home, dragging him outside along with his two sisters and a brother. Out in the street, more people were being rounded up from the neighborhood. The ELAS detachment finally led thirty-five men and women first to the bank of the Ilisus River and from there to a partially built church in the area. The ELAS men found a small house beside the church and decided to use it for the interrogations. They forced the occupants, a family of four, to leave and proceeded to question the prisoners. According to Karlis:

First, they took our clothes and after some perfunctory questioning they marched us in single file for about fifteen minutes to the edge of a large well. At that moment, they fired on us with automatic weapons. A few jumped into the well to avoid the gunfire, most, however were killed or wounded. My brother and I survived because we played dead. I had thick and long hair, which made my head appear larger, so that when an ELAS fired three shots in the direction of my head he missed and I was only grazed by one bullet. I continued to pretend I was dead. The executioners dragged the bodies to the edge of the well, stripped them and tossed them into the hole. When my turn came I could hear them saying "take off his shoes they are new and should not go to waste." I was thrown ten or twelve meters down into the well, my body and face hitting its sides but the corpses of those tossed earlier broke my fall. For a few minutes I kept being struck by the other bodies they were throwing into the well. Not all of them were dead and I could hear a few still moaning. When the ELAS men finished, they tossed stones, pieces of wood, empty cans and other trash in order to fill and cover the well. I was fortunate because I found a curved piece of metal that I held over my head to protect me. After two hours I managed to climb to the top and with considerable effort I moved one of the large stones that had covered the top of the well.[43]

The KKE leadership was appalled by Papadaki's death but made no apologies for the other killings and atrocities. A few days later, Orestes, the sadistic commandant of the Galatsi execution center, was arrested and after a summary trial faced a public execution in Athens. A firing squad also dealt with some of his close associates not too far from the oil refinery, where he had arbitrarily and casually dispensed pain and death, often for no other reason than to claim the clothes or jewelry of the accused. Nikos Zachariadis later denounced the execution of Papadaki, and in the decades following the civil war the KKE absolved itself from all responsibility for Papadaki's execution by continuing to blame the entire episode on Orestes. Phoibos Grigoriadis, an officer in ELAS and one of the early left-wing historians of the Greek civil war, however, admitted "that the murders such as those of Papadaki could not be covered up under any circumstances."[44]

While the KKE punished Orestes, it did not disown Makaronis, the man who either tortured Papadaki to death or, moved by pity, simply shot her. He, along with all the other executioners from the oil refinery, were arrested a few months after the end of the December Uprising and eventually condemned to death. Remarkably, following the cessation of the city's hostilities, they had resumed their civilian vocations. One, employed as a ticket collector, was wearing the sweater of one of his victims, and a relative of the victim identified the garment.

Makaronis was a humble grocer, typical of the thousands of loyal communist cadres, who followed the KKE's directives to the letter, and one of the functionaries who undertook the party's dirty work. In this respect, he was little different from some of the men who filled the ranks of the Security Battalions and was practically identical to those who later tortured confessions and declarations of repentance out of suspected communists. Men like Makaronis who had resented serving at the beck and call of wealthy neighbors or prosperous farmers, or who harbored a grudge against civic officials or had been awed by the expertise of professionals, suddenly were in a position to humble, humiliate, and destroy their "betters."

Such individuals, for the first time in their lives, could exercise power by exploiting the chaotic conditions that prevailed in Athens, but others only did so at the behest of the KKE, which instituted a reign of terror against the wartime collaborators that quickly expanded into a general purge of all vestiges of the political, economic, educational, professional, and cultural establishment of Athens. Astonishingly, the KKE took the decision to implement such a radical and brutal course of action after the tide of battle had turned against ELAS. Part of the motive was revenge; the KKE was striving to punish collaborators and opponents while it still had the ability to do so. The executions also indicated the outline of a clumsy attempt at social revolution by trying to decapitate the old order through the elimination of its current and prospective leaders.

At the very least, the KKE made a concerted effort to destroy all rival Marxist organizations, and during the course of the December Uprising, OPLA hit squads killed dozens of members of the rival Archeiomarxists organization as well as followers of Trotsky. The Archeiomarxists originally formed a secret group within the Socialist Labor Party, which later became the Greek Communist Party. In 1924, the KKE expelled the Archeiomarxists, who, in turn, went on to establish their own political party. Their membership, during the interwar period, often surpassed that of the KKE.[45]

Another consideration is that such vicious policies were born out of fear. By the third week of December, even the most optimistic Greek communist must have realized that it was no longer possible to overcome the British defenses in the center of Athens and that it was only a matter of time before ELAS would concede defeat.

In the event, the highpoint of the ELAS advance against the British and Greek forces in Athens came on the night of 15–16 December 1944. After the collapse of any prospect for a diplomatic settlement with the British and the Papandreou government, ELAS prepared for an all-out offensive against the British positions in the center of Athens. The objective was to overwhelm the enemy by striking simultaneously against the British defenses from three different directions. Concurrent assaults were a difficult feat for well-trained and disciplined armies, but next to impossible for the haphazardly organized ELAS forces. When ELAS launched the attacks on the night of 15–16 December, the assaults were not synchronized, and the British were able to defeat them piecemeal. During the course of the battle, British armored cars and tanks easily shifted from one sector to another, giving the hard-pressed infantry additional firepower at critical moments in the fighting.

ELAS troops, on the other hand, did manage to break through on the east flank of the British lines. In the late night of 13 December (two days ahead of the main ELAS offensive), about 1,000 ELAS troops stormed the area of the Infantry Barracks, which were the quarters of the British armored brigade and a few other units. The ELAS unit succeeded in penetrating very close to the barracks by using troops dressed in British and Greek police uniforms. By the time the defenders realized the ruse, ELAS had captured half the barracks, but instead of trying to capture the British artillery and mortars, they diverted their attention to burning and looting the supply dump as well as killing the civilian radio operators. In the morning the Second Battalion (King's Royal Rifle Corps), supported by armor, cleared the barracks, inflicting heavy losses on ELAS.

Once again, however, rumors of ELAS atrocities were further chipping away at the presumed moral superiority that the left-wing forces had enjoyed from the beginning of the battle. This time a story was circulating among the soldiers of the Fourth Division that the body of a noncommissioned officer of the Parachute Brigade attached to them had been found in a horrible state. The man had had his legs and arms cut off and then was buried alive. The paratroopers became outraged, and although they had taken over 120 ELAS prisoners in the previous engagement, after this alleged atrocity the number of prisoners fell off considerably.

Despite the determination of ELAS to capture the barracks and the high casualties this engagement inflicted on both sides, the attack failed. Although ELAS enjoyed numerical superiority and was fighting on familiar ground, it could not successfully make the transition from guer-rilla warfare to conventional battle. As long as ELAS had engaged in hit-and-run, sniping, sabotage, and other irregular tactics, it could inflict significant losses on the British and hope to bring about a political out-come to the December Uprising.

The failure of the ELAS offensive spelled the end of any prospects for a military victory in Athens and hence the collapse of the left's effort to in-fluence events in Greece. From this point, Scobie's forces grew stronger, with the increasing flow of reinforcements, while those of ELAS grew progressively weaker each passing day. Toward the third week of Decem-ber, two new British divisions as well as a brigade of the Fourth Indian Division and several miscellaneous units arrived in Phaliron Bay and be-gan the process of relieving the beleaguered British forces in Athens. A new officer, Major-General "Ginger" Hawkesworth, was given command of the new forces as well as operational control of all the British and Greek government units. Except for rushing to the rescue of a sector un-der immediate threat and slowly opening a link with the center of Athens, Hawkesworth's corps did not launch an all-out offensive.

The storm of criticism in Britain as well as in the international commu-nity over British intervention in Greece had forced Churchill to attempt a compromise resolution of the crisis with EAM-ELAS. Churchill, joined by Anthony Eden, the foreign secretary, made the difficult journey to Athens on Christmas Day to preside over a conference that included representa-tives of the Papandreou government, the KKE, EAM, and ELAS.

The meeting took place in the Greek foreign ministry from 26 to 27 December, in a bleak room with no heat and lit by hurricane lamps, while sporadic gunfire accompanied the proceedings.

Unfortunately, none of the parties saw any reason to make serious concessions and reach any kind of agreement to end the fighting. The British terms remained the same—ELAS had to disarm and evacuate Athens and the surrounding area. For their part, the KKE-EAM-ELAS delegates remained intransigent, and refusing to concede defeat, they did not accept the British demands. Furthermore, they insisted on a predominant role in any coalition Greek government. It may be that they did not appreciate the scale of British reinforcements or were counting on international pressure, especially from the Americans and Soviets, to force Churchill to accept a compromise that left them with ELAS intact and in control of Athens.

The conservative politicians, but especially the royalists and the ultra-right-wing cabals that had emerged during the uprising, were not in a hurry to see the British stop demolishing EAM-ELAS. When the conference began, some of them tried to walk out rather than sit with the "bandits" and were only prevented from doing so by the British. They were not to be disappointed. After fruitless negotiations for over two days, the meeting broke down. The only point of agreement was the future appointment of Archbishop Damaskinos as regent, pending the outcome of a referendum on the future of the Greek monarchy. It fell on Churchill, upon his return to London on 29 December, to convince a very reluctant George II to accept the Greek cleric as regent. It was not a pleasant task for Churchill, who, according to Roy Jenkins, "had to spend half the night (with Eden) bludgeoning the stubborn Greek King into accepting a regency."[46] Eventually, Churchill had to tell George II that "if he did not agree the matter would be settled without him and that we would recognize the new Government instead of him."[47]

In the meantime, some of the communist political leadership, chose to grapple with the inevitable consequences of military defeat by a means so terrible that afterward even the most stalwart defenders of EAM-ELAS were hamstrung to find excuses for the conduct of the left. In a fit of shortsightedness the KKE decided to take hostages in order to incarcerate and punish collaborators (who the left claimed had been allowed to remain at large and protected by the Papandreou government) and as retaliation for the prisoners taken by the British and the Greek government forces.[48] The fateful decision was taken around the middle of December, in a secret meeting of senior communist leaders at the home of Mitsos Partsalidis, secretary of EAM's central committee. Partsalidis' house was out of the way and set within a large garden, an ideal location for confidential discussions. Only a few of those present opposed this drastic action, and afterward orders were given to EAM-ELAS as well as the various organs of the KKE, such as OPLA and the National Civil Guard, to round up hostages. A quarter of a century later, Kaiti Zevgou, who had taken part in the decision, wrote in her memoirs: "Instead of sitting down and analyzing which people should be taken and under what conditions, some of our members, at times, simply set an artificial number and filled it. Many mistakes were made, which considerably damaged our reputation. We are still paying today for these consequences."[49]

A little later, Zevgou had an opportunity to see the consequences of her decision as well as that of her colleagues:

> One day I was on the road to the party headquarters at Chasia and shared a ride with Chrysa (a member of the KKE's Central Committee). I could see something in the distance moving like a snake on the ground. A few moments later we understood it was a column of hostages, which was coming from the direction we were going. Both Chrysa and I were shocked. We turned our heads the other way and remained silent. The spectacle was unsettling. A column of people exhausted and worn out by fatigue with despair on their faces, herded by armed guards on the other side of the column. I still remember that the head of the column was a very old man who was barely dragging his feet. As I said above, it was one of the mistakes of the movement. The reaction (the Right) exploited such mistakes to cover up the orgy of terror that spilled out after December and continues, whenever it can, until today and will not allow the national schism to end.[50]

The voices of the victims, however, are rarely heard above the din of re-criminations and finger pointing over the December Uprising.[51] Despina Makka-Photiadi was a proud woman devoted to her family, friends, and the close society of Athens. She came from a family of well-to-do professionals, who ensured she received an excellent liberal education, and she could speak German, English, French, and some Italian. In the great debate over monarchy, she remained for the rest of her life a committed Venizelist and opposed the return of the king. In 1940–1941, she was a volunteer nurse, and during the occupation she labored in the soup kitchens of the Greek Red Cross.[52] Effectively, Despina's liberalism and antimonarchism did not set her too far apart from the general goals of EAM. Her daughter had been a member of the left-wing organization for one year. Her reward for surviving the famine and the exigencies of foreign occupation was to be taken as a hostage by the KKE. Toward the end of her life she decided to compile her experiences as an attempt to make sense of that terrible ordeal.[53]

Her poignant account begins with the joy of liberation, which was all too brief, and the outbreak of the December Uprising. From her home in Psychiko, a suburb of Athens (without radio or telephone and with limited travel to the city), she and her friends could only get snippets of news of the events in Athens. In the first week of December, Despina noticed that some acquaintances who were members of EAM started acting strangely, and one of them warned her daughters to leave as soon as possible. After 20 December, Despina to her horror watched as the Communist National Civil Guard started rounding up men and a little later also women as hostages. Her turn came a few days later. A group of ELAS men came to her, and when she inquired what they wanted, they replied, "You and your two daughters." The men then said, "You have five minutes to get ready, bring two blankets and if you have food ready bring it along."[54] From this point on, life as Despina and her family understood it vanished; she and her daughters became hostages at the whim and mercy of the KKE:

> They organized us in a column of three across, the men were placed ahead of the women and we proceeded along Kiphisias Boulevard. The sky darkened and a light rain began to fall. As we headed towards the mountains a strong wind began to flail our faces but the guards yelled at us to move faster. We passed the suburbs of Galatsi and Kypseli and only when we reached a small town in the late evening, they stopped and allowed us to rest on the sidewalks and on the ground. There we sat in the cold December night. Eventually, they led us to an abandoned community center where we spent the night.[55]

Despina and her daughters, along with dozens of other women whose names had been placed on a list of suspected reactionaries, were forced to walk for days. At first, they left behind well-known suburbs northwest of Athens, and then they headed further north into unknown parts of the hinterland past small villages in the mountains. In some places, the locals were kind and offered the hostages what little food or milk they could spare. As they moved from place to place, the column grew longer. The guards had little sympathy for the hostages, and whether they were old, young, pregnant, handicapped, or sick, those who could not join the column were shot, stabbed, or on some occasions beaten to death.

A group of Royal Air Force prisoners, who fared little better under ELAS captivity, witnessed one of these wretched civilian columns: "Mostly old and elderly men, women and children, they were all scantily clad and most without shoes. Some were leaving bloody footprints in the snow. Like drunken cowboys urging on a herd of cattle, their guards repeatedly fired shots over their heads. An old man collapsed moaning. He was shot and thrown into a ditch." Nicoloidis Fortis, an architect at the Athens Town Hall, was one of the hostages, and he remembers, "We were compelled to march thirty miles a day. Children were taken from their mothers because they were unable to keep up." He saw two women murdered, the first because she had hidden thirty gold sovereigns in her clothing and the second because she failed to make that known to the guards.[56]

For Despina and her daughters, the ordeal came to an end in the first week of January, when both sides began negotiating a truce, but for some of the other hostages the agony went on until the end of the month. After the collapse of the talks on 26–27 December, General Hawkesworth launched a major offensive on 3 January 1945 that drove ELAS from Athens in just two weeks. On 11 January 1945, delegates from ELAS met with General Scobie and asked for an armistice. ELAS agreed to evacuate Athens and Boiotia as well as fall back twenty-five miles from Thessaloniki. Although Scobie and Hawkesworth preferred to push their offensive until ELAS was completely destroyed, political considerations and events beyond their control spared the left the humiliation of total collapse. The German Ardennes offensive had threatened to break through the Allied lines, and even though it failed, the British needed to reinforce their armies on the northwestern Europe front. They could not afford the public relations nightmare of continuing to fight EAM-ELAS, which, for most of the world, represented the Greek resistance. After protracted negotiations the British, the Greek government, and the KKE-EAM-ELAS formally ended the Battle of Athens with the conclusion of the Varkiza Agreement on 12 February 1945. The agreement, ultimately, achieved little in the long run, except to end the fighting in Athens. Both sides could claim victory—the British and the Greek government because they had actually won the battle, and the KKE-EAM-ELAS because they had not lost the war, but merely one campaign.

The December Uprising left Athens in shambles with thousands of people homeless and a large number of its citizens permanently scarred and bitterly divided. Despina begins her unpublished memoir by lamenting, "As long as I live [she passed away in 1990] I will never forget December of 1944. I, along with thousands of other Greeks who suffered a great deal, believe that Greece should not forget that cursed month, which unleashed a great storm that was brewing for years."[57]

During the thirty-three days of fighting, the once proud neighborhoods of Kolonaki, which had been synonymous with upper-class privilege, were squeezed from all quarters by the fighting and reduced to a beleaguered enclave. In December 1944 the ELAS attacks pressing toward the center of Athens and the fashionable districts such as Kolonaki also symbolized the assault of the left against the political hegemony of the traditional political and economic establishment.

In 1944, however, the authority of this elite was in tatters. The ravages of the occupation, along with the chaos of liberation and civil war, had humbled and distorted the once affluent and influential Athenian families. The powerful groups and individuals who had reigned over Greece before the war, and whose imprint was stamped on all aspects of Greek political (whether republican or royalist), economic, and cultural life, had been decimated by the occupation and rendered almost irrelevant by the resistance. During the crisis, the village peasants and the humble folk of the working-class districts fighting with ELAS were ever so briefly the masters of Greece and Athens. Astonishingly, for the first time in the Greek political dynamic, the village ruled the city.

The survivors of the middle and upper classes clung to whatever represented the old political authority, whether this meant following the monarchy, the provisional government, the British, or even the ultra-right-wing paramilitary bands that had sprouted just prior to liberation. Still others sought another alternative by trying to leave the country, although there were few places in the world that were accessible, except for the very wealthy. Just about all of the Greek shipping magnates, for example, had escaped to London and New York. Young women, however, discovered that marriage to foreigners offered one of the few practical avenues of escape from the prospect of a grim economic future in war-torn Greece. To these women, British officers and even ordinary soldiers were a passport to a fresh start, especially since many wrongly assumed that any man from the United Kingdom was also wealthy and a member of the British aristocracy. Later, in the case of Americans, there was the equally mistaken notion was that they were all fabulously rich. After liberation, during and after the December Uprising, just about every social occasion in Athens included its share of what Michael Ward, one of the few SOE officers in Athens at the time, called the "Kolonaki girls, almost all known to each other and encountered repeatedly at party after party . . . gyrating on the floor with their British boyfriends. There was something exotic about going out with a foreigner and escaping in the mildest way the strict control exercised by many middle class parents, and to be frank, there was the chance of marriage to an Englezaki (Englishman)."[58]

At first, dozens, then hundreds of these young, mostly middle-class, women managed to walk down the aisle with their trophy Englishmen and later were transported to Britain to begin their new lives. Dodis also recalls that language was not a barrier:

In the spring after the Dekemvriana [December Uprising] I went to work (after school) at a British Officers' Mess as an interpreter. By then I was sixteen years old. Few people knew English then in Greece. At the canteen my main occupation turned out to be interpreting for couples who were planning to get married. The Greek girls didn't know any English and, of course, the British soldiers didn't know a word of Greek. Yet, they were intending to get married. The girls wanted to know where the men lived and how well off they were. The British soldiers presented a rosy picture. In other words, they told them a bunch of lies and that is why most of the girls returned within a year or two. As it was natural the girls were hoping for a better life in England. The only girl I know who didn't return to Greece was my husband's sister. She braved it in Flixton, outside Manchester, in quite poor conditions until her family was able to send her financial help. She stayed married and still is with Frank.[59]

According to Ward, who also acquired a Greek bride, most of these unions did not survive more than "a year or two and the majority of these women decamped back to Greece."[60]

Individually and collectively, the Greek war brides were symptomatic of the social distortions that buffeted Greek society in the postwar period. Perhaps they may be viewed as a metaphor for the relationship between the British and the Greek right. Eventually, and to some extent because of the December Uprising, the conservative element of Greek society, including that of Athens, was reconstituted and reinvigorated after 1945 as the "new right." By the end of 1944, the old monarchist-Venizelist schism had mutated beyond recognition, and its adherents melted into the forces of either the left or the right.

Prior to the occupation, the Venizelist-republican and the royalist factions had monopolized the Greek political scene. Although Greek liberalism and antimonarchism had become synonymous with the Venizelists, it did not necessarily mean that all the members of the Venizelos faction subscribed to liberal convictions and loathed the monarchy or that every royalist rejected liberal ideas. Rather, personal rivalry and competition for power often blurred their ideological differences, and on occasion, they easily shifted from one group to the other. The parties and factions of the left, on the other hand, were small and marginal in prewar Greek society. During the period of the resistance, however, the roles were reversed, and the influence of the left overshadowed that of the traditional political parties.

At the same time, membership in the left or right did not necessarily emanate from defined constituencies of liberals, socialists, communists, royalists, or conservatives. In this context, it is difficult to determine the ideological proclivities of those who joined EAM as well as of those who fought for ELAS. Yet it is evident from the extant sources that many who followed EAM-ELAS did so out of patriotic and nationalist motives. The same can be said of those who supported the other resistance organizations. For example, ELAS and EDES included a large number of professional and monarchist officers, while approximately another thousand, many of them republicans, joined the notorious Security Battalions. After liberation, thousands of resistance fighters, regardless of their ideological proclivities, were labeled leftists simply because they had fought with ELAS or participated in EAM. Ironically, this stigma included the professional officers in ELAS, most of whom had been loyal to the crown, just as thousands of republicans decided that the monarchy was the best guarantee against communism and went over to the royalist camp. Hence, the fear of communism and professional opportunism converged in the emergence of the new right and contributed to the establishment of the anticommunist Greek state.

Furthermore, the unwillingness of the British, because of political considerations, to inflict total destruction on ELAS meant that the left could count on the support of a large body of men and women for support. Arguably a large number of ELAS and EAM followers accepted defeat and attempted to reintegrate into society—some did, but a great many could not avoid persecution by their political opponents. The failure of the succession of governments in the aftermath of the December Uprising to effect even a modicum of reconciliation and their inability to control the lawlessness of the right-wing gangs roaming the countryside practically paved the way for another confrontation. The next, and final, round of the civil war (1946–1949) was the most destructive and left deeper wounds and divisions in Greek society, which have lingered into the twenty-first century. However, the legacy of the last round of the Greek civil war is also intertwined with the onset of the cold war and East-West rivalry between the United States and the Soviet Union.

5

THE INTERNATIONAL CIVIL WAR

Greece's fate is in your hands.

〜PRIME MINISTER SOPHOULIS
TO GEORGE MARSHALL
15 OCTOBER 1948

MAJOR NICHOLAS MOUSKOUNDIS, THE HEAD OF THE GREEK
General Security Service in northern Greece, kept his office sparse. The
plain desk, chair, and file cabinet barely intruded into the solitude of the
room. It was a space devoid of any personal paraphernalia, with the exception of a large icon of Jesus Christ hanging on the wall directly behind the major's chair. A God-fearing man, he attended church services
every Sunday, regardless of circumstance. Major Mouskoundis was Spar-
tan in his habits, taciturn, and short on diplomatic skills. He was over-
weight and bald, but still known as a man who got things done. He also
had a reputation as a fierce nationalist and as a fanatical anticommunist.[1]

On a blazing hot afternoon in August 1948 a man in his early thirties
was sitting on a hard straight-backed chair in the director's office of the
Thessaloniki General Security Service. Grigoris Staktopoulos, the man
sitting on the chair facing Mouskoundis, had been a journalist up until

the time he became a pawn of the General Security Service. In 1948, before the Security Service picked him up, Staktopoulos was making a modest living as a stringer for Reuters, the British wire service, and as a reporter for the Greek newspaper *Macedonia*. In fact, he had achieved little in either his personal or his professional life to distinguish himself. According to some accounts he was "an unpretentious run-of-the-mill journalist, conscientious as a reporter but only modestly ambitious and not very imaginative, gentle to a fault, a bachelor much tied to his mother and sisters, for whom he was the principal means of support."[2] Individuals less well disposed to Staktopoulos described him as "restless, egotistical at times, something of a show off . . . who 'always pretended to know everybody and everything and was ready to tell you so, especially if you were a foreigner.'"[3]

Staktopoulos had been educated at the elite American-run Anatolia College, where he became fluent in English. His education enabled him to work as a translator and interpreter.[4] During the occupation, he was one of the hundreds of thousands of EAM followers and like some had drifted to the KKE; not an ideologue or a committed Marxist, he had joined in order to secure employment as a journalist. Edmund Keeley, who wrote one of the few accounts in English of the Polk affair, writes of Staktopoulos: "To ensure the family's sustenance he was apparently ready to work for almost anybody of whatever political persuasion who would use his special qualifications as an English-speaking newspaperman."[5] Although Staktopoulos' past was not remarkable, it was sufficient to cast him in the role of prime suspect for the assassination of the American George Polk, the CBS Middle East correspondent.

There are several versions of Polk's last hours in Thessaloniki, but none have provided a satisfactory explanation of why the American journalist disappeared and was not seen again until his lifeless body was found floating in the Thessaloniki harbor. One theory has it that Polk had arrived in Thessaloniki on 7 March 1948 after his plane had been diverted from the Kavalla airport, his original destination, because of heavy rain. He proceeded to make some indiscreet inquiries about establishing contact with KKE members, who could secure for him an interview with

Markos Vaphiadis, the commander of the Greek Democratic Army (the name of the Greek communist forces fighting in the new round of the civil war that had broken out in the summer of 1947). Polk had paid a visit to the American consul, who warned him against making any attempts to contact the insurgents or travel to territory controlled by them. Next, he contacted Randall Coat, the British information officer reputed to have links with the rebels; Coat, again depending on conflicting accounts, either threw Polk out of his office or encouraged him by saying that he could help Polk.[6] A few days later Polk vanished, and Coat was transferred to Oslo, Norway, and his secretary to Australia, a fact lending credence to the subsequent conspiracy theories that have continued for more than half a century after the Polk murder.[7]

In the course of his inquiries, Polk met with several other journalists as well as British, American consular, and UN officials. On one occasion, at the bar in the Mediterranean Hotel, Helen Mamas, a Greek-American and stringer for the Associated Press, introduced Polk to Staktopoulos and a Greek liaison officer with the United Nations Special Committee on the Balkans (UNSCOB). After a few drinks, Polk, Mamas, and a few others went on to dinner. Later Staktopoulos called Mamas to get the exact spelling of Polk's name as well as of the names of the other American correspondents, in order to report the visit of the foreigners to the city in the newspaper *Macedonia*, which was a professional courtesy common among journalists in Thessaloniki.[8]

At 11:00 P.M. on 7 May, Polk and the others left the restaurant, at which point Polk headed down a street toward his hotel. Later, the hotel porters testified that they had seen Polk return at 1:00 A.M. Leaving his room very early the next day (Saturday), Polk dropped in on an acquaintance at the U.S. consulate and went on to visit Randall Coat at the British information office. In the afternoon he telegraphed his wife, Rhea, to expect him in Kavalla on Monday or Tuesday. On Saturday evening at 7:00 he had a drink at his hotel bar with Gerald Drew, the American delegate to UNSCOB, and his wife. The hotel staff noticed that Polk left the hotel at 11:00 that night, returned fifteen minutes later, and left again at 12:45 A.M.

That was the last time anyone ever saw Polk alive. A week later, the American's bloated body surfaced in Thessaloniki Bay, plunging the Greek authorities into a fruitless search for the culprit or culprits responsible for killing the American. The list of suspects who, directly or indirectly, may have had some link to delivering Polk to his murderers was a long one.

The news of George Polk's death also brought the remote Greek civil war directly to America. The impact of radio news, which had emerged in its own right as a new form of media during the Second World War, added considerable intensity and drama to an otherwise obscure event. The killing of this American journalist put a face to the conflict, which for most people in the United States was as impersonal as it was remote. Americans became outraged. Howard K. Smith, from CBS, reported that Polk's death was "deliberate execution . . . planned to be spectacular, planned to intimidate. If the murderers are not discovered, an invisible but inevitable pressure of intimidation will rest on every American correspondent abroad."[9] The Greek government quickly attributed Polk's murder to the communists and thus absolved itself of any responsibility. However, Greek officials underestimated the public outcry in the United States, and the failure to produce the killers provoked accusations of cover-up.

The American Overseas Writers' Association, led by Walter Lippman, offered a $10,000 reward for any information on Polk's murder and procured the services of William Donovan, the former head of America's OSS, to undertake a separate investigation. Donovan, with much aplomb, traveled to Greece and intimidated, cajoled, and flattered the representatives of Greek security. Afterward he announced that they were "handling the case satisfactorily."[10] It was only when George Marshall announced that he was going to Greece to look into the situation himself that the Greek authorities produced Grigoris Staktopoulos.

On 14 August 1948 at 2:30 in the afternoon, two nondescript men approached Grigoris Staktopoulos while he was waiting to board the trolley. One of them tapped him on the shoulder and demanded, "Your identity card." Staktopoulos, realizing that the men were plain-clothes police, complied instantly. After scrutinizing the document, one policeman said, "Come to the Security Service for an identification [check]."[11] Staktopoulos could hardly refuse, and for him and his family the journey to hell had begun. He was held and questioned for months, and in addition, the Security Service picked up his mother and his two sisters—their crime was suspicion by association.

Almost six weeks later Staktopoulos was sitting tied to a chair in Mouskoundis' office and staring into a blinding light. He could barely follow the major as the policeman slowly circled him like a vulture circles its prey and kept repeating, "You are involved, you are involved"; then in a soft voice the major intoned, "I will save you." Ignoring his prisoner's denials, the major continued to hover, resuming the chant, "You are involved, you are involved," and then in a hush he whispered in Staktopoulos' ear, "I will save you. I could have had you disappear any time when you were returning home late at night, but you are fortunate that your mother has had a son killed in the war."[12]

Staktopoulos, the victim, and Mouskoundis, the tormentor, performed this ritual for weeks. Afterward, the major's assistants subjected Staktopoulos to further interrogation, which in the parlance of the General Security Service meant torture. The "interrogation" varied from day to day and was inflicted according to the whim of each inquisitor. Staktopoulos was compelled to stand for hours and then made to suffer sleep deprivation. Subsequently, he was tormented with hunger and thirst, followed by severe beatings with truncheons and knuckledusters. Occasionally, Mouskoundis got physical with Staktopoulos, forcing him to stand with his back against a wall and then grinding down on his toes or kneeing him in the groin. On other days, Staktopoulos would be hung upside down in his cell; later he was tortured with electric shocks to the soles of his feet.[13]

Astonishingly, both victim and tormentor knew that Staktopoulos was innocent, Staktopoulos because he had not committed the crime and Mouskoundis because he had fabricated the evidence that implicated the unfortunate journalist. Yet, in the turbulent and almost surreal environment of the 1946 Greek civil war, which had begun two years earlier, guilt or innocence was not germane—sacrifice for the fatherland was the relevant issue. During the course of the civil war, the ultra-Greek right usurped patriotism as an absolute virtue exclusive to itself. The word *ethnikophron,* which translates as "nationalist-minded," encapsulated how the right labeled itself; more precisely it defined people in black and white terms as either godless communists or *ethnikophrons.* In this political and religious climate, individuals, when challenged by the authorities, had to prove that they were not communists and to demonstrate their "nationalist-minded" credentials.

Staktopoulos could establish he was nationalist-minded by admitting to the murder and serving the interests of the Greek state. "You have an obligation to the fatherland to confess," demanded Constantine Rendis, Minister of Public Order.[14] The minister, anxious to see a speedy end to the Polk affair, had made a snap visit to Thessaloniki to confront Staktopoulos. Unfortunately, the victim refused the honor of sparing the fatherland further difficulties by confessing to a crime he had not committed. For his impudence, Mouskoundis and his aides devised new, and more imaginative, techniques of persuasion. They forced him to strip and proceeded to yank slowly the hair on his chest and back, one at a time. This painful exercise was only a prelude to another, and much more excruciating, torment. Using wire, they tied his wrists to his elbows and his knees to his ankles, then his arms to his legs. Afterward he was laid out on the floor of his cell. In a short time, Staktopoulos began to struggle against the binding in response to intense pain, but the movement only made it worse, and soon his cries reverberated in the corridor.[15] He passed out, and when he finally came around, disoriented and terrified, his remaining courage shriveled. He agreed to confess that he had lured Polk to a secret meeting with two communist assassins who shot the American on a small boat in the harbor. The investigation, confession, and subsequent trial did little credit to the Greeks, the Americans, or the cause of justice. On 21 April 1949, a jury that deliberated for less than three hours found Staktopoulos guilty as an accessory to murder after the fact. He was sentenced to life imprisonment and received a pardon twelve years later.

Someone had to answer for the death of George Polk, and at all costs the Greek state had to be absolved of any and all responsibility. Polk had challenged the veracity and integrity of the Greek government at a time when American-Greek relations were still fragile, but of paramount importance to Greece. For by 1948, U.S. military and economic aid was all that stood between victory and defeat for the Greek government forces in the ongoing civil war. To the coterie of old royalist politicians and former republicans-Venizelists, each time George Polk produced an exposé of the corruption and the heavy-handed policies of the Greek government, he negated the cause of anticommunism that often served as a mask for otherwise incompetent and self-serving politicians.

Ultimately, the publicity swirling around Polk's murder, the Donovan investigation, and the direct interest of the Truman administration had induced the Greek authorities to force a confession from Staktopoulos in order to link the death of the American journalist with the struggle against the communist insurgency. In the summer of 1946, the third round of the Greek civil war had broken out and by 1947 was turning Greece into a zone of confrontation between the USSR and the United States. In that context, Polk's murder at the hands of the rebels was convenient as it was symbolic of the communist threat to Greece as well as to the United States.

A critical factor that made the third round of the civil war almost inevitable was the failure of the right-wing governments, which became increasingly conservative after 1945, to deal, in a nonpartisan manner, with ordinary people labeled as left-wing. In the aftermath of the December Uprising, these regimes could not or would not differentiate between the leadership and the hard-core elements of the left-wing resistance organizations, on the one hand, and ordinary Greeks who did not subscribe to any particular ideological agenda, on the other. Moreover, the leaders of the right, by their actions and their failure to contain the ultra-right extremists, compounded this error by driving the point home that anyone not with them was automatically against them. In so doing they had to invalidate the resistance as a factor in the war against the Axis.

The right needed to negate the role of the resistance in order to obscure the activity of the collaborators, particularly the Security Battalions. The officers of the armed forces, police, gendarmerie, judges, prosecutors, district prefects, mayors, civil servants, journalists, and others who (willingly or under duress) had served the Axis were vulnerable to charges of collaboration, if not treason, and had been indiscriminately hunted down by the left during the December Uprising as vestiges of the occupation. Consequently, for these men and women institutionalization of the resistance meant that the proverbial sword of Damocles would continue to hang over their heads for the foreseeable future. Hence, while the rest of Europe recognized and celebrated the contribution of the groups and individuals who had opposed the German and Italian occupation, the Greek state refused to acknowledge the contribution of the resistance until 1981.[16]

The persecution of the left during the period of White Terror (1945–1946), consequently, affected a large segment of Greek society and forced many to seek refuge in the communist-led bands forming in the mountains. Rex Leeper understood this and in his 1945 annual report on Greek affairs warned Ernest Bevin, the new British secretary of state for foreign affairs, that Greece was quickly becoming dangerously polarized:

> The Right, in a vengeful mood, urged on the police, who were only too willing, to arrest thousands of the Left-wing supporters, many of them innocent of anything but socialist sentiments expressed in somewhat intemperate language; others, no doubt, guilty of murders, though even in these cases, owing to the circumstances of the civil war, it often proved difficult to produce conclusive evidence. . . . A favourite charge, on which many respectable citizens were arrested, was "moral responsibility" for murders, i.e. in most cases membership, under the occupation, of EAM resistance and local government committees, or of People's Courts, which had condemned to death people described by EAM as "traitors" and by their opponents as "peaceful citizens opposed to communism." The courts were not able to deal with the rush of work, and thousands of EAM supporters remained in the overcrowded gaols awaiting trial, often for much more than the statutory six months.[17]

On 25 August 1945, under British pressure, the Greek government introduced a partial amnesty to release those not accused of murder, but it made little impact. Three weeks later, on 17 September, the minister of justice reported that 16,700 were still in prison, of which 14,252 were awaiting trial, and only 1,949 had actually been set free by the amnesty.[18] Remarkably, although not so for the times, out of the 16,700 inmates only 2,896 were ever convicted of collaboration. In 1952, the number of collaborators still incarcerated was 1,275 out of a prison population of 28,000. Over the course of 1945, 80,000 adherents or suspected sympathizers as well as members of left-wing organizations faced prosecution.[19] In contrast, partisans of ultra-right-wing groups, collaborators, and officers who had served in the Security Battalions were permeating the security apparatus of the state, the police, and the armed forces. After the March 1946 general election, the drift to the extreme right was further accelerated by the inclusion in parliament of men who had openly supported the puppet occupation governments.

The officers and men of these notorious forces were a living symbol of everything that had gone wrong with the political establishment during and immediately following the occupation. After liberation, most of them were placed in a detention camp in Goudi (outside of Athens) and the more senior officers in Averoff prison. In November, the British had begun to release some of the officers from Averoff prison and brought others to Egypt. According to an OSS report, former members of the Security Battalions were slowly being integrated into regular Greek army units. Another American intelligence report indicated:

EAM's fear, and it is a real one, is that not only will ELAS be dissolved and disintegrated but that there will be no popular national army in the true sense. Not only are the ex-Tsoliadhes [Gestapo-controlled Greek secret police] and members of the Security Battalions being trained as units but there is a strong tendency to place Royalist and ex-Metaxist officers in high-ranking positions.[20]

The December Uprising created the impetus for the mass release and employment of almost all the incarcerated collaborationist officers. Ultimately, 12,000 of those who had served in the Security Battalions were enrolled in the national guards formed during the December Uprising.

However, just two years after the December Uprising, the United States inherited not only Britain's responsibilities in the Mediterranean and the Near East, but also their role as patrons of the Greek right. The withdrawal of the British from Greece in early 1947 and the proclamation of the Truman Doctrine a few weeks later meant that the Americans officially assumed Britain's international responsibilities; therefore, U.S. intervention in Greece was not only new, but unpredictable. After a century of accommodating and ingratiating the British, Greek politicians were not accustomed to the new "superpower," and they were unfamiliar with the quirks and peculiarities of their new protectors. The murder of an American journalist, however, did not portend well for the new relationship. George Polk may have been disagreeable—and, to some extent, a puzzle to right-wing Greek politicians—but he was an American just the same. Thus, the Greek regime felt compelled to get a confession from Grigoris Staktopoulos that put the blame squarely on the communists.

The Staktopoulos family, like hundreds of thousands of other families, had been swept up in the conflagration of the 1946 Greek civil war. This latest round of fratricide was part of the cycle of civil war and retribution that had hijacked the lives of Greeks since occupation. After liberation, a combination of fear, mistrust, desperation, and competition for political control between the left and the right had ignited into the Battle of Athens in December 1944. The toll on the Greek state was high. The fighting stymied any efforts to rehabilitate the economy of the country and retarded most attempts at providing a modicum of subsistence to the thousands left homeless and destitute by the earlier ravages of the Second World War. The wreckage (even by the industrial-scale standards of the Second World War) was overwhelming.

In 1948, the year that Polk was killed and almost four years after liberation, the economic plight of the country and the hardships confronting the population were staggering. The 2,000 villages that had been destroyed by Axis reprisals and the civil war remained in ruins. Almost one quarter of all the structures in the country—400,000 buildings—were totally demolished. Almost 1 million people in Greece were struggling as refugees or displaced persons. The Athens sprawl, characteristic of the congested capital today, is one of the civil war's legacies, triggered by the influx of hundreds of thousands of homeless villagers and refugees from the interior of the country.[21]

By 1948, a combination of uncontrolled forest fires and foraging for wood to use as fuel in some areas decimated 75 percent of the forests and trees. State finances were practically nonexistent, and Greece was drowning in an avalanche of paper currency generated by the inflationary policies of the occupation authorities.[22] Yet liberation had made little impact, and the Greek currency continued to plummet unabated. In March 1948 Greek currency traded at the rate of 170,000,000,000,000 drachmas to a single British gold sovereign.[23] The cost of living by the end of the Greek civil war in 1949 would be almost 250 times higher than during the period prior to the occupation. The levy in human losses was equally appalling. A conservative estimate places the number killed, as a result of the war, at close to 0.5 million and another 880,000 disabled by disease. In other words, out of a population of just over 7 million, approximately 19 percent suffered a violent death or incurred chronic disabilities.

The third round of fighting had broken out in the summer of 1946 as a response to the reign of terror that cascaded across the country in retaliation for the December Uprising. Effectively, the period of White Terror from February 1945 to September 1946 created the momentum for the last phase of the civil war because it left the adherents of EAM-ELAS and the KKE little choice except to fight or face heavy-handed persecution for an indefinite period of time. The scale of retaliation by ultra-right-wing gangs against the partisans of the left was not only widespread but remained unchecked, especially outside of Athens and the other major urban centers. The authorities could not, or would not, intervene in thousands of situations where fanatics of both political extremes indulged in beatings, looting, rape, and murder.

The story of Andreas Patrikios is one example of how the vicissitudes of occupation and the politics of the resistance impacted one family. Patrikios was born and raised in the provincial town of Patras. He graduated from university a short time before the outbreak of the Second World War. In 1942, like many young men, he went to the mountains to join ELAS and fight against the Axis. However, his legal training was more valuable to ELAS, and Patrikios was made a judge. In this capacity he had the task of determining the guilt or innocence of collaborators and those accused of treason against EAM-ELAS. According to one of his relatives, Patrikios tried very hard to dispense even-handed justice, but every so often the local ELAS leadership overruled him and executed innocent men and women.[24]

In the meantime, the Germans and Security Battalions constantly harassed Patrikios' family. Soon after the occupation, the local right-wing X organization paid a visit to Angeliki, his older sister, on her farm. A couple of them punched and kicked her in the stomach, thighs, and head. They tormented her for hours, until she was unconscious. In the months following the outbreak of the 1946 civil war, while Patrikios was still in hiding, the ultra-right-wing group went after Kratitira, his younger sister. This time, they hauled the young girl to the town plaza of Lower Achaia and beat her publicly and then tossed the almost lifeless body to the side of the street. Witnesses to the spectacle cheered and egged on the girl's tormentors; however, some sympathetic bystanders afterward provided first aid, thereby saving her life.[25] Patrikios hid in his cousin's house (spending most of the time on the roof), and when it got too dangerous in Patras he joined his sisters in Athens—they had moved to the capital to escape the persecution meted out to the families of ELAS veterans as well as members of the KKE.

For months Patrikios, tired and suffering from tuberculosis, wandered from place to place in Athens. He managed to evade capture by remaining indoors and using the small laundry room in his sisters' house as a hiding place. Eventually, due to either betrayal or carelessness, he was arrested. First, he was imprisoned on the island of Zakynthos and then transferred to Averoff prison in Athens. He had to be hospitalized for a few months because of the tuberculosis. He tried to defend himself, and despite his own difficulties he provided legal help to other inmates. Ultimately, it was all to no avail. The military court found him guilty and he was executed a few months before the end of the civil war in 1949.[26] Judging by similar cases, Patrikios' trial itself would have been less than a formality and mirrored identical tribunals that had fanned across Greece, supposedly to bring communists and traitors to justice.

A few weeks after the Polk murder, Kenneth Matthews, the BBC correspondent in Greece, witnessed a military tribunal sitting at a women's detention center and by reconstructing the proceedings offers a rare peek into the absurd and crude attempts at this kind of justice:

> The general presiding [asks the accused]: "Where do you come from?"
> The woman witness: "From Thessalonica."
> "What is your work?"
> "I am a doctor."
> "How long have you practiced in Thessalonica?"
> "Twenty years."
> "Then since you have some experience and are besides a qualified scientist, you will be able to tell us: is Thessalonica a Greek or Bulgarian city?" The question, like those devised by the inquisitors of the Holy Office, was framed to disclose whether the witness preserved a Greek and Christian soul or whether she was given over to the abomination of Communism. She replied:
> "I don't know."
> The Bishop of Volos (a member of the tribunal): "Kill her, my general! In the name of religion, kill her where she stands!"[27]

A large number of women in Thessaloniki and Athens as well as in dozens of small cities and towns went through a similar experience because their male family members were in hiding or had joined the communist forces. Many of them also suffered imprisonment or execution as a result of malicious neighbors or duplicitous spouses. Mary Henderson, who served as a Red Cross nurse and had occasion to visit the women prisoners, writes:

> As we were leaving the camp a pretty little woman called Fotini—Greek for light—grabbed my arm and begged for help. "I am only here," she blurted out, "because my husband wanted to be rid of me. He wanted to be free to marry his mistress, Vromokoritso the dirty girl—so he told the

police that I was a Communist. I am no Communist, just a broken-hearted woman. What should I do?" Her big, black eyes veiled with tears searched for mine—for help. "How can I prove that I am not a Communist now that I am in prison?" . . . As I looked back at Fotini's black, imploring eyes I longed to be able to help—but how?[28]

A great many of the women in prison, especially those from the villages, were bereft of any understanding or commitment to Marxism but just the same had participated in the fighting. In another of Henderson's experiences as a nurse visiting the women's detention center, she recalls how Ekaterina, a young peasant girl, "after an incoherent explanation of her symptoms and how she did not want anyone to know—ran into the toilet and a few minutes later gave birth to a premature baby on the pink ladies' cloakroom floor."[29]

The baby did not survive, and Ekaterina, who had been arrested for hiding a gun under her skirt, most likely languished in prison for months before being formally charged with a crime. Thousands of young women, like Ekaterina and Fotini, were swept up by the tumultuous events of Greece in the 1940s and uprooted from the security of the traditional village life. For them the resistance had been an opportunity to escape the asphyxiating role prescribed for women in both the rural communities of Greece and the large urban centers. They had fought the Axis and afterward the British; some of them, like Ekaterina, had smuggled weapons or had volunteered to act as decoys during the December Uprising so that ELAS snipers could pick off British and Greek soldiers.

They paid a heavy price for participating in EAM-ELAS because with the defeat of the left in December 1944 these women effectively became displaced persons within their own country. After breaking the bonds of tradition and religion by abandoning their families they could not return to the village; at any rate, it is doubtful if the small and tightly knit communities would take them back. In some cases, the shame of prison, suspicion of unacceptable sexual behavior, and pregnancy out of wedlock meant that most of these women were doomed to remain unmarried and thus constituted an unacceptable economic and social burden to their families. Consequently, the third round of civil war in 1946 had offered a large number of these women an avenue of escape from the uncertainties of attempting to reintegrate into mainstream society, this time by joining the Greek Democratic Army (the name of the communist forces in 1946–1949) assembling in the mountains.

Young men also faced stringent social and economic liabilities as well as the stigma of antinationalism and anti-Greek behavior for participating in ELAS. In a society as small as Greece's in which citizens were categorized and catalogued by the police and security services so that their "file" followed them the rest of their lives, the labels of communist, anarchist, Slav, Arvanitis (Greek-speaking Orthodox Albanians), traitor, atheist, or a combination of some of the above had economic as well as political consequences. A bad file barred an individual from employment in the civil service, large companies, and even domestic work. Later on, it prevented people with such files from emigrating. In the 1950s and until the collapse of the military junta in 1974, emigration was only possible after a prospective candidate obtained a certificate of "nationally correct views" from the police. Without this certificate, not only was employment difficult, but marriage, baptism of children, and church-sanctioned burials were also denied unless an individual produced the document of "political correctness."

In the heat of the moment thousands of young men, caught in the notion of a better future sponsored by EAM, had fought the British in the streets of Athens to stay the return of the prewar political and economic establishment. For ELAS veterans who had fought the German occupiers, the fighting in December was an extension of the resistance; for others, particularly the younger and less battle-experienced men of the ELAS reserve units in the capital, the Battle of Athens represented a watershed in the political future of Greece. Almost all these younger men came from the working-class districts of Athens. Some of these foot soldiers of the December Uprising may have fought for a new and better way of life, some because they were communists, but many others simply joined to take advantage of an opportunity to improve their present circumstances. Rex Leeper, the British ambassador, lost his housemaid because she went off to find her son "who was with ELAS, a mere boy who had gone because he was offered food, pay and a uniform."[30]

Poorly disciplined and ill equipped, they were no match for the well-trained British forces, and more often than not their enthusiasm led them to make great offensive surges followed by an overreaction to their defeat, which often contributed to the killing of innocent civilians. On the evening of 4 December, Mary Henderson had been entertaining a few friends, including some British officers, and as they were leaving her home she writes, "I heard a loud splat of bullets hitting the pavement outside. . . . The sniper on our roof was our cook. We never saw him again."[31] Did the cook, like many house servants, waiters, laborers, and shoeshine boys, see ELAS as a means of "class warfare" and use his position to assist the cause? There are examples of doormen admitting snipers into exclusive apartment buildings and maids smuggling weapons across the British lines to their relatives and friends in ELAS. There are even more illustrations of university students as well as doctors, lawyers, military officers, architects, and other professionals from the middle class fighting for ELAS that counter the notion of a class division as a major factor in the conflict.

Ultimately, it was not only that the EAM-ELAS supporters advocated the establishment of a socialist or communist state; rather, many insisted on justice—particularly the arrest, trial, and punishment of the collaborators—and a level playing field in addressing the constitutional problem. For the most part, they got nothing with respect to the former and very little with the latter.

In 1945, the Plastiras government established military committees to select officers for the new army, which went on to appoint 228 who had served with the Security Battalions and 221 ELAS veterans. Despite the apparent impartiality of this selection, succeeding governments between 1945 and 1949 tended to discriminate in favor of officers from the Security Battalions rather than ELAS. In fact, the Greek general staff, with few exceptions, placed officers with service in ELAS on the inactive list.[32]

After the end of hostilities in January, the Greek government continued to use former Security Battalion forces to maintain security in the countryside. The cruel absurdity of this situation was that the personnel of the Security Battalions, in the guise of national guard units, now had responsibility for establishing law and order in large areas of Greece that had supported EAM-ELAS. Effectively, the former collaborationist forces were simply given license to settle scores against the left. In September 1945, however, the national guard was withdrawn from active service and replaced by the reorganized gendarmerie, leaving the former Security Battalion officers unemployed, with the exception of the 224 already appointed in the new army. This professional setback was only temporary; the outbreak of hostilities in 1946 and the radical changes taking place within the new armed forces created a fresh opportunity for them to gain admission into the army.

During this period (1945–1946), secret leagues and associations honeycombed the officer corps. The structure of most of these clusters was shadowy, and some groups only represented a loose collection of officers with common professional interests. To a great extent, the development of these factions was a reaction to constant political intervention in the armed forces after 1945. The parade of short-term governments in the post–December Uprising period only served to intensify the insecurity of the officers as each regime promoted its followers in the higher commands. Former Venizelist officers who had accepted the monarchy and had been readmitted into the armed forces were the most vulnerable group. The Plastiras government had reinstated many former republicans at the expense of royalists, but the limited tenure of this regime left them professionally exposed. Meanwhile, the royalist faction saw many of its senior members lose their posts to former republicans, and they responded by forming their own organizations to protect themselves from retirement or dismissal.

Beginning early in 1946, ultra-right-wing royalist officers, who favored the king because they believed that monarchy was a safeguard against communism, were gaining control of the national army. To enforce their brand of nationalism, these radical conservative officers had created a secret organization, which came to be known by its acronym as IDEA (Sacred Association of Nationalist Officers). IDEA quickly spread its tentacles within the officer corps and infiltrated the general staff as well as the headquarters of the new army divisions. In the summer of 1946, representatives of IDEA took the initiative and persuaded the minister of defense to admit into the army officers who had served with the Security

Battalions. The reason, according to George Karayiannis, the unofficial biographer of IDEA, was that these officers were not only capable professionals but also fanatical anticommunists. In addition, they had considerable experience in counterinsurgency warfare, first under the Germans and later under the British during the December Uprising.[33]

Sadly, many of those officers now excluded from the armed forces bore the brunt of the White Terror, and a year later many of them took up arms to create the Greek Democratic Army. In response, the Populist Party government of Dimitrios Maximos, in collaboration with the military, established three detention camps on the islands of Makronisos, Gioura, and Trikeri in 1947. There were supplementary detention centers on other small islands, but the first three camps were set up to deal with three categories of leftists and suspected communists: Makronisos for military personal, usually officers and men who had served with ELAS; Gioura for politicians; and Trikeri for men and women from areas under the control of the communist bands. Makronisos achieved considerably more notoriety than the other two prison islands and became linked with some of the most savage treatment inflicted on leftists or suspected leftist prisoners during the civil war. From 1947 to 1950, 1,110 officers and 27,770 soldiers passed through Makronisos, labeled "the new Dachau" by the left.[34]

Perhaps more galling for the professional officers who by fighting for ELAS had wrecked their careers in the postwar army was that in many cases the men who condemned them to these horrible islands had either actively collaborated with or passively acquiesced to the Axis. In 1947, over 10,000 suspected leftists and communists were rounded up in the larger urban centers and swept into the detention centers and prisons on the mainland as well as the islands. Many of the men who could have filled positions of responsibility in the armed forces and police services instead were forced to languish in prison or submit to a process of political rehabilitation on Makronisos. One historian, Artemis Leontis, describes it thus:

> Greek Government officials nicknamed it the "National Baptismal Front" because they imagined this to be the place where prisoners of the

Greek civil war would wash themselves into more conservative citizens. Philosopher and politician Panayiotis Kanellopoulos called Makronisos the place where Greeks could built new Parthenons, because there, on an island best suited for grazing, prisoners were forced to build out of local materials in a span of three or four years not only administrative buildings, villas, and a club for their persecutors but also a factory for non-alcoholic beverages, a radio station, a convalescence area, kitchens, water reservoirs, roads, six churches, four theaters—where their ideological rehabilitation was to take place—arches, statues, bas-reliefs, monuments with shells and mosaics, as well as miniature versions of the Parthenon and Hagia Sophia.[35]

The lot of the inmates, because they had been officers and soldiers, was harsh and designed to break their spirit. The object of the torture, random beatings, mock executions, and mindless daily drudgery was to force the inmates to sign a declaration of repentance, followed by public denunciations of communism. The prisoners who agreed to be saved from the clutches of "atheist-Marxism" could also demonstrate their sincerity by joining in on the beatings and torture of fellow inmates who had held out against embracing "love of country and religion" by rejecting Godless communism.

In the interim period, a number of veteran ELAS officers (a precise figure is impossible to determine) joined approximately 5,000 men and some women whom the KKE had sent to safety in communist Yugoslavia, Bulgaria, and Albania. The largest percentage was concentrated in Buljkes, northeast of Belgrade, which served as a military training camp for the KKE courtesy of the Yugoslavs. During the winter of 1946, small groups infiltrated into northern Greece and, linking up with bands of leftist guerrillas hiding in the mountains, conducted occasional raids either to secure supplies or to exact revenge against ultra-right-wing gangs.

The problem of lawlessness was further compounded as increasing numbers of ELAS veterans left their homes throughout 1945 and 1946 for the protection of the rugged terrain in parts of northern Greece, in the Peloponnesus, and on some of the Aegean islands. Although ELAS had surrendered an impressive number of weapons as part of the Vark-iza Agreement, an almost equal number were hidden and used by the leftist bands forming in the mountains for self-defense and for attacking police stations, villages, and other targets of opportunity.[36]

The KKE did not sanction the increasing and widespread banditry or encourage its members to join the bands operating in the mountains. Although the communist press made references to the guerrilla activity of former ELAS members, the leftist publications suggested that the people who had taken to the hills did so to escape the White Terror in the cities. According to Ole Smith, the specialist on the KKE, "There is no doubt that the KKE, throughout 1945 and early 1946, held the view that the struggle was political, and thus had to be fought in the cities, mass organizations, trade unions, and agrarian cooperatives."[37]

Certainly, the defeat of ELAS in the December Uprising left the KKE leadership in disarray and the party organization in shambles. Accord-ing to some estimates, at the time of liberation in October 1944, mem-bership in the KKE had peaked at 400,000, but dropped off to 200,000 after the debacle in December.[38] However, the critical political problem confronting the KKE in 1945 was the first postwar parliamentary elec-tion planned for early 1946. The parties of the left as well as the KKE demanded a thorough revision of the electoral lists as a precondition for taking part in the elections. According to Smith's analysis, "[T]hey did not wish to create the impression abroad that elections could be held in the existing anarchical situation. Since there were no indications that the government would carry out a revision or establish law and order, the Center and the Left were inclined to boycott the elections."[39] The decision not to take part in the March election, ultimately, proved a se-rious mistake for the KKE, which in tandem with the increasing scale of violence in the Greek countryside as well as the transformation of the international environment generated the momentum for civil war in Greece.

Indeed, 1945 had been a defining year for Greece and for the rest of the world. At the Yalta Conference in February 1945, Stalin quietly continued to accept the so-called Percentage Agreement with respect to the British and Soviet spheres of influence in the Balkans. During the meeting of the

Big Three at the Yalta Conference (4–11 February 1945) to discuss the shape of postwar Europe and Asia, Churchill and Stalin disagreed over Poland, but not over Greece, which the Soviet leader continued to accept as part of the British sphere. In a matter of months all that changed. Roosevelt died in April and Churchill was swept from office in July, leaving Stalin, the only remaining member of the Big Three, to enjoy the fruits of victory.

Furthermore, when the Second World War came to an end, with the defeat of Germany in May and Japan in August, the international relations dynamic, forged out of the necessity of war, gradually shifted. The United States and the Soviet Union were rapidly undergoing metamorphoses into superpowers; the Grand Alliance that had achieved so much in the war was quickly unraveling in peacetime, susceptible to new fears and suspicions. By the time Truman and Atlee met with the Soviet leader in Potsdam (17 July–1 August 1945), Stalin had become less conciliatory and chided the British over the Greek government's breaches of the Varkiza Agreement, the document which had ended the December Uprising. He surprised the British and Americans by demanding a Soviet presence in the Aegean, with a naval base either at Thessaloniki, Alexandroupolis, or the Dodecanese Islands. Stalin then pressed for a revision of the Montreux Convention on the Dardanelles and the Bosphorus Straits to facilitate Soviet access to the Mediterranean, arguing that it was no less unreasonable than Britain's control of the Suez Canal. He also demanded that Turkey surrender the frontier provinces of Kars and Ardahan to the Soviet republics of Armenia and Georgia. Meanwhile, throughout Eastern Europe and the Balkans the Soviets were already imposing communist or people's democracies.

Yet, despite Stalin's advantage of position and the fact that the Red Army occupied large parts of Europe, he would just as quickly withdraw these claims in the face of opposition from his Anglo-American allies. Stalin agreed to withdraw the Red Army from Vienna as well as pull out of Iran, while failing to force the British out of Syria.[40] Regardless of these compromises, the perception of the Soviet juggernaut gobbling up the rest of postwar Europe was beginning to take hold. After George Kennan's famous "long telegram" from Moscow in 1946, the notion that the West must contain communism—and therefore stop Stalin in Greece and Turkey—became the idée fixe in Washington. Greece became a concern because the anticommunists in Washington could point to an actual communist insurgency taking place; Turkey was seen as another domino, one that could set off a cascade of Middle East petroleum-producing countries coming under Soviet influence and control.

Meanwhile, Greek communists were finding it exceedingly difficult to navigate along the fine line between armed struggle and legitimate political pressure. Their entreaties to Stalin for diplomatic, let alone military, support (at least for most of 1945) seemed to fall on deaf ears. According to Peter Stavrakis, "The Soviets seemed to be content with probing the British influence in the Balkans, most likely knowing that it was coming to an end."[41] Stalin was determined to avoid a breach with the British over Greece. Immediately after the December Uprising, he had even forbidden Grigori Dimitrov, his faithful Bulgarian satrap, to grant asylum to the defeated ELAS fighters. A delegation of Greek communists, led by Mitsos Partsalidis, visited Moscow in the middle of January 1946 to sound out the Soviet leadership with respect to assistance in the immediate future but failed to secure an audience with Stalin. The only tangible response Partsalidis could bring back to Greece was a message from the central committee of the Communist Party of the Soviet Union that the KKE was to "[t]ake part in the elections now. Later, review the situation. In accordance with the way it develops the center of gravity may move as necessary, either to legal methods or to armed struggle."[42] In November 1946, Andrei Zhdanov, the head of the Cominform (the Information Bureau of the Communist Parties), deliberately did not even mention Greece in his address on the anniversary of the Bolshevik Revolution.[43]

A little later, and certainly by 1947, Stalin was prepared to sanction some, albeit defensive, military action by the Greek communists. This can be extrapolated from the decisions of the KKE in early 1946, which called for a military response to the White Terror. At the crucial party meeting in February 1946, Zachariadis, the KKE general secretary, stated that, "since our enemies are continuing the one-sided civil war, we will answer with the same means—weapons. Now has come the time for us to make the historic decision for armed struggle."⁴⁴ Ole Smith concludes:

> The most reliable interpretation is . . . that it was decided to build up gradually a partisan movement, starting from the groups already in the mountains. Where local conditions allowed, the movement should develop; and from the countryside the partisans should aim to put pressure on the government for political reforms. The partisan movement was to be regarded as a defensive weapon first; if the government did not give in, and a democratic development should prove impossible, then the partisan groups should play a more active and offensive role. . . . In essence this seems to have been the KKE policy that was presented to the CPSU (Communist Party of the Soviet Union) by Partsalides in Moscow, and acknowledged by the CPSU representative: that the KKE should wait and see, use both parliamentary and legal methods, and armed action depending on circumstances and opportunity.⁴⁵

After the meeting, the KKE dispatched a number of well-known ELAS officers to organize the disparate bands of resistance fighters who had sought the protection of the mountains. When the shift from uncoordinated raids and counterreprisals to full-scale civil war took place, however, is not clear, but what is certain is that by fall of 1946 the KKE leadership was pulling together all the various guerrilla bands operating in the mountains and amalgamating them into a coherent military force. Even at this point, the KKE still held back from committing its forces to a full-scale conflict. On the night prior to the general election of 30–31 March 1946, a communist band attacked the small town of Litochoro on the eastern slopes of Mount Olympus. Although traditionally, the first blow of the third round of the Greek civil war is marked by this particular event, the assault, according to Markos Vaphiadis, the subsequent commander of the Greek Democratic Army, was meant to frighten the Greek government into making concessions.

Effectively, the KKE committed piecemeal to war over a period of nearly two years, from the winter of 1945 to late 1947. A major factor for the hesitancy was that throughout 1946, the KKE leadership continued to

remain uncertain about the attitude of the Soviet Union. In the meantime, the boycott of the elections marginalized the KKE politically, leaving the initiative to right-wing factions to dominate the makeup of the
postwar governments and in the process destroy the influence of EAM in
Greek society. The increasing lawlessness, moreover, provided the excuse
for these regimes to restructure Greece as a centralized and authoritarian
state. In addition to reviving Metaxas' instruments of repression, such as
the use of internal exile and the infamous declarations of repentance
extorted from prisoners, they established extraordinary courts martial
throughout Greece, which by summary procedures condemned thousands of people to prison or the firing squad for crimes against public security. David Close calculates that these tribunals operated over the three
years of the civil war, "sentencing over 2,000 people to be executed, and
several thousand more to be jailed for offenses as trivial as the reported
slandering of prominent public officials."[46] Other scholars estimate that
the number of those condemned to death during this period reached as
high as 7,500, with 3,000–5,000 political prisoners being executed.[47]

The legal framework that facilitated the imprisonment and execution
of captured communist insurgents as well as their supporters in the
cities or those suspected of sympathizing with the guerrillas was established by the newly elected Populist Party government on 18 June 1946,
a few months after the elections. The first article of Resolution C "on
extraordinary measures concerning the public order and security,"
passed by the Greek parliament, imposed the death penalty for those
who intended to "detach a part of Greece from the whole of the country."[48] This was clearly directed at communists because of the KKE's
support for an autonomous Macedonia. On 27 December 1947 the government put forward Compulsory Law 509 to address "security measures of the state, the regime, and the social order, and the protection of
citizens' liberties."[49] Effectively, this legislation banned all leftist parties
and organizations and imposed the death penalty on those who were
"seeking to apply ideas, which overtly aim to overthrow the regime or
the established social system by violent means, or aim to detach a part
from the whole of the country."[50]

The consequences for ordinary Greeks trapped in the maelstrom of the civil war could be catastrophic. The police used their new authority to hunt down anyone suspected of supporting the rebels and established a wide-range network of informants. The owners of kiosks, who by law had to be disabled military veterans (or their offspring), were a good source of local intelligence and could categorize individuals simply by indicating if they purchased left- or right-wing newspapers. The authorities could also coerce the proprietors of coffeehouses to inform on their customers or lose their license. The burden of arrest and punishment fell primarily on the KKE members in the cities and towns, who could easily be identified by the kiosk and coffee shop owners, by malicious neighbors, or by those who had suffered at the hands of the left during the occupation and the December Uprising. Proof of guilt or innocence was at the discretion of the local extraordinary court. For example, Koula Eleftheriou was accused of recruiting guerrillas under the pseudonym of Maria. The only evidence against her was the accusation of a member of the gendarmerie who was alleged to have collaborated with the Axis forces during the occupation. The court found Eleftheriou guilty and sentenced her to death on 1 May 1947. Five days later she was executed. Although the twenty-four-year-old Eleftheriou was a member of the KKE, her complicity in aiding the insurgency is not certain.

Others were catapulted into the chaos of postwar Greece not because of ideology but through happenstance. Three such examples were Leo, Kostas, and Andreas Katsuris from the small village of Lidouri in the Peloponnesus. The lives of the three brothers were indelibly changed by occupation and civil war. By all the economic standards of the times, the Katsuris family was prosperous. Their father had followed the well-trodden path of many Greeks at the turn of the century who migrated to the United States to seek their fortune. He eventually ended up in Vancouver, Canada, and his monthly remittances enabled the family to live comfortably and build a large house. The boys received their primary and secondary education, but their studies came to an end with the Axis occupation.

In the winter of 1942–1943, Andreas and Kostas left the village, along with other young men, to take part in the resistance. Kostas joined

ELAS and Andreas was trained by EAM to be a teacher. Leo, four years younger than Kostas, remained behind: "I didn't join the partisans, I was young, slim, I didn't have the stamina to go there (to the mountains). While Kostas was crazy already from high school." Leo, however, often risked his life taking food and water to the local ELAS units hiding in the nearby mountains. Kostas took part in numerous firefights against the Germans and was wounded in August 1944.

After the occupation and the defeat of ELAS in the December Uprising all three brothers were marked men. Leo tried moving to Athens in order to study medicine, but his connection to the left via his brothers' participation in ELAS made it impossible. The authorities already had a file on him. In the spring of 1947, Leo had to present himself to the induction board in his village—failure to do so was a capital offense. Unfortunately, just as he arrived one of the dozens of ultra-right-wing gangs suddenly appeared and seized all the men who had shown up for the induction board. "They had lists of names," Leo recalls, "saying who was linked with the left. They sent away all those not on the list and forced the rest of us to stand in the village plaza and stare at the sun. Slapping us whenever we lowered our eyes and yelling 'look at the sun.' I got away because my father's brother worked for the English. The others were forced in trucks and taken to Amphissa, where they were driven mad from the beatings." After his escape Leo made his way back to Athens and eventually reported for military service. Because of his file he was classified as suspect and sent to internal exile on the island of Ikaria.

Four months later he was released to serve in the army and was assigned to the Ninth Infantry Division. Leo's older brother, Kostas, was studying law while recovering from his wound in Athens. After the outbreak of the White Terror he could not bear the thought of beatings and internal exile and decided to make his way to the Greek Democratic Army. Andreas, like Leo, was caught and sent to an island camp, but unlike Leo he served his time in the infamous Makronisos. Thanks to a sympathetic officer, Andreas was released from captivity, but after reaching the mainland he was seized by a right-wing gang and shot. For years the family did not know Andreas' fate. They received letters from acquaintances claiming to have spotted Andreas, but the young man had been buried by the side of the road in an unmarked grave.

For the duration of the civil war Leo and Kostas were fighting on opposite sides and under different conditions. Kostas was made an officer in the Greek Democratic Army and made responsible for recruitment and training. Leo, along with 600 other men, was assigned to a special battalion for suspected leftists. They were often given the thankless task of walking over suspected minefields or were haphazardly committed to particularly dangerous missions. "One time they sent us to the Albanian border," recounts Leo. "Our battalion incinerated a village and killed a bunch of Albanians in a guardhouse. Then we built some defenses on high ground in order to outflank the partisans returning to their hideouts in Albania. But we failed and we couldn't go any further and the Albanians attacked us. Four hundred out of six hundred men in our battalion were killed."

During this time, Leo was fully aware that Kostas was across the line, high up in the rugged mountains intersecting Albania and Greece. "When we reached the Albanian border, you could see a lot of people: partisans walking on the Albanian side. But I knew from my mother that Kostas had joined the Greek Democratic Army and where he was located. Every now and then, our mother received a letter from Kostas, which was sent from the front to Yugoslavia, then to my father in Vancouver, and finally to my mother in Athens." Leo's, Kostas', and Andreas' destinies were shaped by circumstances unfolding in London, Washington, and finally in Moscow.

In 1947, Stalin modified his position and was prepared to allow the KKE to secure aid from nearby communist states, particularly Yugoslavia. Stalin's change of mind was partly in response to Marshal Tito's support of the Greek communists and partly in reaction to the Truman Doctrine. In effect, the escalation to full-scale civil war in Greece was a direct by-product of Soviet and American rivalry and the development of regional factors linked to Tito's machinations for territorial aggrandizement. The Yugoslav leader was planning to incorporate the Greek territory of Macedonia as well as to establish a Balkan federation to include Bulgaria and Greece, all of which was not possible without a sympathetic government in Athens. Although Tito did not think very highly of the

Greek communists, they provided him the means by which he could alter the balance of power in the Balkans in favor of Yugoslav hegemony. In 1950, KKE general secretary Zachariadis claimed that the KKE had decided for military action after "Tito and his clique promised us the most substantial aid. This played a decisive role in our decision because in Yugoslavia, the main factor in the Balkans at that time, our new revolutionary movement did not have an opponent who could pose insurmountable obstacles."[51]

In fact, Tito and his close associates bragged about the impending fall of Greece. Furthermore, when Zachariadis arrived in Moscow in May, two months after Truman had made his pivotal speech to the joint session of Congress requesting aid for Greece and Turkey, Stalin was ready to help the Greek communist insurgency. According to declassified Soviet documents, Soviet policy with respect to the 'the Greek question' was, at this point, a reaction to the Truman Doctrine which had been proclaimed earlier in March 1947 and viewed by the Kremlin as a direct threat to the USSR from the south.[52] The Truman administration was also convinced that Stalin was planning to exploit the insurgency to incorporate Greece and Turkey within the communist sphere in order to expand Soviet power to the Mediterranean and the Middle East. These fears were further enhanced by the ongoing Chinese civil war and the completion of Soviet domination over most of Eastern Europe. The Americans, consequently, made their first foray into supplanting Britain as an interventionist power and did so in the complex and murky world of Balkan politics.

When Americans (under the auspices of the OSS) first became involved on the ground in Greece, they were obliged to tread carefully around the British. In December 1944, an OSS report noted that, up to that point, "both the Soviet and American Governments [had] tended to recognize British primacy in matters concerning Greece."[53] Looking back on the structure of OSS Athens during this same period, OSS officer Gerald Else reflected, "Our tactics in Athens were based on the principle of 'out of sight, out of mind': we were friendly with such British officers as we came in contact with, but we did not go out of our way to attract their attention."[54]

In these early days, the Greek left as well as others greeted the Americans as fellow combatants in the cause of independence, as champions of self-determination, and as allies against the British imperialists. By December 1944, the British believed that the Americans and the Soviets in Greece were trying to gain popular support at home, and that their calls for self-determination "may arouse considerable sympathy in the Allied countries. The British fears were reinforced by the large crowds gathering before the American embassy and crying 'Long live Roosevelt,' while others assembled at the British Embassy with signs reading 'British soldiers: Let us choose our own government.'"⁵⁵ Reports from the period of the December Crisis are peppered with stories of Americans being shot at because they had been mistaken for British soldiers, along with similar incidents. One memo conveys an event in which pot shots were taken at an American jeep:

> The ELAS people had not recognized the jeep as American—it was not flying a large flag at the time. When they saw who it was they stood up, dropped their rifles, cheered America and Roosevelt to the echo, and others in the street went and procured a good-sized flag from some family whose heirloom it was. So we now fly it on all voyages. . . . These difficulties do not exist once you get into uncontested ELAS territory: nothing but cheers, hand-clapping, and smiles.⁵⁶

Early views expressed by Americans in Greece had been sympathetic to those who joined the KKE and did not assume that all Greek communists were puppets of the Soviet Union. An OSS report from January 1945 noted that:

> From all that I can see, the problems of Greece—and I think Greece is only a miniature of Europe—go deeper than almost any of the brains that are on deck to solve them. A real issue has been posed here, and most people, at least on the Government side, are looking it squarely in the back of the neck. Most of the politicians around the G[rande] B[retagne] are worrying chiefly over losing their jobs. The rightists are inclined to

think that everything will be jake if the British will take a good strong line and clean up the Communists now, while the cleaning is good. The idea of cleaning up the situations that are giving the Communists their following does not seem to occur to them. For example, really whacking off the heads of even a few collaborationists, or really shelving the Security Battalions. Meanwhile more and more people in the country at large are either disgusted or terrified by the methods of the Communists, but where are they going to find any leadership outside of the Red brethren? The democratic and conservative forces in the country are just plain bankrupt for leadership, that's all.[57]

Even before the Truman Doctrine was announced in March 1947, British-American relations had gone full circle. The British were highly anxious to secure U.S. support for Greece and did all they could to avoid antagonizing the Americans,[58] and Washington had begun to play an advisory role to the Greek government. In January 1947, Truman sent an economic mission to Greece, headed by Paul Porter, to offer advice on what Truman saw as the Greek government's disastrous financial behavior. The Greek government had evidently begun selling gold "across the counter," and Truman felt that financial collapse was imminent. In addition to offering advice, Porter was also to report back to Truman on exactly what foreign aid would be needed to keep Greece from slipping into an abyss of bankruptcy and, consequently (as Truman saw it), communist control.[59] The United States had also, by this time, participated in two Allied missions: the Allied Mission for Observing the Greek Elections (AMFOGE) and AMFOGE II.[60]

By early 1947, the British, after expending their economic resources to defeat Nazi Germany and Imperial Japan, were financially exhausted. The Labour government of Clement Atlee that had replaced Churchill's in 1945 could not resuscitate the British economy as well as wage a new struggle against Soviet encroachment in Europe and the Middle East. The specter of a long-drawn-out competition with the USSR was simply beyond Britain's capabilities in economic or military terms. As a result, a message was sent by the British embassy to the

American State Department on 21 February 1947, dramatically altering America's role in Greece. The message announced the end of British aid to Greece and Turkey and expressed the hope that the United States would step into the vacuum.[61] This and subsequent messages from the British communicated the impression that, if the United States did not assume Britain's place, the entire Middle East and the Balkans would shortly fall to the Soviets.[62]

The American president was profoundly concerned by the situation as presented by his advisers and agreed with them that urgent action was necessary. With the help of his assistants, Truman formulated an intricate and far-reaching aid scheme for Greece and Turkey. Although this plan included military assistance, Truman's vision of aid to Greece and Turkey was based on economic and financial support, which he saw as fundamental pillars of democracy. Truman's legislation covered "authorization for the President to transfer to Greece military and other supplies . . . to procure for Greece military and other supplies, to detail military and civilian personnel of the United States Government, and to train Greek personnel." A mission was to be sent to Greece to oversee the expenditure of American funds and, in addition, to "assist the Greeks in the planning and execution of reconstruction projects, improvements of public administration and agricultural recovery, control of wages and prices and programming the sale or other disposition of government purchased supplies." Although the initial financial allotment was to cover the period up to 30 June 1948, the "authority granted with respect to the foregoing is not limited as to time and may, therefore, continue in effect after" that date.[63]

The implementation of such a massive peacetime aid program was unprecedented and represented a fundamental change in American foreign policy. As Truman put it, should Greece and Turkey fall to communist and totalitarian forces, it would "undermine the foundations of international peace and hence the security of the United States."[64] Truman recognized this critical turning point. "It means," he said, "the United States is going into European politics."[65] George Marshall echoed the significance of this new responsibility to students at Princeton University in 1948:

> You should fully understand the special position that the United States occupies in the world geographically, financially, militarily, and scientifically, and the implications involved. The development of a sense of responsibility for world order and security, the development of a sense of overwhelming importance of the country's acts, and failures to act in relation to world order and security—these, in my opinion, are great "musts" for your generation.[66]

The Truman Doctrine was described in broad terms as a remedy to international problems created by the withdrawal of Britain from the international stage. As such, it could be applied to countries other than Greece and Turkey in the future. Greece and Turkey represented, in the Balkans and the Middle East, respectively, key spheres of Western influence which were now vulnerable to communist pressures. As a result, these countries were the focus of the Truman plan at its outset. What lay beyond this temporary intervention in these two countries had unspoken implications which reach into the present day.

The Truman administration expressed various motivations for altering its international policies and forming the new doctrine. These included the ideological stance in support of self-determination; fears that increased communist influence in the Balkans could shift the international balance of power; and, strategically, the need to take a more interventionist role internationally, and to protect American interests in the Middle East. In essence, Truman was putting into practice George Kennan's idea of "containment." The Truman administration's internal papers from prior to the announcement of the doctrine primarily focus on the communist threat as the mitigating factor in extending aid to Greece and Turkey. Some members of the government recommended stressing this threat to Congress and the public to gain their support, but in the end much of the anticommunist rhetoric, which had been written into drafts of Truman's public announcement, was removed from the final speech.[67]

Having conceived of a line of action, they were faced with convincing the Congress and the American public that aid to the remote countries of Greece and Turkey was a necessity to America. In 1947, Congress had a Republican majority and was antagonistic toward the Truman administration in general, and toward excessive expenditure in particular. On 27 February 1947, Truman called a meeting with several senators and members of the House to announce his plans. Secretary of State Marshall spoke first and was followed by Undersecretary Dean Acheson, who felt Marshall had not made a strong enough impression. Acheson described the situation as being at a point "where a highly possible Soviet breakthrough might open three continents to Soviet penetration. Like apples in a barrel affected by one rotten one, the corruption of Greece would affect Iran and all to the East."[68] The impact made by these speeches was powerful enough to sway the group, which urged the president to address Congress with the same frankness they had been treated to by Marshall and Acheson.[69]

Once Truman had gained the support of his advisers, the group made a combined effort at concocting a persuasive argument with which to win over Congress and the public. It was decided that an appeal from Greece would be key in engaging the humanitarian and charitable instincts of Congress and the American public. Such an appeal was indeed presented, but it was written by the State Department, in tones most likely to charm American citizens, and then given to the Greek chargé d'affaires, Paul Economou-Gouras, to be signed by the Greek government and returned to America.[70]

A complex campaign was launched to engineer the perfect speech with which to approach Congress. For this address, Truman and his advisers decided to stress the preservation of democracy as the primary motivation for the aid plan (even though neither Greece nor Turkey had in place what could be considered a strictly democratic government). The U.S. government wanted to avoid underlining the oil motive, for fear of seeming cynical, and to avoid belaboring an anti-Soviet message, for fear of instigating war with the Soviet Union.[71] Thus, the focus was on "freedom," "democracy," and "self-determination," and the appeal, ostensibly from the Greek government, was cited as the instigation for Truman's plan to provide aid.[72]

On March 12, 1947, Truman made his broadcast speech to Congress, announcing, "I believe that it must be the policy of the United States to support free peoples who are resisting attempted subjugation by armed minorities or by outside pressures."[73] Such ambiguous references to "armed minorities" (communist guerrillas) and "outside pressures" (the Soviet Union) were puppet terms that served mainly to polarize and generalize the situation to Congress, without explicitly antagonizing the Soviets. Congress' initial reaction was influenced by frugality and caution. Some accused Truman of attempting to divide the world into spheres of influence, others of being aggressive, and still others of being intemperate and reactionary.[74] Truman's legislation finally passed three months later.

Ultimately, the American perception of the Greek and Turkish situation centered on the notion of the "domino effect," in which Greece and Turkey would fall to the communists, causing a chain reaction of Soviet expansion through the Middle East. Marshall poignantly expressed the American fear in his 27 February 1947 speech to Truman and his advisers:

> Our interest in Greece is by no means restricted to humanitarian or friendly impulses. . . . If Greece should dissolve into civil war it is altogether probable that it would emerge as a communist state under Soviet control. Turkey would be surrounded and the Turkish situation . . . would in turn become still more critical. Soviet domination might thus extend over the entire Middle East to the borders of India. The effect of this upon Hungary, Austria, Italy and France cannot be overestimated. It is not alarmist to say that we are faced with the first crisis of a series which might extend Soviet domination to Europe, the Middle East, and Asia.[75]

The oil motive, as mentioned above, must also have preoccupied the American government. Military demands for petroleum had vastly increased during the war, and America was undergoing a general shift toward the use of oil and natural gas. Under fear of oil shortages, Secretary of the Interior Harold Ickes urged that "nothing must be left undone" in the effort to secure overseas oil for the United States.[76]

In 1947, after the approval of Truman's request, the United States had to decide exactly how they were to step into Britain's place—how deeply involved to be, and through what methods. The policy the president out-lined, which became known as the Truman Doctrine, resulted in Amer-ica sending financial aid, as well as various American advisers, to Greece. On 24 May, the first group of American military advisers arrived in Greece as part of the U.S. Army Group Greece (USAGG). It was their responsibility to make recommendations regarding the management of the Greek general staff, the Greek army, and the gendarmerie. The Tru-man administration considered but decided against direct American mil-itary involvement, fearing that such a presence would "give substance to the communist charges of American aggression."77

The official U.S. line was that American military advisers were not to engage in fighting or actively command troops. Their position, like that of the OSS in Athens before them, remained ambiguous, despite the clar-ification of American policy toward Greece. When General William Livesay, director of USAGG, briefed the first twenty American officers going into the field, he told them, "[G]o out among the troops and see what is going on." "Neither your actions nor your talk" should put you in the light of a "combatant. . . . You carry no arms. Your conduct, if you are caught in an operation, is more or less entirely up to you. The thing for you to do is to take cover. You are not armed and you take the best cover you can and see what you can but don't get involved in the combat."78

Despite the careful instructions and stringent intentions, stories of Americans participating in the fighting soon seeped into the U.S. media.79 In February 1948, United Press correspondent Dan Thrapp re-ported from Thessaloniki that Colonel Augustus Regnier, the command-ing officer of a U.S. army detachment, "personally led a Greek platoon up a mountain slope under heavy machine fire." Regnier apparently said that he "took the lead when the Greek major commanding the battalion was hesitant about pushing his troops forward in the face of heavy fire." Reg-nier reportedly asked the Greek major, "Will you go forward if I do?" to which the major responded, "Sure, pal." Regnier then "led one platoon to the topmost mountain peak south of the lake, though [he] had to hit the dirt often."80 Before CBS correspondent George Polk was murdered, he reported to the U.S. embassy in Athens that he had been told by a U.S. colonel in Thessaloniki that American military advisers were leading the

Greek troops because "their commanders from the brigade level up were 'not worth a damn.'" Response to this allegation was described by journalist Constantine Poulos as "half a dozen feeble denials, a brief flurry of censorship on the part of the American Mission for Aid to Greece, and Colonel Regnier's transfer out of Thessalonica."[81]

Despite the largesse of U.S. military assistance the Greek army was unable to crush the insurgents quickly, while the communist forces, by their very survival, could claim cheap victories. In fact, the new Greek army and its commanders lacked experience in dealing with guerrilla warfare, since many Greek officers who had remained loyal to the Greek government-in-exile during the occupation had either sat out the war or joined the Greek forces in the Middle East. In both cases, these officers had been trained in conventional warfare only. In addition, many of the higher-ranking officers were former republicans who had been dismissed for their role in the military coups of the 1930s.[82]

This problem was further compounded by the low morale of the conscripts, many of whom deserted at the first opportunity. In fairness to the general staff, the Greek army only existed on paper in January 1946, and the few units that could be organized were hastily deployed in July 1946. According to the official history of the Greek army (which was only made available after 1998), most of the new recruits were considered communists or sympathetic to the left; also, many of the new units had been infiltrated by KKE cadres and could not be trusted.[83]

Under these circumstances, the Greek general staff tried to deal with the insurgency by creating defense perimeters around major cities and towns, leaving most of the countryside to the KKE bands. Unfortunately, this tactic tied down the Greek army in static defense positions and left it exposed to the hit-and-run tactics of the communist forces. The ensuing military quagmire forced the Greek high command to rely even more on paramilitary units and parapolice forces, whose actions in the field were marked by incidents of banditry and revenge killings. The general staff also constituted self-defense units in towns and villages by simply providing rudimentary training in arms and leaving these hapless forces to fend for themselves among the better-trained and -equipped communist bands. These tactics yielded negligible results, except for the limited information gathering that the self-defense units provided to the army and gendarmerie. Occasionally, the local defense units exceeded their authority to settle old scores and in some cases expropriated the property of left-wing sympathizers. By the beginning of July 1946, the situation had deteriorated significantly and right-wing reprisals claimed 780 killed and 5,677 wounded, along with over 28,450 cases of torture.

However, this did not deter the KKE from maintaining extensive clandestine networks of informants, sabotage groups, assassination squads, propaganda units, and even mine-laying operations in Greek harbors during the period of the civil war. The Greek Democratic Army, the new name for the communist insurgents since October 1946, also indulged in excesses and was responsible for thousands of executions, kidnappings, and torture incidents—and in a last desperate measure, the abduction of children. Whenever the Greek Democratic Army was forced to retreat from occupied areas, it often took along thousands of children without their parents. The KKE argued that they were rescuing the children from the misery of war, but the government claimed, usually with considerable justification, that the children had been kidnapped. By the end of the war, approximately 28,000 children had been taken out of Greece and only 10,000 were eventually returned.[84]

The initial strategy of the KKE was to isolate Macedonia, Greece's northern province, and use it as a staging ground to continue the war in the rest of the country. Until they could accomplish this, they had to rely on Yugoslavia, Bulgaria, and Albania for logistical support, bases of operations, and safe havens for retreat after engaging the Greek army. To a great extent, Yugoslavia carried the main burden of supplying the insurgents as well as providing staging areas for the Greek Democratic Army's hit-and-run tactics. Part of the strategy also included the use of Macedonia as a resource region to sustain the Greek Democratic Army in the field. The insurgents often requisitioned much food and many livestock at the expense of the villagers. These expropriations and the forced recruitment of young men and women caused severe shortages of both foodstuffs and workers in the region. John Koliopoulos argues that "these were not the actions of persecuted and desperate men: they were part of a drive to force the authorities to their knees by destroying the productive capacity of the region and drive all who could bear arms into the mountains."[85] These acts, combined with the negative accounts of deserters and government propaganda, eventually eroded support for the KKE.

The choice of Macedonia also had the advantage of securing easy access to supplies from Yugoslavia and Bulgaria as well as a steady stream of Slavo-Macedonian recruits. The KKE could also count on moral and material support from the residents of the region who had settled as refugees from Asia Minor. The Slavic element in northern Greece was generally hostile to the Greek authorities, and many believed that they could form an independent Macedonian state, or failing that, that they could merge with the People's Republic of Macedonia in Yugoslavia if the KKE emerged victorious in the civil war. Consequently, the high proportion of Slavo-Macedonians in the Greek Democratic Army, in addition to proposals for detaching parts of northern Greece, underscored the claims of the propaganda machine in Athens that the KKE not only represented external interests but also was itself foreign.

During the course of the civil war, the Greek Democratic Army averaged approximately 20,000 men and women (who throughout the civil war represented at least 25 percent of the insurgent forces), while the Greek army continued to expand, reaching 132,000 men in the last year of the conflict.[86] According to U.S. sources, in order for the insurgents to sustain an army of 20,000 in the field it was necessary to replace the force three and a half times. In terms of the quantity of personnel, the ranks of the Greek Democratic Army swelled in 1946–1947, at the expense of the Greek army, which lost conscripts who ran off to join the insurgents. However, in the long run this was not a major loss since many of these recruits had been raised from the older prewar classes and proved unsuitable for counterinsurgency operations.[87] After 1947, the Greek army was able to replace the lower-quality recruits with men who were younger, better trained, and much healthier. The Greek Democratic Army, on the other hand, had to rely on older deserters and conscripted peasants who fled at the first opportunity. Over the three years of conflict, consequently, the age and quality of the Greek Democratic Army's officers and soldiers continued to deteriorate unabated.[88]

In 1949, the Greek Democratic Army switched from guerrilla tactics to conventional battles, with disastrous consequences, to bring about a quick end to the war. The change from small mobile units of insurgents striking at the Greek army over a broad area was one of the consequences of the Stalin-Tito split in 1948 and one that sealed the fate of the Greek communists. Stalin could no longer abide Tito's growing stature in the communist world and growing independence from Moscow. In February 1948, the Soviet dictator summoned Tito to Moscow, but he declined, and Stalin vented his fury on the Yugoslav delegation, composed of Milovan Djilas, Edvard Kardelj, and Vladimir Bakaric. After railing at them over the proposed Balkan Federation of Yugoslavia and Bulgaria, Stalin turned to the Greek situation, Djilas recalls in his memoirs:

> "The uprising in Greece will have to fold up. Do you believe" he turned to Kardelj "in the success of the uprising in Greece?" Kardelj replied, "If foreign intervention does not grow, and if serious political and military errors are not made." Stalin went on, without paying attention to Kardelj's opinion, "If, if! No, they have no prospect of success at all. What, do you think that Great Britain and the United States—the United States, the most powerful state in the world—will permit you to break their line of communication in the Mediterranean? Nonsense. And we have no navy. The uprising in Greece must be stopped, and as quickly as possible."[89]

After this tirade, Tito's relationship with Stalin was finished. It also destroyed any chance that the Greek communists may have had to achieve even a partial victory. Stubbornly, Zachariadis, despite the critical dependence of the Greek Democratic Army on Yugoslavia, clung to the Moscow line. Because of this, he needed a quick victory before Tito could cut off the Greek communist forces from their supplies in Yugoslavia. Unfortunately, Zachariadis had neither the military skill nor sufficient resources and personnel to successfully wage a conventional battle. In the summer of 1949 Zachariadis shifted completely from guerrilla tactics to positional warfare. For the next two months, the Greek

Democratic Army constructed strong defenses in the Frontier Corner around the Vitsi massif as a jumping-off point for offensive operations in Greece. The area encompassed approximately 250 square miles, with Albania in the rear and Yugoslavia in the north. Steep mountains, strewn with rocks and cut by valleys with thick forests, marked the region, which made it ideal defensive terrain. The communists built concrete emplacements for their artillery, which they covered with barbed wire and reinforced with machine guns. Now, for the first time in the war, the Greek army confronted the now static communist forces along a broad front of approximately forty miles.[90]

The Greek Democratic Army had about 7,000 troops concentrated in the Vitsi bastion and another 5,000 in the south positioned along the Grammos Mountain Range. Another 3,000 troops were located in close proximity to the main force—a total of 15,000 men and women. The Greek army, thanks to massive U.S. aid, was able to field over 160,000 troops and managed to attack before Zachariadis could deploy all his forces. On 5 August 1949 three divisions of the Greek government forces attempted a diversionary attack against the communist defenses in Grammos in order to mask the primary offensive aimed at Vitsi, but after one week of fighting they made little progress. Leo Katsuris, who took part in the diversionary attack against the Grammos defenses, remembers that his division struck deep behind the flanks of the rebels and some units crossed the border into Albania. "The moment we crossed," he recalls, "the Albanians attacked us and as our unit fell back towards the Greek frontier we stumbled on a minefield. We lost 400 men that day."[91]

On 10 August, the main offensive of the Greek government forces, consisting of another three divisions, struck the Greek Democratic Army in Vitsi in a three-pronged attack. The fighting was bitter and the communists clung grimly to their positions along the mountainsides and in the valleys, but the superior firepower of the Greek army eventually overwhelmed the insurgents. Although the Greek government forces killed and captured over 2,000 rebels, their victory was not complete because a large number escaped to Albania, Bulgaria, and Yugoslavia.[92]

The Grammos stronghold, however, continued to hold out, and on 25 August the Third Corps of the Greek army launched a fresh offensive, this time supported by fifty-one Curtiss Helldivers armed with cannon, machine guns, and rockets and able to drop two napalm bombs with pinpoint accuracy. The insurgents fought stubbornly and, using the advantage of terrain and camouflage, at first repulsed the Greek government forces. The craggy rocks and precipitous Grammos mountaintops provided excellent cover for the defenders and almost insurmountable obstacles for the attackers. Greek soldiers, on both sides, hunted each other on the barren hillsides, but once again the firepower of the Greek army and the sheer weight of numbers prevailed. Greek government artillery pounded the communist positions, and the Helldivers machine-gunned the defenders; where bullets and soldiers could not reach, napalm incinerated any further opposition. After only one day, the insurgents began to give way, and the government forces captured several of the heights. On 27 August, Mount Grammos fell to the Greek army; the rebel forces fell apart, and soon about 8,000 were fleeing across the border into Albania. The Yugoslavs had already closed the border to the Greek communists, and the Albanians now began to restrict their movements as well; only the Bulgarians were prepared to support the insurgents.

Despite the defeats at Grammos and Vitsi, Zachariadis was prepared to continue the struggle in a long guerrilla war, but Stalin intervened and ordered the Greek communists to declare a cease-fire. The Greek civil war had by the early fall of 1949 become a dangerous luxury for the Soviets in their overall policy toward the West. In early October a flotilla of small boats (chartered by the British Secret Service), carrying twenty-six Albanian freedom fighters, landed on the coast of Albania with the aim of overthrowing the country's communist regime. Little came of it and upon reaching the shoreline they were ambushed.[93] Similar attempts by parachute drops had also failed, and years later Kim Philby, the notorious communist mole in Britain's intelligence service, hinted that he had betrayed the operations to his Soviet masters. There is little doubt, however, that Stalin was unsettled by the Anglo-American efforts to undermine the Albanian regime in response to Albania's support of the Greek insurgents. Furthermore, he was still smarting from Tito's defection and becoming increasingly apprehensive over U.S. maneuvers to encourage a Greek-Yugloslav-Turkish anti-Soviet Balkan pact.[94]

On 16 October 1949, the insurgents' radio station announced a temporary halt to the fighting in order to prevent the destruction of Greece. The voice of the Greek communists then proclaimed that the Greek Democratic Army had not given up but was forced to back down temporarily due to the material advantage of the Athens government and Tito's treachery. A few isolated pockets of resistance continued throughout the fall, but otherwise the Greek civil war sputtered to an end. A little later, Soviet ships steamed into the harbors of Albania and collected the remnants of the Greek Democratic Army; among them was Kostas Katsuris, who would remain for almost twenty years in exile. He was one of the lucky ones; many others spent the rest of their lives in remote parts of the USSR, and only a few eventually trickled back to Greece after the Greek government declared a general amnesty in 1982.[95]

Epilogue: Shadows Cast from Yesterday

FULL CIRCLE:
FROM GREECE TO
VIETNAM

THE IMMEDIATE CIRCUMSTANCES SURROUNDING THE MURDER of American journalist George Polk may never come to light. But the wider background—the conflict that fueled the ongoing civil war in Greece and set the stage for his death—was the new kind of war that was reshaping the postwar world in 1948. In this respect, Polk was one of the first American casualties of the cold war. The tally for the Greeks was considerably higher; perhaps as many as 158,000 lost their lives as a direct result of the civil war. Losses in the Greek army reached 11,000 killed, while the Greek Democratic Army lost over 38,000.

Soldiers and guerrillas weren't the only ones—or even the majority—of those who suffered. Seven hundred thousand people, 10 percent of Greece's population, fled from their homes or were forcibly relocated by the Greek authorities in order to deny the communists recruits and supplies from the mountain villages. U.S. advisers had inspired this strategy of shifting populations and relocating entire communities; later, it was applied with much less success in Vietnam. Close to 50,000 Greeks were condemned to exile and almost 28,000 children were abducted or forced to flee Greece with the communist forces to the Balkan communist states. Eventually, only 10,344 were repatriated after the war.[1] The rest faced a dreary life in the orphanages of the Eastern Bloc countries. Nicholas Gage's book *Eleni*, the poignant account of his mother's fatal struggle to save her children from such a fate and his odyssey to find his mother's killers, offers a unique insight into the tragedy.

Ultimately, the civil war gutted Greece's postwar reconstruction for at least a decade, while the rift between the right and the left handicapped Greek society for another half century. The prospect of a "Red Acropolis" for most Greeks was fundamentally unpalatable. Often, when the communists took control of a village or neighborhood, they held people's trials, carried out summary executions, demanded requisitions, forcibly recruited young men and women into the ranks of the insurgents, and kidnapped children, leaving a bitter legacy in their wake. However, the overreaction of the authorities in the form of Black Terror—meted out by military tribunals dispensing justice based on innuendo and gossip and followed by the application of torture, prison, and the degrading declarations of repentance—in turn generated sympathy for the communists and contributed to a prolonged war.

From 1946 to 1949, the Greek communists, averaging fewer than 20,000 forces (and those only after 1947), engaged the Greek army in a successful guerrilla campaign, and only when they switched to conventional battle tactics did they suffer complete defeat. Yet the military lessons of the Greek civil war were obscured by the impact of America's political success. The United States had "won the hearts and minds" of the Greeks. The occasional flurry of "anti-Americanism" in present-day Greece is fallout from the time of the Greek Colonel's Junta (1967–1974) and the Turkish invasion of Cyprus in 1974, events believed by some Greeks to have been orchestrated by the United States.

America emerged, out of the Greek civil war, not only unscathed politically but also victorious in its first indirect showdown with the Soviet Union. However, as historians have since learned, the showdown was in fact unnecessary: Stalin had little interest in Greece and even less inclination to confront the United States in the Balkans, but American policymakers were convinced that they had stayed the fall of the first domino to global communism. Further opportunities to halt Soviet and Chinese expansion presented themselves, including, eventually, Vietnam. As historian Howard Jones explains, "America's experience in Greece provided a glimmer of a policy that would later become known in the 1950s as 'nation building.'"[2] After North Korea attacked South Korea in 1950, Truman declared, "Korea is the Greece of the Far East. If we are tough enough now, if we stand up to them like we did in Greece three years ago, they won't take over the whole Middle East."[3]

The stalemate in Korea further reinforced the notion of a worldwide communist conspiracy, with countries such as Greece serving as frontline states in the global conflict. In 1952 Greece and Turkey were admitted to NATO, and in the fall of that year the Americans established military bases in both countries. The formation of the Greek anticommunist state was complete. The U.S. bases became a symbol of America's commitment to fighting communism not only on the battlefield but also within the social and political fabric of individual states. Accordingly, the Greek example served as a model for America's intervention in Central and South America, in the Middle East, and, perhaps most dramatically, in Vietnam. In 1950, the U.S. chargé d'affaires in Saigon, in a report criticizing the French failure to contain the Vietminh, wrote that for the United States it "may eventually become necessary to assume some responsibilities in Indochina as in [the] case of Greece, the threat of spreading Communist political contagion East and West . . . should influence our action." He went on to recommend "limited use of U.S. force" and "our going as far as we did in Greece and farther than was ever announced we could go."[4] In the same year, John Foster Dulles, the secretary of state, even before the Korean War, connected the situation in Asia, and particularly Southeast Asia, with that in the Middle East. He concluded that the fall of Greece to the communist rebels would have resulted in the encirclement of Turkey and ultimately the Soviet domination of the eastern Mediterranean and the Middle East.[5]

In 1957, Dwight D. Eisenhower, claiming that he understood the lesson learned from the Greek civil war, agreed to expand the U.S. role in Vietnam. Henry Cabot Lodge Jr., the American ambassador to the United Nations, also claimed, "We of the free world won in Greece . . .

and we can win in Vietnam."[6] The Greek-Vietnam nexus, however, was not confined to the Republicans: According to his speechwriter Theodore Sorensen, John F. Kennedy "[a]t times compared the Vietnam War to the long struggles against Communist guerrillas in Greece and Asia."[7] Likewise, in his memoirs, President Lyndon B. Johnson considered the Truman Doctrine in Greece part of America's international inheritance and his justification for committing additional U.S. forces in Vietnam, stating, "In 1947 the British were able to pass on to us their responsibilities in Greece and Turkey. In 1954 the French knew they could transfer the problem of Southeast Asia's security to our shoulders." For American cold warriors, the U.S. experience in Greece—a successfully fought proxy war featuring a counterinsurgency campaign against communist guerrillas and marked by the use of napalm—became a model for involvement in Vietnam.

The failure of the United States in Vietnam is complex and beyond the scope of this study. Two decades of war in Vietnam caused 58,178 U.S. deaths and, in the process, triggered social and political upheavals whose aftershocks continue to reverberate to this day. Presidents Johnson and Nixon committed substantial ground forces to fight the war on behalf of the South Vietnamese and learned to accept increasing American casualties. However, the American presence in Greece and in Southeast Asia is differentiated by the willingness of most Greeks (despite later anti-Americanism) to welcome U.S. intervention in their civil war.

There is little doubt that the Truman Doctrine saved Greece from slipping into the Soviet sphere, and Greece thus escaped decades of economic and cultural stagnation. Yet the U.S. grand strategy of containment retarded and distorted the political evolution of Greece. Indeed, after Greece became a member of NATO, the role of the Greek armed forces was to act as a trip wire to alert the Americans of sudden Soviet attack against southeastern Europe. Greece became a military assembly center for a confrontation between the United States and the Soviets during the cold war. The cold war threat conveniently dovetailed with the memory of 1946–1949 communist insurrection and was exploited by the conservative regimes in Athens to suppress legitimate dissent in the name of allied security.

In the years after 1949, the KKE remained an outlaw organization, and ultra-right-wing gangs tormented anyone suspected of leftist activity. Greek schools and universities excluded any course on the resistance or the civil war from their curriculum—Greek history came to an abrupt halt with the glorious victories of the Greek army in Albania in 1940–1941. References to the 1946–1949 period described the conflict as the "bandit war" and as part of Bulgarian and Albanian plots inspired by the Soviets to destroy Greece. Nonetheless, the Greek electorate in the 1960s supported moderate politicians and began to edge toward electing center-left coalitions. These tendencies alarmed the monarchy and the army, both of which maintained independent relations with the United States, and plans were set in motion to preempt the election of a government that appeared too far away from the right. Ironically, the man who elicited such fears was centrist politician George Papandreou, the man who defeated EAM-ELAS and the KKE in the December Uprising. In April 1967, the army seized control of the state and imposed a military dictatorship. For seven years, the military dictatorship applied all the instruments of fear and repression against the left and the moderate right. The prison islands were once again filled to capacity, the torture chambers were reactivated, and a web of informants spied on Greeks at home and abroad.

For most Greeks the cruel legacy of the civil war began to dissipate slowly after the collapse of the junta in 1974, accelerated by the election of the Pan-Hellenic Socialist Movement (PASOK) in October 1981, the first Socialist Party to rule Greece, and by the recognition of the resistance a year later. During the 1990s the schism between the left and the right blurred beyond recognition: In 1989, an ecumenical government that also included the conservative and communist parties had already breached the last barriers of mistrust, fear, and hatred that had polarized Greek society since the occupation.

However, the shadow of the civil war continues to linger, and occasionally emotions flare up in response to events in the Balkans. The breakup of the Yugoslav Federation in 1990 and the possibility of the establishment of a Macedonian state (across the border from the Greek province of Macedonia) caused waves of hysteria in Greece and throughout the Greek diaspora. The overreaction to the breakup of

Yugoslavia and the exaggerated fears of a Balkan conflagration spilling into Greece were, in fact, a reflex reaction from the civil war legacy.

The proponents of the splinter Yugoslav Macedonian Republic were a faint echo of the Greek communist insurgents. Although the Greek Democratic Army represented all sectors of society in Greece, the majority came from parts of northern Macedonia where ethnic Greeks had been a minority. During the occupation, a substantial number of Slavo-Macedonians or Slavophones had collaborated with the Axis and particularly with the Bulgarians.[8] After the occupation, fearing retaliation, and at the very least systematic repression, many gladly volunteered to fight for the communist insurgency and by 1949 made up the majority of the communist rebel army. Accordingly, for a great many Greeks living in the north, especially those in western Macedonia, the issue of Slavo-Macedonians was directly linked with the memory of the civil war. After the initial nationalistic brouhaha in 1992, the Greek population reconciled itself to the prospect of a Slavic state with some kind of Greek name, and the memory of civil war edged closer to oblivion— except for a small number of aging radicals whose struggle against the ultra-right in Greece had metastasized into terrorism.

On Thursday, 19 July 2002, on the sleepy island of Lipsi in the eastern Aegean, a small example of the recent transformation of the right-left rift unfolded. On that day this island of just 650 inhabitants served as the setting of a drama that had been unfolding for twenty-seven years. A force of 700 police and soldiers descended on the sun-drenched island to capture a solitary figure. Navy divers were in the waters close to shore, navy gunboats hovered a few hundred yards from the island, and commandos circled overhead in a helicopter. The authorities were taking few chances. The target of the military exercise was Alexandros Yiotopoulos, the leader of the left-wing terrorist group 17 November. Yiotopoulos went quietly, with little resistance. His neighbors were stunned. Few could have believed that this man was responsible for twenty-three murders and had masterminded one of the longest surviving terrorist organizations in the world.

November 17, the name adopted by his Greek Marxist-Leninist terrorist group, had bedeviled the Greek authorities, along with the intelligence services of the United States, Great Britain, France, and Interpol, for close to thirty years. The organization had inaugurated its activities in 1975 by killing Richard Wells, the CIA station head in Athens, and for the next twenty-seven years November 17 maintained a steady pace of assassinations. Their targets included a hodgepodge of intelligence and military personnel serving in Greece, from the United States and Great Britain, Turkish diplomats, Greek tycoons, and politicians. Each killing was followed by a long communiqué replete with Marxist-Leninist slogans that were more in sync with the late 1940s than with contemporary Greece. These sensational murders strained and at times embittered Greece's relations with the United States and Great Britain.

Prior to Yiotopoulos' arrest November 17 had remained an enigma and immune to penetration. For almost three decades, speculations had run rampant in Greece concerning the mysterious group. Theories ranged from the preposterous to the ridiculous. Some argued forcefully that November 17 was the pet child of PASOK (the Greek socialist party), which dominated the Greek government from 1981 to 2004. Others even suggested that the terrorists were members of Greece's military, which explained the skills and weapons knowledge of the group. Still others advanced the idea that the members of November 17 were not Greek at all but agent provocateurs and, depending on the conspiracy theorist, had been sent by the Americans, the British, the Soviets, or even the Turks. There was no end to the theories, and each murder by the group spawned new allegations and allusions to new conspiracies. On 19 July 2002 and in the days that followed, all the rumors were finally silenced by facts.

The arrest brought instant relief to Greece's socialist government and incredulity to those few who had known Yiotopoulos as a student in Paris. The newspaper testimonials from Greek academics and intellectuals who had also earned their radical spurs in the French student movement in the 1960s all identified Yiotopoulos as a poor, unassuming fellow. Most agreed that he was interested in left-wing causes and had been a member of the more extreme Greek student organizations that had sprouted up in reaction to the military junta in Athens. No one remembered him as a fanatic.

Lipsi is a small island, part of the Dodecanese Archipelago, drenched in sunlight and surrounded by pebble beaches. The island is home to fishermen, summer tourists, and the few businesses that cater to them, along with a growing population of Greek professionals who are dotting the Aegean islands with summer homes. These professionals are the generation of European Union Greeks and are uninhibited capitalists— even when they vote for the Greek socialist party. Prosperous and mostly apolitical, few are concerned with the memory of the Greek civil war, to say nothing of Marxist-Leninist ideology. In this context, Yiotopoulos is an aberration, a creature of the 1930s rather than a citizen of the twenty-first-century European Union.

In fact, Yiotopoulos is one of the unfortunate prisoners of the Greek civil war legacy. His story and that of his father, Dimitris, are tales of futility and pain, poverty and fear, and finally violence, representing two generations of the human flotsam from the political and military convulsions that raked Greece before and after the Second World War.

Dimitris Yiotopoulos was a member of that strange and compulsive group of political animals who emerged out of the labor and student movements in Athens and Thessaloniki in the early twentieth century. Most of these men and women gravitated to radical politics and organizations as the only avenue of escape from a life of dreary poverty and insignificance. Yiotopoulos senior quickly emerged as the leader of the Archive Marxists, a splinter group of the KKE named after the leftist periodical *Archives of Marxism,* and joined the Trotskyite movement in Paris.

The Greek Archive Marxists splintered several more times, as some members refused to follow Yiotopoulos' ideological shifts within the political spectrum of the left. During the occupation and in the early months of liberation, they were hunted down by the KKE, whose leadership actually believed that this obscure group posed a deadly threat to the Greek Communist Party. The executioners of the OPLA, the dreaded security service of the KKE, took particular delight in dispatching Archive Marxists by slicing their throats with the tops of tin cans, and they massacred at least 600 Archive Marxists during this tumultuous period.

After the Second World War, the elder Yiotopoulos returned to Athens and led the few hundred remaining Archive Marxists who had defied the grisly efforts of the KKE. For a short time he served as an adviser to the Greek minister of education, but he ended up dying in obscurity in 1965.

Dimitris' son, Alexandros, inherited his father's complex sense of social justice and gravitated to the French radical student movement as a student in Paris during the 1960s, eventually coming to lead one of the most ruthless and long-standing terrorist groups in Greece's post–civil war history. Why did Alexandros Yiotopoulos choose the path of urban terrorism? Whatever the ultimate reason, his clandestine and deadly activities of the past decades had exorcised his father's failures and allowed him and his followers to replay a civil war that had expired long before.

By 2003, the year of Yiotopoulos' dramatic arrest on Lipsi, the civil war that had loomed so large in Greek society was finally slipping into the pages of history. But the three rounds of civil war had left their mark on several generations of Greeks. Supporters of the resistance against the Germans had been marginalized by the official denial of the resistance, which the Greek right linked with each phase of insurgency. Others had faced years of persecution because they were identified with the left. Likewise, the chaos of the December Uprising and the depredations of leftist guerrillas had left a bitter legacy long after the physical scars had faded. But for millions of Greeks caught in the crossfire between the two sides, who lived through the agony of a society riven by civil war, and who saw their country become a proxy battlefield for a global war of ideologies, the memories of the civil war remain etched in consciousness, no matter how many years have intervened.

NOTES

Introduction

1. For a detailed and compelling account of the trial and execution see Stelios Protaios, *E Diki ton Ex* (Athens: Chrisima Vivlia, n.d., passim). Protaios includes, along with his own account, the minutes of the extraordinary court martial. Michael Llewellyn Smith, in his study of the Greek expedition in Turkey, *Ionian Vision: Greece in Asia Minor 1919–1922* (Ann Arbor, Michigan: University of Michigan Press, 1973), includes some discussion (in English) on the trial and execution of the Six.

2. There is some confusion about whether Hatzianestis was degraded. Protaios (p. 819) states that according to some accounts Hatzianestis removed his own epaulets; others claim he was degraded in prison. Smith (p. 328) relies on A. F. Frangoulis (*La Grèce, son statut international, son histoire diplomatique*, 2nd edition, 2 vols., Paris, n.d.), who was not present but was closely associated with the condemned men. According to this version, the degrading was to take place just before the execution, but as the officers approached the general to remove his military insignia, he ripped off his epaulets and decorations. Proteus writes that most of the eyewitnesses of the execution did not comment on this. One interesting fact is that Hatzianestis was wearing a civilian trench coat, which casts some doubt on the theory that the general suffered this final humiliation just before the firing squad ended his life.

3. This came none too soon for Protopapadakis, who lay in the makeshift grave with part of his brain lying beside him. The scene of the helpless Protopapadakis lying on the ground spattered with brains and blood so unsettled General Lambros Spais, deputy commander of Athens and a member of the Revolutionary Committee, that years later he still could not forget the execution. He omitted any details of it in his memoirs but conveyed the frightful scene to Spiros Markezinis, a Greek historian.

Chapter 1

1. George II returned in 1935 after a fraudulent referendum restored the monarchy.

2. On 28 September, part of the main army (12,000) marched into the capital in good order (Smith, *Ionian Vision*, p. 314).

3. The court martial began deliberations in the Greek parliament on 13 November and concluded with guilty verdicts on 28 November. The court martial consisted of ten officers, headed by General Alexander Othonaios.

4. Upon arrival in Athens, the leaders of the coup ordered the arrest of Dimitris Gounaris, Nikolaos Theotokis, Petros Protopapadakis, Nikolaos Stratos, and Admiral Michael Goudas, whom they planned to execute immediately and then declare a general amnesty. They also had arrested Prince Andrew, one of Constantine's younger sons. After protests from the British and French ambassadors, they decided to wait. Subsequently they arrested Georgios Baltazzis, General Georgios Hatzianestis, and Xenephon Stratigos. All were found guilty, six condemned to death, and two (Goudas and Sratigos) sentenced to life imprisonment, but they were released after a few years.

5. This particular version of Andrew's escape is supplanted by a more fanciful and dramatic report in which Talbot persuades Plastiras to have Pangalos personally escort Andrew to the British warship. Pangalos was considered a hardliner and an implacable foe of the monarchy and its supporters; thus his presence guaranteed Andrew's safety.

6. If Andrew had indeed been executed it would have affected the British royal family. Andrew was the father of Philip, later Duke of Edinburgh and Queen Elizabeth's consort. Prince Philip was one year old in 1922.

7. The name means "lighthouse." The lighthouse district in Constantinople served as the center of the Orthodox church and the residence of the wealthy Greeks.

8. L. S. Stavrianos, *The Balkans since 1453* (New York: New York University Press, 1958), p. 111.

9. On this point see Bernard Lewis, *What Went Wrong? Western Impact and Middle Eastern Response* (Oxford: Oxford University Press, 2002), passim).

10. Most of the diaspora communities in Europe were small in numbers and eventually assimilated or returned to Greece. The communities that remained in the Ottoman Empire were considerably larger and greater in number than even the population of Greece in 1830. Those in Russia were also significant in size at least until 1917.

11. Petropoulos, *Politics and Statecraft in the Kingdom of Greece, 1833–1843* (Princeton: Princeton University Press, 1968), pp. 28–30.

12. Petropoulos, *Politics and Statecraft in the Kingdom of Greece*, p. 29.

13. For an erudite and exhaustive study of the factions and their role in the period of 1833–1843, see Petropoulos' *Politics and Statecraft in the Kingdom of Greece*.

14. Cyprus as well as the Italian-occupied Dodecanese and northern Epirus (southern Albania) remained as the three outstanding issues of Greek foreign policy until the end of the Second World War. In the postwar settlement of the Treaty of Paris in 1947, Greece took possession of the Dodecanese Islands but failed to secure Cyprus and northern Epirus.

15. The republic was proclaimed on 25 March 1924, the anniversary of the outbreak of the Greek War of Independence.

16. The purge of royalist officers in 1922 was followed by the dismissal of 1,800 republican officers because of the unsuccessful coups of 1933 and 1935 (André Gerolymatos, "The Role of the Greek Officer Corps in the Resistance," *Journal of the Hellenic Diaspora*, Vol. 11, No. 3, Fall 1984, p. 71, note 7).

17. A critical factor in the victory of the Populists was the boycott of the elections by the Venizelists.

18. According to the American ambassador, Lincoln MacVeagh (*Ambassador MacVeagh Reports: Greece, 1933–1947*, ed. J. O. Iatrides, Princeton: Princeton University Press, 1980, p. 60), the number given for the monarchist vote was higher by a margin of 400,000 votes than the total vote cast by all parties in any previous election. Hagen Fleischer (*Stemma kai Swastika*, Athens: Papazisis, 1988, p. 54) adds that the Danish ambassador in Athens commented that the entire process was a farce and "the greatest comedy performed on the European scene for a long time."

19. J. S. Koliopoulos, *Greece and the British Connection 1935–1941* (Oxford: Oxford University Press, 1977), p. 6.

20. The breakdown of seats in the new parliament of 1936 was 143 Populists, 141 Liberals (Venizelists), and 15 Communists (G. Dafnis, *I Ellas Metaxy Dyo Polemon 1923–1940*, 2 vols., Vol. 2, Athens: Ikaros, 1974, p. 402).

21. Koliopoulos, *Greece and the British Connection*, p. 40.

22. Dafnis, Vol. 2, p. 423 ff.

23. Metaxas confided in his diary that the country was on the eve of a communist revolution. Communist propaganda, he wrote, had already infiltrated the civil service and threatened to paralyze the state, and it had started eroding the discipline of the armed forces. See Ioannis Metaxas, *To Prosopiko tou Imerologio*, P. Vranas (Vol. 4, 1933–1941), pp. 222–223, 4 August 1936 (Athens: Ekdoseis Gkobosti, 1951–1964).

24. Metaxas considered this the successor to the classical and Byzantine civilizations. There are several works in Greek on the Metaxas' dictatorship, but as Koliopoulos (*Greece and the British Connection*, p. 51) points out, they are either polemics against Metaxas or apologias for his regime. A reliable addition to the bibliography of the period is *Praktika tou Diethnous Istorokou Synedriou, I Ellada 1936–44: Diktatoria, Katochi, Andistasi*, ed. Hagen Fleischer and Nikolas Svoronos (Athens: Morphotiko Institouto ATE, 1989). Also see P. J. Vatikiotis, *Popular Autocracy in Greece 1936–41: A Political Biography of General Ioannis Metaxas* (London: Frank Cass, 1998), for a recent study of the Metaxas regime.

25. Metaxas, *Imerologio*, Vol. 4, p. 553; also in Vatikiotis, p. 156.

26. J. Kofas, *Authoritarianism in Greece* (New York: Columbia University Press, 1983), pp. 53–54, however, argues that the Metaxas regime evolved from a conservative dictatorship to an authoritarian quasi-fascist state. By 1938, Kofas writes, Metaxas had purged most of the royalists from his government and replaced them with his own followers, thus gradually becoming independent of the king.

27. J. S. Koliopoulos, "Esoterikes Exelixeis apo tin Protin Martiou os tin 28 Octovriou 1940," *Istoria tou Ellinikou Ethnous: Neoteros Ellinismos apo 1913 os 1941* (Athens: Ekdotiki Athenon, 1978), p. 393, attributes the passivity of the politicians to several factors based on the weakness of the parties and their inability to galvanize popular opposition to the dictatorship. Some in the Liberal Party even entertained the hope that Metaxas would reinstate the cashiered Venizelist officers. Another consideration was the fear that the reaction of Metaxas to vociferous opposition would be to create his own party.

28. Gerolymatos, "The Role of the Greek Officer Corps in the Resistance," p. 71.

29. Anticommunist policy was nothing new in Greek politics. Previous administrations had been as fervent in combating communism. Between 1929 and 1932, the Venizelos government had made 11,000 arrests resulting in 2,130 convictions (A. Elephandis, *I Epangelia tis Adinatis Epanastasis: K.K.E. kai Astismos ston Mesopolemon*, Athens: Themilio, 1976, p. 256).

30. A month after the declaration of martial law, the authorities apprehended the general secretary of the KKE, Nikos Zachariadis. By April 1938, all members of the politburo had been arrested, with the exception of George Siantos (John Loulis, *The Greek Communist Party, 1940–1944,* London: CroomHelm, 1982, pp. 4–5).

31. Fleischer, Stemma, p. 128. D. G. Kousoulas, *Revolution and Defeat: The Story of the Greek Communist Party* (London: Oxford University Press, 1965), p. 130, places the figure at 45,000; Loulis, *The Greek Communist Party,* p. xiv, Table 1.

32. According to the official history of the KKE, *Syntomi Istoria tou KKE, Meros A 1918–1949,* eds. Istoriki Epeitropi tou KKE (Athens: Synchroni Epochi, 1988), p. 142, the process of decapitating the leadership of the party was completed in November 1939 with the arrest of Siantos and George Skafida. Approximately 2,000 communists were imprisoned throughout the period of the dictatorship (Aggelos G. Elephandis, *I Epangelia tis Adinatis Epanastasis,* Athens: Themelio, 1976, p. 257).

33. According to D. H. Close, "The Police in the Fourth of August Regime," *Journal of the Hellenic Diaspora,* Vol. 13, Nos. 1 and 2 (1986), p. 93, two departments of the gendarmerie, the Eidiki Asfalia (Special Security) and the Yeniki Asfalia (General Security), formed the political or secret police responsible for counterespionage and anticommunism.

34. Loulis, *The Greek Communist Party,* p. 4; D. G. Kousoulas, *KKE: Ta Prota Chronia, 1918–1949* (Athens : Elliniki Euroekdotiki, 1987) p. 158.

35. On the underground activities of one prominent member of the KKE during this period, see V. Bartziotas, *Exinda Chronia Kommounistis* (Athens: Synchroni Epochi, 1986), pp. 151–153. Some of these cells established contact with noncommunist underground organizations, including that of a group of serving officers who had socialist sympathies (Elephandis, *I Epangelia tis Adinatis Epanastasis,* p. 245).

36. Bartziotas, *Athens 1986,* pp. 159–168; A. Phlountzes, *Akrovafplia kai Akronafpliotes* (Athens: Thermilio, 1979), pp. 213–216 and passim; S. Linardatos, *I 4i Au-*

goustou (Athens: Ekdoseie Dialogos, 1975), pp. 415–417; A. Stinas, *Anamniseis: Evdominda Chronia Kato apo ti Semaia tis Sosialistikis Epanastasis* (Athens: Dithnis Bibliothiki, 1985), pp. 235–238; Markos Vafeiadis, *Apomnimonevmata,* Vol. 1 (Athens: Diphros, 1984), pp. 308–311.

37. Elephandis, *I Epangelia,* p. 258, remarks that the collective imprisonment of the communists enabled many of them to form lasting personal relationships, thus solidifying their unity and their affiliation with the KKE.

38. R. Vansittart, *The Mist Procession* (London: Hutchinson and Company, 1958), p. 289.

39. Athens Dispatch No. 281, FO 371/20390.

40. Koliopoulos, *Greece and the British Connection,* p. 60.

41. Metaxas, *Imerologio,* Vol. 7, p. 359, 19 March 1939.

42. War Cabinet: Chiefs of Staff Committee, "Greek Co-Operation Report," 22 September 1939, FO371/23782R7921.

43. Metaxas, *Imerologio,* Vol. 4, p. 406, 13 November 1939. In December, Metaxas confided again in his diary that he was pleased with the state of affairs of Greece considering what was going on in the rest of the world (Metaxas, *Imerologio,* Vol. 4, p. 412, 31 December 1939).

44. FO 371/24910.

45. FO 371/24982.

46. *Documents on Foreign German Policy* (referred to hereafter as DGFP), Series D, Vol. 11, No. 323, "Directive 18," p. 530.

47. DGFP, Series D, Vol. 11, No. 511, "Directive 20: Operation Marita."

48. Part of the inducement for the Greeks to accept the presence of British intelligence representatives was their role in organizing secret meetings between British and Greek military authorities. B. Sweet-Escott, *Baker Street Irregular* (London: Methuen, 1962), pp. 61–62.

49. Sweet-Escott, *Baker Street Irregular,* pp. 60–62; N. Hammond, *Venture into Greece: With the Guerrillas, 1943–1944* (London: William Kimbers, 1983), p. 13; Anonymous, *Report on SOE Activities in Greece and the Islands of the Aegean Sea,* Appendix I, "Origin and Constitution of SOE," p. 1; R. Clogg, "The Special Operations Executive in Greece," *Greece in the 1940s: A Nation in Crisis* (Hanover and London: University Press of New England, 1981), pp. 110–111.

50. Clogg, "The Special Operations Executive in Greece," p. 111; Anonymous, *Report on SOE Activities in Greece and the Islands of the Aegean Sea,* Appendix I, "Origin and Constitution of SOE," p. 1. MIR attempted to make contact with groups hostile to the Metaxas regime. In the summer of 1940, a MIR agent went to Crete to meet with General Emmanouil Mandakas, a leading opponent of Metaxas, in order to prepare for a possible rebellion in Crete in the event that the Greek government gave in to Axis pressure. Unfortunately the agent was caught, causing some embarrassment for the British diplomats in Athens (Clogg, "The Special Operations Executive in Greece," p. 110).

51. C. Woodhouse, *The Apple of Discord* (London: Hutchinson, 1948), p. 37. In *The Struggle for Greece 1941–1949* (Chicago: Ivan R. Dee, 1976), p. 29, however, Woodhouse emphasizes that the SOE gave priority to recruiting cashiered republican officers since "such officers were readily available . . . and were perhaps thought not to be as dangerous politically as the Communists."

52. Hammond, *Venture into Greece*, pp. 13–14.

53. Clogg, "The Special Operations Executive in Greece," p. 11.

54. Anonymous, *Report on SOE Activities in Greece and the Islands of the Aegean Sea*, p. 21.

55. Anonymous, *Report on SOE Activities in Greece and the Islands of the Aegean Sea*, Appendix II, "Directives," p. 5.

56. Colin Gubbins, who became the executive director of the SOE in 1943, also adopted the concept. Gubbins was particularly impressed by the Poles and the Czechs, who had organized secret armies, and he believed that these could serve as a model for other countries in occupied Europe (Sweet-Escott, *Baker Street Irregular*, pp. 47–48).

57. Koliopoulos, *Greece and the British Connection*, p. 214; FO 371/29862.

58. "Greek Military Situation," FO 371/24884 R 74320.

59. DGFP, Series D, Vol. 12, No. 195, "Directives of the High Command of the Wehrmacht," p. 338 ff.; F. H. Hinsley et al., *British Intelligence in the Second World War: Its Influence on Strategy and Operations*, 4 vols. (New York: Cambridge University Press, 1979–1993), Vol. 1, pp. 347–348.

60. John Keegan, *The Second World War* (Toronto: Penguin Press, 1989), p. 152.

61. Martin Van Creveld, *Hitler's Strategy 1940–1941: The Balkan Clue* (Cambridge: Cambridge University Press, 1973), p. 158.

62. The British had assumed (from their discussions with Papagos on 21 February 1941) that Papagos would abandon the Metaxas Line and use those forces to hold the Aliakhmon Line. When the first elements of the BEF arrived in Greece on 5 March, however, Papagos refused to withdraw his forces to the Aliakhmon Line because he feared the political repercussions of abandoning Macedonia and Thrace to Bulgaria. Instead, he recommended that the British commit their forces piecemeal to reinforce the Macedonian frontier. This suggestion proved unacceptable, and a compromise was reached that left the BEF defending the Aliakhmon Line with the support of three Greek divisions (Great Britain Cabinet Office, *Cabinet History Series: Principal War Telegrams and Memoranda 1940–1943*, Vol. 1, "Middle East, From the Occupation of Cyrenaica to the Fall of Keren and Harar," Nos. 39, 40, 69, 73).

63. Papagos was convinced that by keeping a defensive position that included Macedonia and Thrace as well as the port of Thessaloniki, the Yugoslavs could be induced to deploy their forces in southern Yugoslavia and protect the flank of the Greek army. At the very least Papagos believed that he would have sufficient time to withdraw his forces to the Aliakhmon Line if the Yugoslavs remained neutral.

Another important consideration for the Greek commander-in-chief was that by not defending Macedonia and Thrace, he would be abandoning Greece's second largest city, and most probably the entire region would fall under Bulgarian control. At this time, Bulgaria was Greece's greatest rival in the Balkans, and abandoning any national territory to a traditional enemy would have had severe political repercussions.

64. Hinsley, *British Intelligence in the Second World War*, Vol. 1, p. 361.

65. Great Britain Cabinet Office, Vol. 1, Nos. 36, 39; Sir Llewellyn Woodward, *British Foreign Policy in the Second World War*, Vol. I (London: HMSO, 1970), p. 511.

66. Woodward, *British Foreign Policy in the Second World War*, Vol. 1, p. 526.

67. Evacuation of the BEF began on the night of 24–25 April and continued for the next five nights. See S. W. Roskill, *The War at Sea 1939–1945, Vol. 1: The Defensive London* (London: HMSO 1954), p. 436.

68. Tsolakoglou initiated unauthorized discussions with Sepp Dietrich, the commander of the Adolf Hitler Division, and surrendered his forces on 20 April 1941.

69. The British Mediterranean Fleet provided a force of six cruisers, twenty destroyers, and thirty other ships to facilitate the evacuation. The Royal Navy, at a cost of two destroyers and four transports, rescued slightly over 50,000 men.

70. Papagos requested that he should be relieved of his command and put on the retired list. According to Koliopoulos (*Greece and the British Connection*, p. 292), the reason given for Papagos' resignation was that no one should be left in a high position who might make terms with the Germans. The Foreign Office, however, interpreted the resignation of Papagos and the dismissal of the Greek general headquarters as an indication of the Greek government's lack of trust in the general (Koliopoulos, *Greece and the British Connection*, p. 292; FO 371/29820 R 4615).

71. The surviving Greek fleet included one old cruiser, nine destroyers, one torpedo boat, five submarines, and one depot and repair ship. In addition to the fleet, some land forces had been evacuated or made their way to Egypt along with 900 air force personnel, of whom 200 were pilots (FO 371/29816 R 74220).

72. E. Tsouderos, *Gnomes kai Logoi* (Athens: Aetos, 1946), p. 73; FO 371/33167 R 1362; Fleischer, *Stemma*, p. 179.

73. P. Papastatis, *British Policy Towards Greece during the Second World War 1941–1944* (Cambridge: Cambridge University Press, 1984), pp. 8–9.

74. The constitution of 1911 was a variation of that of 1864, when Prince George of Denmark became King George I of Greece. In 1924, after the abolition of the monarchy, the constitution was again revised, but in 1935, with the restoration of George II, the constitution of 1911 was reinstated. In 1936, Metaxas, with the support of the king, suspended eight articles of the constitution and set up the dictatorship.

75. FO 371/33160, p. 59ff.; GAK E 13.

76. On 30 March 1942, the leaders of the prewar political parties, with the exception of Kanellopoulos and Tsaldaris, signed an agreement stating that the constitutional problem would be addressed after the war by a referendum

(Emmanouil Tsouderos, *Ellinikes Anomalies stin Mesi Anatoli,* Athens, 1945, pp. 47–48; Fleischer, *Stemma,* pp. 159–160).

77. Fleischer, *Stemma,* pp. 157–159; J. Petropoulos, "Traditional Political Parties of Greece during the Axis Occupation," *Greece in the 1940's: A Nation in Crisis,* ed. J. O. Iatrides, Hanover and London, 1981, pp. 27–28.

78. The famine took a greater toll of life than the war of 1940–1941, all the bombings, the casualties from resistance activity, and the victims of reprisals exacted by the Axis forces (Fleischer, *Stemma,* p. 194).

79. Emmanouil Tsouderos, *O Episitismos 1941–1944: Mesi Anatoli* (Athens: Papazisis, 1948), p. 3. On the reaction to the famine by the Greek government-in-exile, see GAK File A6-A17; B1-B4; E1-E3.

80. As early as June 1941 Tsouderos began to argue that a blockade would have serious implications for Greece. He accepted the policy of denying the enemy any supplies of food, but he pointed out that the situation in Greece would become desperate and that a way around the problem was to supply Greece through the International Red Cross or even simply by sending food secretly and unofficially (Tsouderos, *Logoi,* pp. 17–18 and passim). Fleischer (*Stemma,* p. 206, note 58) suggests that Tsouderos has received a great deal of criticism for his role in the crisis but that for the most part he has been blamed for the delays of food shipments from Turkey caused by R. Raphael, the Greek ambassador in Istanbul.

81. Another possible source of supply acceptable to the British was Russia, but the German invasion in 1941 eliminated that option (Papastratis, *British Policy towards Greece,* pp. 115–116).

82. Why, and if, the British ambassador made such a promise knowing full well the policy of blockade is not known, but the matter of 30,000 tons of grain per month is mentioned by E. Venezis, *Archiepiskopos Damaskinos* (Athens: Estias, 1981), p. 110, note, and supported by Fleischer (*Stemma,* p. 204). Before the war, Greece annually imported 400,000–500,000 tons of grain but the problem was compounded by a poor harvest in 1941 and the additional burden of feeding the BEF. Just before the collapse of Greece, the Greek government had purchased over 350,000 tons of grain from abroad, but most of these supplies had been consumed (Fleischer, *Stemma,* p. 204). According to Peter Hoffmann ("Roncalli in the Second World War: Peace Initiatives, the Greek Famine and the Persecution of the Jews," *Journal of Ecclesiastical History,* Vol. 40, No. 1, 1989, p. 78), a shipment of 47,000 tons of grain from Australia, which was to have replaced what the British forces had confiscated and consumed in Greece, was prevented from reaching Greece.

83. CAB 65/25 WM (42) 5.

84. W. N. Medlicott, *The Economic Blockade,* 2 vols. (London: HMSO, 1978), p. 254. John L. Hondros (*Occupation and Resistance: The Greek Agony 1941–44,* New York: Pella, 1983, pp. 75–77) writes that as food rations rose and fell, "Political agitation against the Axis followed inversely. Under these conditions, the Axis

powers were anxious to cooperate with the relief mission, and they did not hinder the flow of relief." A joint SOE/PWE analysis of the Greek resistance a year and a half later (April 1943) reached the opposite conclusion—that famine as opposed to food shortages hampered vitality and impaired resistance. The report also indicated that the arrival of food shipments actually helped to instigate resistance activity and increase faith in the Allies ("Joint SOE/PWE Survey of Resistance in Occupied Europe," FO 898/97 R 74320).

85. CAB 65/25 WM (42) 5.

86. Th. Saloutsos, *The Greeks in the United States* (Boston: Cambridge University Press, 1964), p. 345 ff., p. 432; Medlicott, *The Economic Blockade*, Vol. 2, pp. 258–259; Hondros, *Occupation and Resistance*, p. 73.

87. This was cited as another consideration in favor of lifting the blockade (CAB 65/25 WM [42] 5). Fleischer (*Stemma*, pp. 194–216) takes the view that the British dragged their feet in deciding to lift the blockade and refused to allow the passage of 350,000 tons of grain purchased by the Greek government before the occupation.

88. FO 371/29817 R 8810. From his first meetings with Churchill and Eden, Tsouderos had brought up the subject of Greek territorial claims but both avoided giving the Greek prime minister any commitments and sidestepped the proposal of an Anglo-Greek alliance (Papastratis, *British Policy towards Greece*, p. 16).

89. The main articles provided that the Greek armed forces came under the command of the Britain's Middle East Theater of Operations, which also became responsible for their organization and direction. On the other articles, see E. Tsouderos, *Diplomatika Paraskinia*, 1950, pp. 164–167, and P. Papastratis, "Diplomatika Paraskinia tis Ipografis tis Stratiotikis Symfonias Vretanias—Elladas stis 9 Martiou 1941," *Mnimon*, Vol. 7, 1979, pp. 178–179.

90. Woodward, *British Foreign Policy in the Second World War*, Vol. 3, p. 383.

91. Woodhouse, *The Apple of Discord*, p. 49.

92. Woodhouse, *The Apple of Discord*, p. 50.

93. W. S. Churchill, *The Second World War: Vol. 5, Closing the Ring* (London: Houghton Mifflin, 1951), pp. 458, 465.

94. Churchill, *The Second World War*, p. 466.

95. Henri Michel, *The Shadow War: Resistance in Europe 1939–1945*, trans. Richard Barry (London: Andre Deutsch, 1972), pp. 53–54; D. Stafford, *Britain and European Resistance 1940–1945: A Survey of the Special Operations Executive, with Documents* (London: Macmillan, 1980), pp. 33–34.

96. DGFP, Series D, Vol. 12, No. 463, p. 722.

97. DGFP, Series D, Vol. 12, No. 463, p. 722.

98. Fleischer, *Stemma*, pp. 117–118.

99. Ch. Zalokostas, *To Chroniko tis Sklavias* (Athens: Estia, 1949), p. 14; Fleischer, *Stemma*, p. 118.

100. Fleischer, *Stemma*, p. 118.

101. FO 371/37216 R 3924). Fleischer (*Stemma*, p. 118, note 7) also points out that half the faculty of the University of Athens and four-fifths of the faculty of the Polytechnic School had studied in Germany.

102. Ch. Christidis, *Chronia Katochis: Martyries Imerologion, 1941–1944*, 1971, p. 5.

103. Christidis, *Chronia Katochis*, p. 10; Fleischer, *Stemma*, p. 121.

104. D. Benetatos, *To Chroniko tis Sklavias 1941–1944*, 1963, p. 28; Christidis, *Chronia Katochis*, pp. 5–6; Fleischer, *Stemma*, p. 121.

105. Raphael Lemkin, *Axis Rule in Occupied Greece: Laws of Occupation, Analysis of Government Proposals for Redress* (New York: H. Fertig, 1973), p. 190.

106. Benetatos, *To Chroniko*, p. 27.

107. Particularly irritating for the Germans, since it was hailed by the British BBC as a major act of resistance in all of occupied Europe (Fleischer, *Stemma*, pp. 119–120). The individuals who took down the German flag were two students, Manolis Glezos and Apostolos Santas (Dimitris Gatopoulos, *Istoria tis Katochis*, Vol. A, Athens: Melisa, 1949, p. 131).

108. Venezis, *Archiepiskopos Damaskinos*, pp. 195–197.

109. FO 371/29909 R 8414; FO 371/29842 R 10894.

110. Hondros, *Occupation and Resistance*, p. 101.

111. E. Myers, *Greek Entanglement*, Gloucester 1985, p. 103; K. Pyromaglou, *O Georgios Kartalis kai i Epochi tou 1934–1957*; Tomos A *1934–1944*, 1965, p. 140. Archbishop Damaskinos concluded that the government-in-exile's neglect of its supporters allowed the communists to seize the initiative and that by the time the government addressed the problem, it was too late (FO 371/37206 R 10450).

112. Fleischer (*Stemma*, pp. 179–181) suggests that the means of accomplishing this was the return of the king (after the war) and that the Tsouderos regime, from the very beginning of its existence in exile, had attempted to exclude from the government all those who opposed the monarchy. Hondros (*Occupation and Resistance*, p. 101) states that the aim of the government-in-exile was to use the officer corps in order to support the monarchy in the postwar period. K. Pyromaglou (*O Georgios Kartalis*, pp. 140–141) also maintains that "the government-in-exile had the express purpose of re-imposing the prewar political system and finds little difference between the puppet governments and that of Tsouderos and the king." On 6 November 1941, Alexander Sakellariou (*Enas Navarchos Th*imatai, Athens: Dimitrakos, 1971, p. 392), the vice premier and commander-in-chief of the Greek fleet, warned Tsouderos that the Greek nation considered the government-in-exile nothing more than the continuation of the Fourth of August Regime.

113. Georgios Tsolakoglou, *Apomnemonevmata*, Athens: Acropolis, 1959, passim; K. Logothetopoulos, *Idou i Alitheia*, 1948, passim; Ioannis Rallis, *O Ioannis Rallis Omilei ek tou Tafou*, 1947, passim; N. Louvaris, "Golgothas enos Ethnous," *Ethnikos Keryx*, 2/4/1950–11/6/1950, passim; Woodhouse, *The Apple of Discord*, p. 27.

114. In April 1940, the number of permanent officers reached 4,980. Later, because of the war, 300 senior cadets from the military academy were prematurely

graduated, and 50 warrant officers were advanced to the rank of second lieutenant, which increased the number of officers to 5,180. The Greek armed forces also included 10,000 reserve officers and 1,150 noncommissioned (A. Papagos, *O Ellinikos Stratos kai i pros Paraskevi tou*, 1945, p. 412; *Archigeion Stratou Diefthnisis Stratou*, "I pros Polemou proparaskevi tou Ellinikou Stratou 1923–1940," Athens: Diefthynseos Stratou, 1969, passim).

115. By the beginning of the war, 4,500 professional officers had been purged from the armed forces. During the war 3,000 of these were recalled to active service, but approximately 1,500, most of whom were of higher rank, were excluded (Gerolymatos, "The Role of the Greek Officer Corps," p. 71 and notes 7 and 8).

116. As a body, the professional active officers suffered a much higher casualty rate than the ordinary soldiers or the reserve officers. According to established figures, casualties among professional officers reached 6.9 percent dead and 9 percent wounded. In contrast, the rate for the reserve officers was 1.7 percent dead (figures not available for wounded), while for the permanent reserve officers (those who had been forced to retire) recalled to active duty, the rate was 1.1 percent dead and 1.8 percent wounded. The lower casualty rate among this group was due to the reluctance of the Metaxas regime to place them in command of combat units (Gerolymatos, "The Role of the Greek Officer Corps," pp. 70–71).

117. K. Pyromaglou, "Ta Tagmata Asphalias," *Istoriki Epitheoresis*, Vol. 6, p. 539. Also, see Konstantinos Th. Bakopoulos, *I Omeria ton Pende Andistratigon: I Zoe ton—Stratopeda Sygendroseos*, 1948, pp. 26–27.

118. See Tsouderos, *Ellinikes Anomalies*, passim; Hagen Fleischer, "The Anomalies in the Greek Middle East Forces, 1941–1944," *Journal of the Hellenic Diaspora*, Vol. 5, No. 3, pp. 5–36.

Chapter 2

1. W. K. Klingman, *1941: Our Lives in a World on the Edge* (New York: Harper and Row, 1966), p. 210.

2. The thousands of young women who joined the left-wing ELAS, on the other hand, eschewed identification with tradition and preferred military attire and, when this was not possible, just ordinary trousers.

3. The SOE had secretly trained about 350 saboteurs in northern Greece and hid three and a half tons of explosives. In the Athens area, seven groups were established with 50 saboteurs and supplied with one and a half tons of explosives. According to a secret SOE report all the groups had accepted money, but only one had agreed to maintain a radio set (Major Ian Pirie's Report, *A History of SOE Activities in Greece May 1940–November 1942*, HS7/268 89846, p. 443).

4. Pirie, *A History of SOE Activities in Greece*, p. 444.

5. Alexatos, although a key figure in the development of espionage, sabotage, and guerrilla activity organizations in Greece, remains a mystery. It is not clear when he

was recruited by the SOE, but it was before the occupation (R. Clogg, "Pearls from Swine," *British Policy towards Wartime Resistance in Yugoslavia and Greece*, ed. P. Auty and R. Clogg [London: The Macmillan Press, 1975], p. 113). According to Fleischer (Athens 1988, pp. 240–241), Alexatos was a smuggler with considerable experience in getting in and out of Greece as well as other countries in the Middle East. Between 1941 and 1942 he brought into Greece funds and instructions for several groups working for different British intelligence services. It is evident from one source (Alexander Levidis, *Yia Hare tis Alithias: Intelligence kai Andistasi* [Athens: Unpublished Manuscript, 1975], p. 29) that Alexatos was sympathetic to the left and of considerable assistance to both EAM and the KKE. In August 1943 Tsimas traveled to Cairo as part of a guerrilla delegation and used the opportunity to look for Alexatos, but to no avail. He concluded that Alexatos was terminated (Fleischer, Athens 1988, p. 241 note 75). Odysseus, however, survived; the reason for his disappearance was that he had resumed his career in smuggling, which continued after the war (Michael Ward, Greek Assignments: 1943 SOE–1948 UNSCOB, [private publication] Athens 1990, pp. 132–133).

6. Pirie, *A History of SOE Activities in Greece*, p. 445.

7. Ward, pp. 254–255.

8. FO 74038 HS5/524.

9. HS 7/151 89846.

10. G. H. N. Seaton Watson, "Afterword," *British Policy towards Wartime Resistance in Yugoslavia and Greece*, p. 289.

11. On the details of the Atkinson mission and problems with the sources concerning this event, see Andre Gerolymatos, *Guerrilla Warfare and Espionage in Greece, 1940–1944* (New York: Pella Publishing Company, 1992), p. 222 ff. and note 3.

12. FO 74038 HS5/524.

13. Alexander Zannas, Athens 1964, p. 73.

14. FO 74038 HS5/524.

15. According to Zannas, *I Katochi: Anamniseis-Epistoles* (Athens: Estias, 1964), p. 74, Atkinson arrived by submarine at Euboia and made his way on foot to Athens. He contacted Zannas through a mutual friend, Panagiotis Sifnaios. Zannas and Atkinson met at the home of Sifnaios, where Atkinson was staying and where he had found refuge in the course of his escape in April.

16. In the summer of 1941, Zannas purchased four bombs from a left-wing or communist organization (for 280,000 drachmas), which he passed on to Nikos Nikolaidis and Stavros Margaritis. Both of these men had found employment at the Athens airport (an important base for the German air force) and wished to try their hand at sabotage. They placed the first two bombs in German aircraft bound for Crete or North Africa and set them to explode one hour after the planes were in the air. The third bomb, however, went off on the ground next to a loaded bomber, which caused the destruction of several aircraft (Zannas, pp. 76–77).

17. Zannas was a link between several groups conducting espionage and sabotage. As the head of the Greek Red Cross, he was under constant surveillance and could only be involved indirectly. He had direct access to Evangelos Evert, the commander of the Athenian police, and to the Archbishop of Athens, both of whom aided many of the different clandestine groups set up in Athens. Zannas' brother, Sotiris, had been an agent of Section D in 1940–1941 but had been forced to leave Greece because of his involvement with the Maleas organization, another group that hid British soldiers and assisted them to escape to the Middle East (Levidis, p. 20).

18. Zannas, p. 77.

19. Zannas, pp. 78–79.

20. At Antiparos, Atkinson was able to operate from the summer home of a Greek lawyer, Spyros Tzavellas (Yiannis Ioannidis, *Ellines kai Xeni Kataskopi,* [Athens: Ekdosis A. Mavridis, 1952], p. 23).

21. Ioannidis, *Ellines,* p. 24; Zaousis, Part B (I), pp. 73–74.

22. Alexander Zaousis, *Oi Dyo Ochthes, 1939–1945,* 3 vols. (Athens: Papazisis, Part B [I]), p. 73.

23. According to Spyro Kotsis (*Midas 614,* Athens 1976, p. 127), the explosives were set for 9:00 A.M. At that time, the ships were usually 500 meters from the harbor, and according to Atkinson's calculation they would sink in deeper water. Fortunately for the population of Milos, the German and Italian authorities assumed the attack was the work of British commandos and did not exact retribution against the inhabitants of the island (Ioannidis, *Ellines,* p. 26; Kotsis, p. 127).

24. In Zannas' account (pp. 78–80), Atkinson had left Antiparos for Egypt by submarine and returned in mid-December 1941 to organize the escape of twenty British and four Greeks. The group in Athens had sent the twenty-four escapees to Anavyso and later to Antiparos, but the Italians captured them. Afterward, the British submarine was also sunk. Ward (p. 180), who was responsible for sending off agents to Greece, relates in his memoirs that Atkinson left Alexandria for Antiparos in October 1941.

25. According to Ioannidis (*Ellines,* p. 26) Atkinson and his associates were betrayed because someone affiliated with the group was disenchanted over a failed affair with a woman and informed the Italians as an act of revenge. Kotsis (p. 127), on the other hand, suggests that the activities of the group had attracted the attention of the Italian garrison. P. E. Konstas, *E Elas, 1940–1950* (Athens: n.p., 1955), p. 246, writes that according to the evidence produced in the postwar trial of the collaborators at Siros, the Italians detected the group through "an unfortunate incident" and by the incredible carelessness of Atkinson, who at one point was fishing by dropping hand grenades in the sea.

26. Konstas, p. 246; Zannas, p. 80; Kotsis, p. 128; Zaousis, Part B (I), p. 74; Sweet-Escott, p. 119.

27. Konstas, pp. 246–247; Zannas, p. 81; Kotsis, p. 128; Zaousis, Part B (I), p. 74.

28. Some received long prison sentences and others were exiled to Italy for the duration of the war; Atkinson and his immediate associates were condemned to death and executed some months later.

29. The others included Captain Theodoros Koundouriotis, the son of one of Greece's most famous admirals and one of the organizers of the Bakirdzis cell; Leon Polymenakos, a distinguished physician and Kanellopoulos's doctor; Panagiotis Klapeas, a well-known lawyer; and two senior officers, Aristidis Pallis and Vasilis Angelopoulos (Kotsis, pp. 128–129). In addition to Kanellopoulos, Bakirdzis' name was included in Atkinson's papers; he, too, had to leave Greece, and Koutsogiannopoulos, a naval officer with the code name of Prometheus II, headed the clandestine cell (Zaousis, Part B [I], p. 75).

30. Konstas, p. 247.

31. Christidis, p. 258, 27 April 1942. Atkinson and those implicated with him were tried in February 1943 (the trial lasted from 9 to 17 February). Atkinson along with Diamandis Arvanitopoulos, Tzavellas, and two others closely affiliated with the group were executed on 24 February 1943 (Konstas, p. 247).

32. According to Zaousis (Part B [I], p. 85), Kanellopoulos had excellent contacts with the officer corps and was in a good position to get Greek officers to participate in a resistance organization. Fleischer (*Stemma,* p. 161) writes that Kanellopoulos had established links with Greek republican officers such as Bakirdzis, Sarafis, and Psaros as well as with monarchists in order to organize a resistance movement. At the same time, Kanellopoulos refused to cooperate with EAM since he opposed the creation of mass-based organizations and preferred the establishment of a number of small, well-organized groups.

33. For an analysis of the attitudes of the Greek political leaders, see Fleischer, *Stemma,* pp. 155–161; Pyromaglou, pp. 215–221.

34. The committee included Thrasyvoulos Tsakalotos, P. Spiliotopoulos, Eust. Liosis, St. Kitrilakis, K. Dovas, and Filippidis (Th. Tsakalotos, *40 Chronia Stratiotis tis Ellados,* Vol. A [Athens: n.p., 1960], p. 369).

35. Tsakalotos, Vol. A, p. 371.

36. Kanellopoulos, *Imerologio,* 8 May 1943.

37. FO 371/37201 R 74220; Kanellopoulos, *Imerologio,* 8 May 1943.

38. Kanellopoulos, *Imerologio,* 5 August 1943.

39. Kanellopoulos (*Imerologio,* 9 May 1943) also adds that information from the intelligence groups in Greece, although transmitted by Greek agents, was received and interpreted by SOE personnel in Cairo, an arrangement that he wished to change in the near future.

40. Kanellopoulos, *Imerologio,* 8 May 1943.

41. GAK, "Apostoli Gama," No. 4; Kotsis, pp. 28–30.

42. GAK, "Apostoli Gama," No. 4; Kotsis, *Athens 1976,* p. 28.

43. Kotsis, pp. 32–37.

44. Kotsis, pp. 56–57.

45. The death of Tsigantes also meant that the first attempt to block the Corinth Canal, code-named Thurgoland, did not materialize. A second SOE team, commanded by Lieutenant Commander Cumberledge, and code-named Locksmith, managed to penetrate the canal and succeeded in laying some mines, especially designed for this operation, but they failed to explode. Unfortunately, Cumberledge and three members of his team were arrested upon their return to the island of Paros. The four were then brought to Athens and later sent to Germany, where they were shot in May 1945.

46. The Italian invasion of Greece further compounded the difficulties of the Greek communists. The general secretary of the KKE, Zachariadis, who was in prison at the time, published a letter on 1 October in the government-controlled communist newspaper *(Rizospastis)* stating that the Communist Party was prepared to accept the direction of the Metaxas regime in the war. On 31 October, he issued a second letter, supporting the government unconditionally in the war with Italy *(Akropolis* 2.11.40; *Rizospastis* 25.10.43; *Saranda Chronia tou KKE 1918–1958* [Athens: Sygchroni Epoch, 1958, p. 744]; Fleischer, *Stemma*, pp. 130–131). In this, Zachariadis, despite the German-Soviet Pact (on the directives of the Comintern to the KKE, see Fleischer, Athens, 1988, pp. 132–133), was supported by the majority of the imprisoned communists and members of the central committee held at Akronafplia. In fact, just prior to Zachariadis' letter the communist inmates of Akronafplia appealed to Metaxas for their release so that they could fight on the Albanian front *(Rizospastis* 28.10.45; *KKE Episima Keimena,* Vol. 4, pp. 14–15). The remnants of the central committee still at large, however, declared Zachariadis' letter false and contrary to communist ideology. The Italian-Greek conflict, they claimed, had nothing to do with the protection of Greece but only served the interests of the British *(KKE Episima Keimena,* Vol. 4, pp. 24–36). However, the policy of the KKE became confused when a month later, Zachariadis published a third letter. This time, he stated that the KKE's support was based on the understanding that the war was antifascist, and after the Greek army crossed the Albanian frontier it became fascist in nature and served British imperialist interests *(KKE Episima Keimena,* Vol. 4, pp. 22–23). After 1949 (and the split of the KKE) the central committee of the KKE concluded that Zachariadis' decision to support the government in 1940 had exceeded the policy guidelines of the Comintern (Fleischer, Athens 1988, p. 133).

47. Zaousis, Vol. B (I), p. 23; Yiannis Ioannidis, *Anamniseis: Provlimata tis Politikis tou KKE stin Ethniki Andistasi, 1940–1945* (Athens: Themelio, 1979), p. 505. A total of 1,350 communists were kept in the following prisons and islands: Akronafplia (600), Agio Stratis (230), Anaphi (220), Aigina (170), and Pholegandros (130); another 500 were in various prisons in the Peloponnese and in Kimolo (36), Gavdos (30), Asvestochori (17), Kerkyra (10), and 30 more in Ios, Siphnos, Pylos, and Amorgos.

48. In this case Kaiti Zevgos, who spoke a little French and German while hiding the fact that they were communists, convinced the German authorities on the island that they were exiled because they had opposed the Metaxas regime. The

Greek commandant of the island also helped by not referring to his inmates as communists. Accordingly, the Germans permitted the exiles to make use of small boats and depart from the island (Kaiti Zevgos, *Me ton Yianni Zevgo sto Epanastatiko* [Athens: Ekdosis Okeanida, 1980], pp. 197–199).

49. According to Bartziotas, *E Ethniki Adistasi* (Athens: Sygchroni Epochi, 1979), p. 74, during the same period seventeen more escaped from other islands, two of whom would play key roles in the resistance: Markos Vafeiadis and Metsos Vladas. In the next two years, adds Bartziotas (p. 74), 400 more managed to escape and reestablish contact with the KKE.

50. Another 400 escaped during the course of the occupation (Alexander Zaousis, Part B [I], p. 23).

51. Twenty-seven inmates of Akronafplia prison, called the Marxist university by the communists, found their freedom by the intervention of the German security services acting through the Bulgarian embassy. They identified themselves as Bulgarian and were released. Many of these were instrumental in the creation of EAM-ELAS and played a key role in the resistance (Fleischer, Athens 1988, p. 142; Bartziotas, *Ethniki Andistasi kai Dekemvris 1944*, p. 74). Some agreed to work for the Bulgarian security services, which acted as a front for the Gestapo, and some, such as Tsipas, may have been Bulgarian agents all along.

52. Fleischer, *Stemma*, pp. 142–143; Ioannidis, *Amamnisis*, p. 506.

53. Thanasis Hadzis, *E Nikiphora Epanastasi pou Chathike*, 4 vols. (Athens: Dorikos, 1982), Vol. A, pp. 121–122 and note 5. The organizational difficulties were resolved with the sixth and seventh plenums of the central committee, and the KKE called upon the Greek nation to form a national liberation front to fight the Axis. According to Hadzis (Vol. A, pp. 118–119), those present represented the reorganized central committee of the KKE. The old central committee dissolved itself (*KKE Episema Keimena 1940–1945*, Vol. 5, Athens, 1979, pp. 58–59).

54. Hadzis, Vol. A, p. 150.

55. In early September Hadzis and Kostas Vidalis met with General Stylianos Gonatas, one of the leading republican officers, and brought up the subject of resistance. The latter not only opposed the concept but threatened the representatives of the KKE personally and stated that he would violently oppose them (Hadzis, Vol. A, pp. 152–153).

56. SKE (Socialist Party of Greece); ELD (Union of Popular Democracy); AKE (Agrarian Party of Greece).

57. The first step toward forming a common front was taken by the Greek labor unions, which, with the support of the communists, formed the National Workers' Liberation Front (EEAM) on 16 July 1941. In addition to its role of looking after the needs of labor during the occupation, EEAM proposed the creation of a common front to instigate resistance (*Avgi* 13 July 1960; *KKE Episima Keimena 1940–1945*, Vol. 5, pp. 66–67; Fleischer, *Stemma*, p. 146). On the establishment of the EEAM, see also Angelos Avgoustidis, "EEAM: The Workers' Resistance," *Jour-*

nal of the Hellenic Diaspora, Vol. 11, No. 3 (1984), pp. 55–67; D. Benetatos, *To Chroniko tis Sklavias* (Athens: Estia, 1963), pp. 51–52. For the entire constitution of EEAM see *St' Armata St' Armata! Chroniko tis Ethnikis Andistasis 1940–1945* (Athens: Giannikos, 1964), pp. 104–105; *KKE Episima Keimena 1940–1945*, Vol. 5, pp. 83–85.

58. Fleischer, *Stemma*, p. 147.

59. According to Hadzis (pp. 272–273), who became the political officer of the central committee of ELAS, the KKE proceeded with the creation of armed bands after exhausting every effort to enlist the cooperation of senior Greek officers. On 2 February 1942, EAM decided that it would initiate the armed struggle against the occupation forces by establishing its own units in the mountains. It was agreed by those present (I. Polydoros, Tsimas, and Hadzis) and afterward approved by Siantos that these forces would be named the National Popular Liberation Army and that the new organization would come under EAM; the central committee of ELAS would receive its direction from the central committee of EAM.

60. Velouchiotis was the nom de guerre adopted by Athanasios Klaras. Klaras was arrested by the Metaxas security service and with the agreement of Zachariadis (according to his brother, B. Klaras, *O Adelphos mou o Aris,* Athens: Dorikos, 1985, pp. 112–113) signed the infamous declaration of repentance. Klaras was not able to substantiate this and during the occupation no one came forward to back his claim; Zachariadis himself was shipped off to Dachau and after the war denounced Klaras. As a result, Klaras was viewed with suspicion by the KKE central committee. According to Benetatos (Athens, 1963, pp. 83–84), the central committee of EAM had not yet made up its mind whether to initiate guerrilla warfare when Klaras on his own initiative formed his band, which was recognized after the fact.

61. In Greek *democratic* also means "republican." Another translation of EDES would therefore be "National Republican Greek League."

62. K. Pyromaglou, *I Ethniki Andistasis: EAM-ELAS-EDES-EKKA* (Athens: Dodoni, 1975), pp. 314–315.

63. The following were listed as the primary goals of EDES: (1) To establish in Greece the basis of a democratic political system of a socialist nature and (2) to prevent by any means the return of the king of Greece and his mob of the 4 August dictatorial regime and to impose on those criminals the severest penalties such as the confiscation of their property as well as the properties of their relatives and their associates during the period of the tyranny.

64. Pyromaglou, *Ethniki Adistasi*, pp. 305–306, 315.

65. Fleischer, *Stemma*, p. 152. In his account of the Greek resistance and his role in EDES, Pyromaglou writes that on 9 September 1941 Plastiras asked him to return to Greece and work with the latter's followers toward establishing a democratic and socialist organization. Upon his arrival in Athens (23 September 1941), Pyromaglou, through the intervention of Gonatas and Ilias Stamatopoulos, met

with Zervas and shortly thereafter agreed to become the general secretary of a five-man governing committee created in October to direct EDES.

66. Pyromaglou, *Ethniki Adistasi*, pp. 314–315; Benetatos, pp. 53–54.

67. *IAEA*, Vol. 4, p. 46.

68. He was the cousin of the poet George Seferis (Woodhouse, 1982, p. 29; Alexandros Levidis, p. 26; Hadzis, Vol. A, 1982, p. 373).

69. The implication in the Greek sources is that contact with Cairo meant contact with the SOE.

70. Levidis, 1975, p. 23 ff.

71. Leonidas Spais, *Peninda Chronia Stratiotis* (Athens: Melissa, 1970), p. 225; *IAEA*, Vol. 4, p. 35; Pyromaglou, *Kartalis*, p. 150; Fleischer, *Stemma*, p. 241.

72. Levidis, p. 27. Fleischer, *Stemma*, p. 241, note 74, who interviewed Levidis, suggests that the British were not prepared to sever contact with EAM and that is why they decided to support only EDES and EAM and exclude those who refused to cooperate with the left.

73. Levidis, p. 30.

74. Fleischer, *Stemma*, p. 241.

75. Alexatos not only brought 7,100 gold sovereigns to the KKE but turned over to them at least one wireless set and helped them repair a second (Ioannidis, *Ellines*, pp. 124–125 and p. 513, note 40).

76. Fleischer, *Stemma*, p. 242, notes 76, 77, and 78, bases his account of this episode on a series of articles published in the newspaper *Akropolis* by both Zervas and Koutsogiannopoulos; see also *Report on SOE Activities in Greece and the Islands of the Aegean Sea*, Cairo 27/6/45, p. 53.

77. Woodhouse, 1982, p. 21.

78. C. M. Woodhouse, *Something Ventured* (London: Granada, 1982), pp. 40–41.

79. Woodhouse, *Something Ventured*, p. 43. This statement is disputed by Hadzis (Vol. A, p. 377), who claims that the central committees of the KKE, EAM, and ELAS were more than willing to cooperate with the British.

80. *OKW Diaries*, Band II, p. 141.

81. Over the next two years, the SOE established eighty missions in Greece, which employed 611 officers and other ranks. During the same period the SOE's intelligence activity was carried out by 600 British and 3,000 Greek agents (*Report on SOE Activities in Greece and the Islands of the Aegean Sea*, pp. 7, 17).

82. Woodhouse, *Something Ventured*, p. 54.

83. "Political Aspects of the Greek Resistance Movement," FO 371/37201 74220 R 2050, p. 123.

84. "Political Aspects of the Greek Resistance Movement," FO 371/37201 74220 R 2050.

85. "Political Aspects of the Greek Resistance Movement," FO 371/37201 74220 R 2050.

86. "Political Aspects of the Greek Resistance Movement," FO 371/37201 74220 R 2050, pp. 116–117.

87. "Resistance Groups in Greece," Minute by Dixon, 7 March 1943, FO 371/37201 74220 R 2050. Dixon went so far as to recommend that all SOE activity be suspended in Greece.

88. FO 371/37201 74220 R 2332.

89. Woodhouse had prompted Zervas to send a friendly message to the king of Greece on the occasion of Greek National Day, 25 March. To Woodhouse's surprise (London, 1982, p. 64), Zervas went even further and in the telegram assured George II that if the British so desired he would accept the return of the monarch with or without a plebiscite. Initially this was kept secret, and according to Pyromaglou (*Kartalis*, Vol. A, p. 544), had it become known right away it would have led to the break-up of EDES.

90. Clogg, "Pearls from Swine," p. 175. The SOE used this message from Zervas to prove to the Foreign Office that it was not supporting only antimonarchist resistance organizations (FO 371/3717194 R 2266).

91. FO 371/37201 74220, R 2322.

92. "Political Aspects of the Greek Resistance Movement," FO 371/37201 74220, R 2050.

93. On the strength of these forces, see Hondros 1983, pp. 117–118, 144–145.

94. The report was written in June 1943 by J. M. Stevens, who had returned to Cairo from a fact-finding mission in the Greek mountains in which he tried to assess the merits of ELAS and EDES. Stevens concluded in his report (*British Reports on Greece 1943–44,* "Report of Lt.-Col. J. M. Stevens on Present Conditions in Central Greece," ed. Lars Baerentzen, Copenhagen: 1982, pp. 16, 24) that ELAS was poorly led, since it had mounted a campaign against regular Greek officers but by the summer of 1943 was attempting to attract such men into its ranks.

95. In each village, EAM had set up four organizations: the local EAM central committee, which supervised all political and resistance activity; a group responsible for relief; another responsible for youth; and a division that looked after logistical support for ELAS. The entire EAM apparatus was under the control of the secretary of the central committee, who was usually a member of the KKE. The village secretaries elected a district EAM, which in turn elected regional committees of EAM. Each of the regions then had one representative on the twenty-five-member national central committee of EAM in Athens. Cities, such as Athens and Thessaloniki, had independent representation, and the EAM organizations were based on neighborhood units (Hondros, p. 118).

96. Sarafis, a well-respected republican officer, had initially taken the field with a new band, but it was soon dispersed and he was captured by ELAS. After some hesitation Sarafis agreed to join ELAS and serve as its military commander. By the

summer of 1943, ELAS included 600 professional officers, 1,250 republican officers, and 2,000 lower-ranking reserve officers.

97. Gerolymatos, "The Role of the Greek Officer Corps," p. 75.

98. Although Zervas' message to King George was kept secret, it was leaked to the Antifascist Military Organization (ASO), based in the Middle East, which passed it on to Athens, where it was published in the communist newspapers (Fleischer, A, 1988, p. 393; *Kommounistiki Epitheoresi,* February 1944, p. 15; *Rizospastis,* 15 November 1944).

99. When ELAS captured Sarafis on 7 March 1943, Zervas requested permission from the BMM to effect a rescue, but Myers feared it would lead to a war between ELAS and EDES. He was convinced, however, that Zervas' forces would prove superior and advised the SOE that the destruction of ELAS would have little impact upon the guerrilla war. He also added that this was the last opportunity to check the growing power of ELAS and recommended all-out support for EDES (Fleischer, 1988, p. 391; FO 71/37202 R 4209).

100. D. J. Wallace, "Conditions in Zervas-Held Territory," *British Reports on Greece 1943–44,* ed. Lars Baerentzen, Copenhagen, 1982, p. 120.

101. On the text of the agreement, see Woodhouse, *Apple of Discord,* Appendix C, pp. 299–300.

102. FO 371/37203 R 5573.

103. According to Hadzis (Vol. B, p. 139), another reason the British were forced to recognize ELAS as an Allied force was that they were afraid of complications in the Balkans, since ELAS was coming into contact with Albanian and Yugoslavian partisans and might form a military and perhaps even a political alliance. Hadzis adds that the British recognition of ELAS was considered a significant political victory.

104. Myers, *Greek Entanglement,* p. 228.

105. Operation Animals was one element of a much greater effort, Operation Minced Meat, implemented to persuade the Germans that the Allies had targeted Greece for their offensive in the Mediterranean. See Charles Cruickshank, *Deception in World War II* (Oxford: Oxford University Press, 1979), Chapter 4; F. H. Hinsley, *British Intelligence in the Second World War* (London: HMSO, 1984), Vol. 3, p. 120.

106. Between March and the time of the Allied landings in Sicily, the total number of German divisions in the Balkans rose from eight to eighteen and those in Greece from one to eight (Hinsley, Vol. 3, p. 11, pp. 80, 144–145). According to the anonymous *Report on SOE Activities in Greece and the Islands of the Aegean Sea,* six German and twelve Italian divisions were contained in Greece during this period (*Report on SOE Activities in Greece and the Islands of the Aegean Sea,* Appendix IV).

107. Myers ("The Andarte Delegation to Cairo: August 1943," *British Policy towards Wartime Resistance in Yugoslavia and Greece,* ed. Phyllis Auty and Richard

Clogg, London: Macmillan, 1975, pp. 148–149) had planned to visit Cairo on his own to report to Moyne and discuss the problems of the guerrilla bands, but after he informed Tsimas and Pyromaglou of his trip, both asked whether they could go along. To satisfy EKKA, Myers also had to agree to take George Kartalis. Before Myers could complete the travel arrangements, Siantos, the acting secretary of the KKE, insisted that three other EAM representatives join the group. Although Myers had asked and received permission from Cairo to take Tsimas, Pyromaglou, and Kartalis, when he signaled the SOE about the additional EAM representatives there was not enough time to await a reply.

108. Myers (*Greek Entanglement,* pp. 236–243) proposed that the guerrilla bands be recognized as part of the Greek armed forces and recommended that Andarte liaison officers be attached to the Greek general staff. He also believed that political matters concerning the resistance organizations should be handled by civilian authorities and hoped that the joint headquarters could be divided into two separate departments, with civil liaison officials attached to the Greek government-in-exile. Myers feared that after the intensive guerrilla activity that preceded the Allied landings in Sicily the Andarte bands would grow restless and begin to attack each other. Therefore, he planned to limit the size of the bands but to provide them with light artillery and other supporting arms, in order to raise both the status and the quality of the guerrillas and focus their attention on training, thus avoiding a civil war in the mountains. Before departing from Greece, Myers held several meetings with the delegation that was to travel to Cairo, and all agreed to accept and collectively support Myers' recommendations.

109. Myers, "The Andarte Delegation to Cairo," p. 151.

110. Myers, "The Andarte Delegation to Cairo," pp. 151–152.

111. *Report on SOE Activities in Greece and the Islands of the Aegean,* Appendix III, p. 10.

112. The two Americans were Captain Winston Ehrgott and Lieutenant Bob Ford. In November they were joined by Major Gerald K. Wines, who assumed command of the OSS (Office of Strategic Services) part of the AMM. Between August 1943 and November 1944 the OSS deployed over 400 men in various clandestine operations in Greece and provided the State Department with an independent source of information on the Greek situation. By the end of the occupation, the OSS maintained eight missions: five with EAM-ELAS and one with EDES, while the rest operated independently in several parts of Greece. For the most part OSS personnel in Greece tended to support whichever organization they were attached to, but they had orders to use British communications under the control of a senior SOE officer. However, the secret intelligence group (the OSS intelligence units) maintained independent communications. In September 1943, relations between the SOE, MI6, and the OSS were formalized by a series of

agreements that gave each organization certain geographic spheres of resistibility. Under the terms of these understandings, the SOE was given exclusive control over the Balkans and the Middle East (André Gerolymatos, "American Foreign Policy towards Greece and the Problem of Intelligence, 1945–1947," *Journal of Modern Hellenism,* No. 7, 1990, pp. 157–162).

113. Hondros, 1983, p. 183. In his account of the Greek resistance, Hondros (1983, pp. 175–183) includes a detailed study of Zervas' contacts with the Germans. On contacts between the Greek guerrilla bands and the Germans in general, also see Fleischer (1981, pp. 48–60).

114. Hondros, p. 183.

115. By August 1944, according to General Hubert Lanz ("Partisan Warfare in the Balkans," *Historical Division European Command: Foreign Military Studies Branch,* MS No. P–055a, pp. 21–22), EDES had received considerable material support from the Allies and under strong pressure from the AMM attempted to destroy German units in the region of Epiros. As a result Zervas' forces suffered considerable losses so that by the time of the German withdrawal in October, EDES was down to 8,000 men.

116. In a memorandum to the Foreign Office on 14 October 1943, it was argued that the British had to work with EAM-ELAS since this was the most effective resistance in Greece. The author of the memorandum also stressed that left-wing groups produce much better results (FO 371/37206 R 10177).

117. FO 371/37208 R 1221; FO 371/37206 74337.

118. FO 371/37206 R 10295; FO 371/37208 R 11753, R 11908.

119. CAB 65/40, W. M. (43), Minutes, 22 November 1943.

120. Anthony Eden, *The Reckoning: The Memoirs of Anthony Eden, Earl of Avon* (Boston: Cassel, 1965), pp. 498–499; FRUS, 1943, Vol. 4, 157–158; MacVeagh, 1980, p. 395. For a comprehensive study of American policy toward Greece at least from 1943 see Lawrence S. Wittner, *American Intervention in Greece, 1943–1949,* 1982. Another useful guide in American-British relations over Greece is *Churchill and Roosevelt: The Complete Correspondence,* 3 vols., ed. Warren F. Kimball, 1984.

121. Henderson, *Xenia—Memoir: Greece, 1919–1949* (London: Weidenfield and Nicolson, 1988), p. 61.

122. Hondros, p. 204.

123. Hondros, p. 204.

124. FO 371/37210 R 13883.

125. Hondros, pp. 206–207.

126. Other stipulations included the resumption of supplies to all the guerrilla organizations and the release of prisoners. For the complete articles of the agreement see Woodhouse, 1948, Appendix F, pp. 303–304.

127. The other members of PEEA included several more academics and social democrats, with Siantos serving as the only representative of the KKE. On the

history and organization of PEEA, see Basilis Bouras, *I Politiki Epitropi Ethnikis Apeleftherosis PEEA: Eleftheri Ellada 1944* (Athens: Diogenis, 1983), passim. Bouras (p. 90) argues that the participation of some of Greece's most notable academics indicated that the intellectuals had become supporters of EAM.

128. Hondros, pp. 211–212.

129. L. S. Stavrianos, "Mutiny of the Greek Armed Forces, April 1944," *American Slavic and East European Review,* Vol. 9 (December 1950), p. 307; Harold Macmillan, *The Blast of War, 1939–1945* (London: Macmillan, 1967), p. 571; Fleischer, "The Anomalies in the Greek Middle East Forces, 1941–1944," pp. 26–27.

130. According to Fleischer ("The Anomalies in the Greek Middle East Forces, 1941–1944," pp. 28–29), Venizelos had contacts with the mutineers, and he and the other republican politicians were attempting to use the crisis to topple Tsouderos. By this time, however, both the king and the Foreign Office had become convinced that keeping Tsouderos would aggravate the crisis and found Venizelos the only acceptable alternative.

131. Eighteen of the rebels were condemned to death, but their sentences were commuted to life imprisonment by the Greek government in October 1944. The British imprisoned 6,397 Greek seamen and soldiers in camps in Eritrea and in other detention centers in the Middle East; 2,060 were eventually reinstated in the armed forces but confined to garrison duties, while another 1,450 who were offered amnesty refused and were detained for the duration of the war (FO 371/43714 R 7081; Hondros, p. 214).

132. Hondros, p. 216.

133. The conference had been arranged by Tsouderos before the arrival of Papandreou.

134. Rex Leeper, *When Greek Meets Greek* (London: Chatto and Windus, 1950), p. 51.

135. According to Leeper (p. 54), Papandreou simply managed to postpone the question of the monarchy.

136. A summary of these points is found in Woodhouse (1948, Appendix G, pp. 305–306), and in Leeper (pp. 53–54).

137. Leeper, p. 56.

138. Hondros, pp. 224–226.

139. On 12 June, according to Leeper (pp. 57–58), Papandreou convinced his cabinet to state publicly that it was the view of the national government that the king would return to Greece only after a plebiscite and that the king had agreed to this in advance, both by his letter to Tsouderos on 8 November 1943 and by approving the Lebanon Charter, in which this policy was implicit. George II had little choice but to accept or face the resignation of the government.

140. For a detailed analysis of the tactics of the German military operations, see Hondros, pp. 153–159.

141. Hondros, p. 153.

142. André Gerolymatos, "The Security Battalions and the Civil War," *Journal of the Hellenic Diaspora*, Vol. 12, No. 1 (Spring 1985), p. 17.

143. NARS RG 226:83476; E. Wiskemann, *The Rome Berlin Axis: A History of the Relations between Hitler and Mussolini* (London: Oxford University Press, 1949), p. 278; F. W. Deakin, *The Brutal Friendship* (London: Weidenfeld and Nicolson, 1962), p. 253.

144. Gerolymatos, "The Security Battalions and the Civil War," p. 18.

145. NARS RG 226:83476. Professional considerations were certainly a motive, since the mutinies among the Greek armed forces in the Middle East had caused the removal of many republican officers. A postwar Greek army, it was assumed, would also have to accommodate officers who had fought in North Africa and those who had participated in the resistance, at least with right-wing groups. This would leave little room for officers who had remained outside these forces (A. Stavrou, *Allied Politics and Military Interventions: The Political Role of the Greek Army* [Athens: Papazissis, 1970], p. 24).

146. According to Pyromaglou ("Ta Tagmata Asfalias," p. 543), although the Security Battalions were envisioned as a means of controlling the immediate postwar period in Greece, they were not intended to be used as an anticommunist force. Pyromaglou adds that their use against EAM-ELAS not only betrayed the republican leaders who had supported the establishment of these units but served to divide the republican world in a manner that was irreconcilable.

147. Gerolymatos, "The Role of the Greek Officer Corps," p. 76.

148. Bakopoulos, pp. 34–38.

149. Hondros, pp. 172–173.

150. Hondros, p. 173.

151. Hondros, p. 174. Hondros adds (p. 173) that although EAM-ELAS did not publicly denounce British contacts with the Rallis government, shortly after the outbreak of the civil war they made strong protests to Cairo that British officers were working with collaborators.

152. John L. Hondros, "Too Weighty a Weapon: Britain and the Greek Security Battalions, 1943–1944," *Journal of the Hellenic Diaspora*, Vol. 15, Nos. 1 and 2 (1988), pp. 36–37.

153. FO 371/43706.

154. Gerolymatos, "The Security Battalions and the Civil War," p. 21.

155. General Infante, the commander of the Pinerolo Division, instantly changed sides after the Italian surrender and signed an agreement with ELAS recognizing his unit as an Allied force. The Pinerolo Division had a complement of 12,000 well-equipped men. Within one month, ELAS divided the Italian division into small units that were subsequently disarmed (Woodhouse, *Apple of Discord*, p. 101).

156. Procopis Papastratis, *British Policy towards Greece during the Second World War, 1941–1944* (1984), p. 210.

157. Gerolymatos, "The Security Battalions and the Civil War," p. 21, note 23.

158. The EAM ministers were sworn in on 3 September 1944 and received the following portfolios: Svolos was made minister of finance; Nikos Askoutsis received communications; Ilias Tsirimokos, Militiadis Porphyrogenis, and Zevgos were made ministers of economy, labor and agriculture, respectively; and Angelos Angelopoulos became undersecretary for finance.

159. FO 371/43715 R 12457; Force 133 MEF Reports, GSOE/94506.

160. Harold Macmillan, *War Diaries: Politics and War in the Mediterranean, January 1943–May 1945* (New York: Macmillan, 1984), pp. 524–525.

161. The Greek government was to arrive in Athens on 17 October 1944, but when it was realized that 17 October fell on a Tuesday, the day that Constantinople fell to the Ottomans and therefore was considered unlucky, the arrival was postponed to 18 October. The Greek government was transported by a Canadian ship from Taranto to the island of Poros, where, for the sake of propriety, the passengers were transferred to the Greek cruiser *Averoff*. Although a very old ship and only able to make ten knots, the *Averoff* was the pride of the Greek navy in the Balkan wars and thus had the honor of bringing the Greek government to Athens (Leeper, 1950, pp. 73–74).

162. Force 133 MEF Reports, Ref GSOE/94/505, "Maintenance of Law and Order in Greece."

163. NARS RG 226: L49839; XL 2683; L49838; NARS RG 226: L49839.

164. Gerolymatos, "The Security Battalions and the Civil War," p. 23.

165. According to Hondros ("Too Weighty a Weapon," p. 35), the decisions made at Tehran by Roosevelt, Churchill, and Stalin regarding war crimes worked to the advantage of those who had served in the Security Battalions. The criteria for charging war criminals instituted by the United Nations commission set up by the Allies omitted atrocities committed by traitors or quislings of Allied nations against their own country. The Allies eventually agreed to three categories of collaborators: Allied nationals in German uniform, Allied nationals in military or paramilitary quisling formations, and Allied nationals who actively collaborated but did not take up arms against the Allies. The United States, writes Hondros, wanted to treat members of the first two categories as prisoners of war who would be screened for war crimes and turned over to their national governments for trial. The British chiefs of staff agreed but requested that "after thorough investigation, those found suitable" for incorporation into their national forces or formation into labor units be transferred to their own governments. In 1945 the Greek courts trying collaborators ruled that the formation of the Security Battalions did not fall under the category of collaboration since their function had been to maintain law and order and to act against criminal elements (Gerolymatos, "The Security Battalions and the Civil War," p. 25).

166. On this issue, see Papastratis, pp. 213–216.

167. Gilbert, p. 882.

Chapter 3

1. Churchill's retort to a Labour member of Parliament with respect to the British intervention during the December Uprising (*Hansard*, 8 December 1944, columns 934–947).

2. William H. McNeill, *The Greek Dilemma: War and Aftermath* (New York: Lippincott, 1947), p. 163.

3. The disproportionate number of young women participating in the demonstrations as well as their extreme behavior is a phenomenon mentioned by several Greek and non-Greek witnesses. See Henderson, *Xenia—A Memoir*, p. 122; P. W. Byford-Jones, *Greek Trilogy: Resistance, Liberation, Revolution* (London: Hutchinson, 1945), p. 138.

4. Henderson, *Xenia*, p. 123.

5. There are several accounts of the demonstration at Papandreou's residence. Most of them, however, were either written after the event or are hearsay from almost immediately afterward. It is also indicative of the confusion and mythology of the December Uprising that the explosion caused by the hand grenades was used as evidence by opponents of EAM that some of the demonstrators at Constitution Square were armed. H. Maule, *Scobie: Hero of Greece, The British Campaign 1944–45* (London: Arthur Barker Limited, 1975).

6. Kanellopoulos, *Imerologio*, p. 703.

7. Byford-Jones, *The Greek Trilogy*, p. 138.

8. Byford-Jones, *The Greek Trilogy*, p. 138.

9. Some accounts say that he used an automatic weapon. However, if that had been the case the number of dead would have been much higher.

10. Byford-Jones (*The Greek Trilogy*, p. 139), who generally is evenhanded about the crisis, accounts for the twelve killed. The EAM, ELAS, and KKE sources are not in agreement on the precise number of dead and wounded, but they range from 16 to 54 killed and 140 wounded (on the various sources discussing the December casualties, see Spyros Gasparinatos, *Apeleftherosi, Dekemvriana, Varkiza*, Vol. 1, Athens: I. Sideris, 1998, p. 261, note 16). Panayiotis Kanellopoulos (*Imerologico*, pp. 701–703), a moderate member of the right, claims in his diary that only 11 were killed that Sunday.

11. Byford-Jones, *The Greek Trilogy*, pp. 139–140.

12. Precise numbers are difficult to verify. McNeill (*The Greek Dilemma*, p. 170) suggests that about 60,000 filled Constitution Square; left-wing accounts claim that the total number of demonstrators ranged from 500,000 to 600,000 (see Gasparinatos, *Apeleutherosi, Dekemvriana, Varkiza*, p. 257, note 7).

13. McNeill, *The Greek Dilemma*, p. 170.

14. McNeill, *The Greek Dilemma*, p. 170.

15. The principal sources for the events of 3 December 1944 are W. H. McNeill, *The Greek Dilemma*, pp. 165–171, and John O. Iatrides, *Revolt in Athens: The Greek Communist "Second Round," 1944–1945* (Princeton: Princeton University Press, 1972), pp. 187–194. A personal interpretation of the December Uprising is found in Nigel Clive, *A Greek Experience 1943–1948* (London: Michael Russell, 1985), pp. 152–153, and a more recent analysis is provided by Lars Baerentzen, "The Demonstration in Syntagma Square on Sunday the 3rd of December, 1944," *Scandinavian Studies in Modern Greek*, Vol. 2 (1978), pp. 3–52. Another main source is W. Byford-Jones, *The Greek Trilogy: Resistance, Liberation, Revolution.*

16. The leading editorial in *Rizospastis* on 5 December 1944 underlined that the hundreds of thousands of demonstrators denounced Papandreou as a murderer and claimed that the funeral of Sunday's victims also represented the political and national funeral of the "pathetic" prime minister.

17. Zaousis, Vol. B (II), p. 692.

18. Hadzis (*E Nikiphora Epanastasi*, Vol. 4, p. 215) states that the ELAS men were instructed to use only their weapons in self-defense.

19. Zaousis, Volume B (II), p. 693.

20. Henry Maule, *Scobie: Hero of Greece, The British Campaign 1944–45* (London: Arthur Barker, 1975), pp. 11–120.

21. Maule, p. 126.

22. Conversation with Rigas Rigopoulos. Also see his account of his wartime experiences in *The Secret War: Greece–Middle East, 1940–1945, The Events Surrounding the Story of Service 5–16–5* (Paducah, Kentucky: Turner, 2003), passim.

23. Gilbert, *The Road to Victory*, p. 1100; Fo 371/43736 R 19933: Churchill to Leeper, 5/12/1944.

24. Clive's comments regarding Papandreou were related to the author during a delightful lunch in Athens a few years before Clive passed away.

25. Bartsiotas, pp. 340-341.

26. Hadzis, *E Nikiphora Epanastasi*, p. 211.

27. Hadzis, *E Nikiphora Epanastasi*, pp. 211–212.

28. Richard O'Brien, *Recollections*, p. 2.

29. Gilbert, *The Road to Victory*, p. 1086.

30. Woodhouse, *Struggle for Greece*, p. 119.

31. McNeill (*The Greek Dilemma*, p. 158) suggests that the right wing's opposition to disbanding the Third Brigade was strongly backed by Leeper, the British ambassador, and General Scobie.

32. The *EAM White Book* (p. 24) claims Papandreou stated that "until our regular army is organized, and in order to continue the participation of Greece in the common allied struggle, besides the Mountain (Third) Brigade and the Sacred Squadron there will also be organized from the forces of our national resistance a Brigade of ELAS and a proportional unit of EDES." However, there is no reference to where or under what circumstances Papandreou made these comments.

33. C. M. Woodhouse, *Something Ventured* (London: Granada, 1982), p. 80.

34. Lars Baerentzen, "The Arrival of the Soviet Military Mission in July 1944 and KKE Policy: A Study of Chronology," *Journal of the Hellenic Diaspora*, Vol. 13, Nos. 3 and 4, 1986.

35. Peter Stavrakis, *Moscow and the Greek Communism, 1944–1949* (Ithaca and London: Cornell University Press, 1989), p. 38.

36. Hammond, *Venture into Greece*, pp. 162–163.

37. Woodhouse, *The Apple of Discord*, p. 198.

38. Ioannidis, *Anamniseis*, p. 250.

39. Petros Rousos, *I Megali Pendaetia 1940–1945: I Ethniki Andistasi kai O Rolos tou KKE*, Vol. 2 (Athens: Ekdoseis Synchroni Epochi, 1978) p. 203.

40. Vasos Georgiou, *I Zoi Mou* (Athens: n.p., 1992), pp. 414–416.

41. This is also indicated in the *History of the Great Patriotic War*, Vol. 1 (Moscow: Military Publishing House of the Ministry of Defense of the USSR, 1960–1965), p. 417.

42. John O. Iatrides, *Revolt in Athens* (Princeton, Princeton University Press, 1972), passim.

43. Record of meetings at the Kremlin, Moscow, 9 October at 10 P.M.: Foreign Office Papers, 800/303, folios 227–235, in Gilbert, *The Road to Victory*, p. 991.

44. Record of meetings at the Kremlin, Moscow, 9 October at 10 P.M.: Foreign Office Papers, 800/303, folios 227–235, in Gilbert, *The Road to Victory*, p. 991.

45. Churchill, *The Second World War*, Vol. 6, pp. 196–197.

46. Record of meetings at the Kremlin, Moscow, 9 October at 10 P.M.: Foreign Office Papers, 800/303, folios 227–235 in Gilbert, *The Road to Victory*, p. 991.

47. Churchill, *The Second World War*, Vol. 6, p. 197.

48. Giorgis Vontitsos-Gousias, *Oi Aities Gia tis Ittes ti Diaspasi tou KKE kai tis Ellinikis Aristeras* (Athens: Na Ypiretisoume to Lao, n.d.), p. 12.

49. Record of meetings at the Kremlin, Moscow, 9 October at 10 P.M.: Foreign Office Papers, 800/303, folios 227–235, in Gilbert, *The Road to Victory*, p. 992.

50. Georgiou, p. 408.

51. Woodhouse, *The Struggle for Greece*, p. 14.

52. Ioannidis, *Anamniseis,* p. 267.

53. Ole Smith, "History Made to Fit All Occasions: The KKE View of the December Crisis," *Journal of the Hellenic Diaspora*, Vol. 22, No.2 (1996), p. 67.

54. N. Zachariadis, *Provlimata Kathothigisis* (Athens: Poreia, 1978), p. 80.

55. Vassilis Bartziotas, *I Politiki Stelekhon tou KKE sta Teleutea Deka Chronia* (Central Committee of the KKE, 1950), pp. 13–14.

56. Woodhouse, *The Struggle for Greece*, p. 20.

57. Ole Smith ("History Made to Fit All Occasions," p. 67), one of the most knowledgeable scholars of the KKE, and one who had access to KKE archives, commented that "there is more to this issue than merely the question of Siantos'

role." Smith was convinced that "either the KKE knows the motives behind Siantos' strange behavior during the December events or at least some individuals in the party leadership suspect there were reasons for that behavior which would not be wise to reveal." Whatever these reasons, Smith concludes that the KKE strategy in December 1944 was to avoid a fight with the British and confine the battle against the Papandreou government.

58. Kenneth Matthews, *Memories of a Mountain War: Greece 1944–1949* (London: Longman, 1972), p. 79; Svetozar Vukmanovic, *How and Why the People's Liberation Struggle of Greece Met with Defeat* (London: Merlin Press, 1950), pp. 14–16.

59. Loulis, *The Greek Communist Party*, p. 161.

60. Loulis, *The Greek Communist Party*, p. 161.

61. Woodhouse, *The Struggle for Greece*, p. 115.

62. Ioannidis, *Anamniseis*, p. 339.

63. "Crowd Fired On in Athens," *The Times*, Monday, 4 December 1944.

64. *The Times*, 6 December 1944.

65. "A Tragedy of Errors," *The Times*, Thursday, 7 December 1944.

66. Drew Pearson, "Daily Washington Merry-Go-Round," Monday, 11 December 1944, *Washington Post*. For additional anti-British comments see his column on Saturday, 19 August 1944.

67. Woodhouse, *Something Ventured*, p. 93.

68. Woodhouse, *Something Ventured*, p. 95.

69. McNeill, *The Greek Dilemma*, p. 178.

70. Gilbert, *The Road to Victory*, p. 1056.

71. Ehrman, *Grand Strategy*, p. 61.

72. Ehrman, *Grand Strategy*, p. 61.

73. On the ELAS order of battle see the "secret report" of Makridis in *Pharakos*, Vol. 2, p. 115.

74. Ioannidis, *Anamniseis*, p. 339.

75. Ehrman, *Grand Strategy*, p. 62.

76. On this point see, Ole Smith, "History Made to Fit All Occasions," p. 67.

77. McNeill, *The Greek Dilemma*, p. 175.

78. According to McNeill (*The Greek Dilemma*, p. 179), as late as 12 or 13 December EAM leaders still hoped for a diplomatic settlement.

79. McNeill, *The Greek Dilemma*, pp. 179–180.

Chapter 4

1. Theophilos Frangopoulos, "Betrayals," *The Silent Border* (Athens: Ekdositon Philon, 1995).

2. Today, Ron McAdam is a retired physician living in West Vancouver, but in 1944 he was a second lieutenant with the Eleventh Battalion of the prestigious King's Royal Rifle Corps.

3. Interview with Ron McAdam, January 2004, West Vancouver.

4. Interview with Ron McAdam, January 2004, West Vancouver.

5. Interview with Ron McAdam, January 2004, West Vancouver.

6. Major J. C. H. Beswick, Eleventh Battalion, Liberation of Greece and Civil War, King's Royal Rifle Corps, p. 83, in Wake, H., and Deeds, W. F., *Swift and Bold: The Story of the King's Royal Rifle Corps in the Second World War, 1939-1945* (Aldershot: Gale and Polden, 1949).

7. Major J. C. H. Beswick, p. 87.

8. Major J. C. H. Beswick, p. 87.

9. Part of Minced Meat, the deception operation implemented in the early summer of 1943 to fool the Germans into believing that the Allies were planning an invasion of Greece instead of Italy, included the use of a corpse washed ashore in neutral Spain. Furthermore, the SOE employed women operatives who, out of uniform, did not hesitate to kill the enemy. British commandos, during hit-and-run tactics, rarely took prisoners.

10. Major J. C. H. Beswick, p. 87.

11. Byford-Jones, pp. 198–199.

12. Major J. C. H. Beswick, p. 87.

13. Interview with Ron McAdam, January 2004, West Vancouver.

14. Byford-Jones, p. 169.

15. Byford-Jones, p. 170.

16. Maule, *Scobie: Hero of Greece,* p. 122.

17. Byford-Jones, p. 170.

18. Petros Makris-Staikos, *Kitsos Maltezos, O Agapimenos ton Theon* (Athens: Okeanida, 2000), pp. 133–134.

19. Makris-Staikos, *Kitsos Maltezos,* pp. 201–202 and note 465.

20. Makris-Staikos, *Kitsos Maltezos,* p. 209.

21. Makris-Staikos, *Kitsos Maltezos,* pp. 245–246.

22. Spyros G. Gasparinatos, *Apeleutherosi, Dekemvriana, Varkiza,* Vol.1 (Athens: I. Sideris, 1998), pp. 271–271.

23. Interview with Dione Dodis, October 2003.

24. Correspondence with Dione Dodis, 10 November 2003.

25. Ward, p. 215; correspondence with Dodis.

26. Ward, p. 217.

27. Ward, p. 217.

28. Iakovos Chondrymadis, *E Mavri Skia stin Ellada: Ethnikososialistikes kai Fasistikes Organosis stin Ellada tou Mesopolemou kai tis Germanikis Katochis, 1941–1942* (Athens: Monographia tis Stratiotikic Istorias, 2001), p. 70.

29. K. Kokkoroyiannis, "Dialogos me tin Istoria: Oi Ektelestes tis Ithopoiou Elenis Papadaki," *Labyrinthos,* 7 January 2004, pp. 28–32.

30. Kenneth Matthews, p. 98.

31. George Rallis stated to the author that his father was urged by other politicians to work with the Axis in order to counterbalance the growing influence and power of EAM and the KKE (interview with George Rallis, Athens, 1984). George, however, could not follow his father's decision to collaborate, and he left home, only to return after liberation and support his father, who faced charges of treason.

32. Polybias Marsan, *Eleni Papadaki: Mia Photerini Theatriki Porea me Aprosdokito Telos* (Athens: Kastianiotis Publishers, 2001), pp. 286–289.

33. 15 October 1943, *Elinikon Ema*.

34. 6 December 1943, *Elinikon Ema*.

35. Marsan, p. 345.

36. Marsan, p. 351.

37. Marsan, p. 352.

38. Marsan, p. 360.

39. Marsan, p. 360.

40. Maule, *Scobie: Hero of Greece*, p. 254.

41. Also see Zaousis (*Oi Dio Ochtes*, Vol. B, Part III, p. 776) on the controversy over the Peristeri mass gravesite.

42. Matthews, p. 94.

43. "Ta Eglimata ton Eamokommouniston," *E ELLAS*, Tuesday, 2 January 1945, in Dimitris Garouphalias, *Keimena kai Anamnisis apo ton Tragiko Dekemvrio 1944* (Athens: n.p., 1981), pp. 322–324. On the use of wells as makeshift gravesites for those executed by ELAS, see Byford-Jones, p. 248.

44. Phoivos Grigoriadis, *Emphilios Polemos 1944–1949, (Dekemvris, Chitokratia)*, Vol. 9 (Athens: Neokosmos, 1975), p. 194. Some of the senior communist leaders who had led the KKE during the December Uprising have also attempted to spin the outrageous tale that Orestes was an agent of the British Secret Service and that he killed Papadaki at the service's behest in order to discredit the Greek communists (Vasils Bartsiotas, *Ethniki Adistasi kai Dekemvris,* Athens: Sygchroni Epochi, 1983, p. 403). Others claimed that Orestes came from a good family with solid communist credentials and was the dupe of manipulative mistresses who drove him to commit excesses (Spyros A. Kotsakis, *Eisphora, sto chroniko tic katochis kai tic Ethnikis Adistasis stin Athena,* Athens: Syschroni Epochi, 1986, pp. 211–212). If that is the case, and Orestes was the victim of circumstance, the burden of guilt remains with the KKE. The Communist Party orchestrated the arrests and mass executions and thus created an environment that desensitized young men and women in its ranks and enabled them to commit atrocities.

45. On the persecution and execution of Greek members of the Trotsky organization as well as communists who did not agree with the KKE, see A. Stinas, *EAM-ELAS-OPLA* (Athens: Diethnis Vivliothiki, 1984).

46. Roy Jenkins, *Churchill* (New York: Farrar, Straus and Giroux, 2001), p. 771.

47. W. Churchill, *Triumph and Tragedy* (London: Bantam Books, 1953), p. 276.

48. Gasparinatos, *Apeleutherosi, Dekemvriana, Varkiza*, Vol. 2, pp. 104–105.

49. Kaiti Zevgou, p. 332.

50. Kaiti Zevgou, p. 332.

51. There are no precise numbers of the hostages and they range from as few as 10,000 to 25,000. On the problem of the number of hostages see Gasparinatos, *Apeleutherosi, Dekemvriana, Varkiza*, Vol. 2, pp. 103–104 and note 6.

52. *Reminiscences from December 1944* (Athens: Unpublished manuscript, 1990).

53. *Reminiscences from December 1944* (Athens: Unpublished manuscript, 1990).

54. *Reminiscences from December 1944* (Athens: Unpublished manuscript, 1990).

55. *Reminiscences from December 1944* (Athens: Unpublished manuscript, 1990).

56. Maule, *Scobie: Hero of Greece*, p. 244.

57. *Reminiscences from December 1944* (Athens: Unpublished manuscript, 1990).

58. Ward, pp. 225–226.

59. Correspondence with Dione Dodis, 13 November 2003.

60. Ward, p. 229.

Chapter 5

1. Grigoris Staktopoulos, *Ypothesi Polk: E Prosopiki mou Martiria* (Athens: Ekdosis Gnosi 1984), p. 25. Panayiotis Kanellopoulos, the veteran and well-respected politician, wrote the prologue to Staktopoulos' memoirs. On Mouskoundis' personality, see also Edmund Keeley, *The Salonika Bay Murder: Cold War Politics and the Polk Affair* (Princeton: Princeton University Press, 1989), p. 14, and the less reliable and gossipy account of Kati Marton, *The Polk Conspiracy: Murder and Cover-Up in the Case of CBS News Correspondent George Polk* (New York: Random House, 1990), pp. 166–167.

2. Keeley (p. 131) quotes another source who described Staktopoulos as "a softy, afraid of his own shadow."

3. Keeley, p. 131.

4. Keeley, p. 131.

5. Keeley, p. 132.

6. Keeley, pp. 18–19.

7. Keeley, p. 19.

8. Keeley, p. 22.

9. Jones, pp. 163–164.

10. Jones, p. 164.

11. Staktopoulos, p. 20.

12. Staktopoulos, pp. 86–87.

13. Staktopoulos (pp. 81–90) outlines, in detail, the type of torture he suffered.

14. Staktopoulos, p. 79.

15. Staktopoulos, pp. 88–89.

16. The PASOK government of Andreas Papandreou, recognized the resistance in 1982.

17. British Documents on Foreign Affairs (BDOFA), p. 69.

18. British Documents on Foreign Affairs (BDOFA), p. 80.

19. David Close, "The Reconstruction of a Right-Wing State," in David Close, ed., *The Greek Civil War, 1943–1950: Studies in Polarization* (London, 1993), pp. 156–165; Mark Mazower, "The Cold War and the Appropriation of Memory: Greece after Liberation," in *The Politics of Retribution in Europe: War and Its Aftermath,* eds. Istvan Deak et al. (Princeton: Princeton University Press, 2000), p. 214.

20. NARA, RG 226 Entry 172 Box 4 Folder 227, 4 December 1944.

21. British Embassy estimates, 14 November 1949, FO 371/78373 R 11085.

22. FO 371 72213/R7618, Monthly Intelligence Review, 15 June 1948; Bickham Sweet-Escott, *Greece, A Political and Economic History* (London: Royal Institute of International Affairs, 1954), p. 91.

23. Central Intelligence Agency, "Greece," March 1948, Truman Library, President's Secretary File, Box 259.

24. Author's interview with Efthimia Phanou, Patrikios' niece and the daughter of his third sister, Katina, 15 January 2004.

25. Author's interview with Efthimia Phanou, 15 January 2004.

26. Author's interview with Efthimia Phanou, 15 January 2004.

27. Matthews, p. 187.

28. Henderson, p. 128.

29. Henderson, pp. 127–128.

30. Leeper, p. 112.

31. Henderson, p. 124.

32. *ELAS, Greek Resistance Army* (London: Merlin Press, 1980), pp. 161–162.

33. Gerolymatos, "The Security Battalions and the Civil War," *Journal of the Hellenic Diaspora,* Vol. 11, No. 1, 1985.

34. For a recent study of Makronisos, see Stavros Alvanos, *To Phenomeno Makronisos: Ena Prtognoro Egklematiko Peirema* (Athens: Ellinka Grammata, 1998), passim.

35. Artemis Leontis, T*opographies of Hellenism: Mapping the Homeland* (Ithaca and London: Cornell University Press, 1995), p. 231.

36. As part of the surrender, ELAS handed over 100 artillery pieces, over 200 mortars, 419 heavy machine guns, 1,412 light machine guns, 713 automatic weapons, 48,973 rifles and pistols, and various other types of weapons, radio transmitters, small boats, and thousands of hand grenades. Perhaps an assortment of as many as 40,000 weapons was hidden in the mountains (T. Gerozisis, *To Soma ton Axiomatikon kai E Thesi tou stin Sygchroni Elliniki Koinonia, 1821–1975,* Athens: Dodoni, 1996, p. 794).

37. Ole Smith, "The Greek Communist Party, 1945–1949," in *The Greek Civil War, 1943–1950: Studies in Polarization*, ed. D. H. Close (London: Routledge, 1993), p. 135.

38. Ole Smith, "The Greek Communist Party," p. 135.

39. Smith, "The Greek Communist Party," p. 136.

40. H. Montgomery Hyde, *Stalin, The History of a Dictator* (New York: Farrar, Straus and Giroux, 1971), p. 539.

41. Stavrakis, p. 49.

42. Mitsos Partsialidis, *Dipli Apokatastasi tis Ethnikis Andistasis* (Athens: Themelio, 1978), pp. 195, 199.

43. Vladislav Zubik and Constantine Pleshakov, *Inside the Kremlin's War: From Stalin to Khrushchev* (Cambridge: Harvard University Press, 1996), p. 126.

44. Vasilis Bartziotas, *O Agonas tou Dimokratikou Stratou Elladas* (Athens: Sygchroni Epochi, 1982), p. 28.

45. Smith, "The Greek Communist Party," p. 137.

46. David Close, *Greece since 1945: Civil War and Reconstruction, 1945–1950* (London: Longman, 2002), p. 27.

47. Plymeris Voglis, "Between Negation and Self-Negation: Political Prisoners in Greece," in *After the War Was Over: Reconstructing the Family, Nation, and State in Greece*, ed. Mark Mazower (Princeton: Princeton University Press, 2000), p. 81. Voglis also cites British sources indicating that 3,003 were sentenced to death by the extraordinary military tribunals and later executed, in addition to another 378 by civil courts.

48. Voglis, pp. 81–82.

49. Voglis, p. 82.

50. The second law was in response to the formation of a provisional government by the insurgents in December (Voglis, pp. 81–82).

51. Nikos Zachariadis, *Kainourgia Katastasi, Kainnouyia Kathikonda* (Nicosia: n.p., 1950), p. 38.

52. Ariom A. Ulunian, "The Soviet Union and the Greek Question," in *The Soviet Union and Europe in the Cold War, 1943–1953*, eds. F. Gori and S. Pons (New York: St. Martin's Press, 1996), p. 150.

53. NARA, RG 226 Entry 172 Folder 227, 4 December 1944.

54. NARA, Entry 210, Folder 1, 31 January 1945.

55. NARA, RG 226 Entry 172, Folder 227, 4 December 1944, p. 9.

56. NARA, Entry 16, Folder 110924–110936, 8 January 1945, covering December 1944–January 1945.

57. NARA, Entry 16, Folder 110605–110619, 5 January 1945.

58. Wittner, p. 73.

59. Jones, pp. 29–30.

60. NARA, Entry 421, Folder ABC 400, 336 Greece (20 March 1947), Sec. 1-A, Appendix F.

61. F. C. Pogue *George C. Marshall: Statesman* (New York: Viking, 1987), p. 161.

62. Memo 24 February 1947, FRUS 1947, v, 42-45, quoted in Pogue, p. 163.

63. All quotes in the preceding paragraph cited from NARA Entry 421, Folder 400,336 (20 March 1947), Sec 1-A, pp. 4 and 7. ("Memorandum by the State-War-Navy Coordination Committee to the Joint Chiefs of Staff on Policies for Execution of Assistance Program to Greece," 18 August 1947).

64. Howard Jones, *"A New Kind of War": America's Global Strategy and the Truman Doctrine in Greece* (Oxford: Oxford University Press, 1989), Preface, p.1.

65. McCullough, p. 545.

66. Pogue, p. 162, quoting from text of speech in Marshall's Speech File, ML. Appen, 525–528.

67. Pogue, pp. 165–167; Wittner, pp. 78–79; McCullough, pp. 546–547.

68. Wittner, p. 71, quoting Dean Acheson, *Present at the Creation,* p. 219.

69. McCullough, p. 542.

70. Wittner, p. 73.

71. Wittner, pp. 78–79.

72. The initial draft of this speech was thought by Truman's special counsel, Clark Clifford, to be too weak, while Marshall (who was in Paris, en route to Moscow) found the final draft too aggressive. Truman wanted to avoid sounding as if he was reading an "investment prospectus"; Marshall was known for shying away from heady rhetoric. Various changes were made over the multiple drafts, and some direct references to the Soviets were made obscure, but overall, Marshall was told that the communist threat had to remain tangible in the wording. Pogue, pp. 165–167; McCullough, pp. 545–546.

73. Jones, p. I.

74. Wittner, pp. 80–81.

75. Pogue, p. 164, quoting from FRUS 1947, V, 60–62.

76. Wittner, pp. 17–18, quoting from multiple sources.

77. Jones, p. 94.

78. Jones, pp. 127–128.

79. Jones, pp. 127–129.

80. United Press story in "Note for Record," 11 February 1948 [in P & O 000.7 (TS), sect. I, case 1, Army Staff Records, NA], quoted in Jones, pp. 128-129.

81. Constantine Poulos, "The Lesson of Greece," *The Nation,* 27 March 1948, pp. 343–345, quoted in Jones, p. 129.

82. Andre Gerolymatos, "Greek Democracy on Trial: From Insurgency to Civil War, 1943–1949," in "Democracies and Small Wars," *The Review of International Affairs: Center for Eurasian Studies,* Vol. 2, No. 3, Spring 2003, p. 130.

83. Gerolymatos, "Greek Democracy," p. 131.

84. Gerolymatos, "Greek Democracy," p. 132.

85. John S. Koliopoulos, *Plundered Loyalties: World War II and Civil War in Macedonia* (New York: New York University Press, 1999), p. 254.

86. Edgar O'Ballance, *The Greek Civil War* (New York: Praeger, 1966), p. 196.

87. Gerolymatos, "Greek Democracy," p. 133.

88. Gerolymatos, "Greek Democracy," p. 133.

89. Milovan Djilas, *Conversations with Stalin* (London: Penguin Books, 1962), pp. 140–141.

90. Edgar O'Ballance, p. 196.

91. Author's interview with Leo Katsuris, Vancouver, 8 March 2004.

92. Edgar O'Ballance, pp. 196–197.

93. Richard J. Aldrich, *The Hidden Hand: Britain, America and Cold War Secret Intelligence* (New York: Overlook Press, 2002), p. 163.

94. Ulunian, p. 154. In 1952, Greece and Turkey joined NATO, and between 1953 and 1954, Greece, Yugoslavia, and Turkey concluded a series of treaties laying the foundation for a Balkan pact.

95. Kosta Katsuris emigrated to Canada from the Soviet Union in 1967.

Epilogue

1. Woodhouse, *Struggle for Greece,* p. 209. At least 7,000 of these children along with their parents—most of them Slavs from Macedonia—remained in Yugoslavia (Jones, p. 232).

2. Jones, p. 234.

3. Margaret Truman, *Harry S. Truman* (New York: William Morrow, 1973), p. 461.

4. 1950, Vol. 6, p. 710.

5. John Foster Dulles, *War or Peace* (New York: Macmillan, 1950), pp. 44, 231.

6. William J. Miller, *Henry Cabot Lodge: A Biography* (New York: Heineman, 1967), p. 373.

7. Theodore Sorensen, *Kennedy* (New York: Harper and Row, 1965), p. 745.

8. American Consulate, Salonica, to American Embassy, Athens, 6 November 1946, USNA, 868.00-10-2946.

BIBLIOGRAPHY

Primary Sources

Anonymous, *Report on SOE Activities in Greece and the Islands of the Aegean Sea,* Appendix I, "Origin and Constitution of SOE."

British Documents on Foreign Affairs: Reports and Papers from the Foreign Office Confidential Print General Editors. Paul Preston and Michael Partridge, Part IV from 1946 through 1950, Series F, Europe, Vol. 5, 1946 EDS. Denis Smyth and Andre Gerolymatos (University Publications of America, 2000).

Cabinet Office (Great Britain), Cabinet History Series: Principal War Telegrams and Memoranda 1940–1943, Vol. 1, "Middle East, From the Occupation of Cyrenaica to the Fall of Keren and Harar," Nos. 39, 40, 69, 73.

CAB 65/25 WM (42) 5.

CAB 65/25 WM (42) 5.

CAB 65/25 WM (42) 5.

CAB 65/40, WM (43), Minutes, 22 November 1943.

Central Intelligence Agency, "Greece" March 1948, Truman Library, President's Secretary File, Box 259, December 1944–January 1945.

Documents on Foreign German Policy, Series D, Vol. 11, No. 323, "Directive 18."

Documents on Foreign German Policy, Series D, Vol. 11, No. 511, "Directive 20: Operation Marita."

Documents on Foreign German Policy, Series D, Vol. 12, No. 195, "Directives of the High Command of the Wehrmacht."

Documents on Foreign German Policy, Series D, Vol. 12, No. 463.

Documents on Foreign German Policy, Series D, Vol. 12, No. 463.

FO 371/72213 R 7618, Monthly Intelligence Review , 15 June 1948.

FO 371/20390, Athens Dispatch No. 281.

FO 371/23782 R 7921, Chiefs of Staff Committee.

FO 371/24884 R 74320 "Greek Military Situation."

FO 371/24910.

FO 371/24982.

FO 371/29816 R 74220.

FO 371/29817 R 8810.

FO 371/29820 R 4615.

FO 371/29842 R 10894.

FO 371/29909 R 8414.

FO 371/33160.

FO 371/33167 R 1362.

FO 371/3717194 R 2266.

FO 371/37201 74220 R 2050, "Resistance Groups in Greece," Minute by Dixon, 7 March 1943.

FO 371/37201 74220 R 2332.

FO 371/37201 74220 R 2050, "Political Aspects of the Greek Resistance Movement."

FO 371/37201 74220, R 2050, "Political Aspects of the Greek Resistance Movement."

FO 371/37201 74220, R 2322.

FO 371/37201 R 74220.

FO 371/37203 R 5573.

FO 371/37206 74337.

FO 371/37206 R 10177.

FO 371/37206 R 10295.

FO 371/37206 R 10450.

FO 371/37208 R 11753, R 11908.

FO 371/37208 R 1221.

FO 371/37210 R 13883.

FO 371/37216 R 3924.

FO 371/43706.

FO 371/43715 R 12457.

FO 371/78373 R 11085, British Embassy estimates, 14 November 1949.

FO 71/37202 R 4209.

FO 74038 HS5/524.

FO 74038 HS5/524.

FO 74038; HS5/524.

FO 800/303, folios 227–235 cited in Gilbert, *The Road to Victory*.

FO 898/97 R 74320, "Joint SOE/PWE Survey of Resistance in Occupied Europe."

Force 133, MEF Reports, GSOE/94506.

Force 133 MEF Reports, Ref GSOE/94/505, "Maintenance of Law and Order in Greece."

FRUS 1943.

FRUS 1947, V, 42–45 Memo dated 24 February 1947, "Under Secretary of State to Secretary concerning visit, 24 February 47," quoted in Pogue.

FRUS 1947, V, 60–62, quoted in Pogue.

GAK E 13.

GAK File A6–A17; B1–B4; E1–E3.

GAK, "Apostoli Gama," No. 4.

HS 7/151 89846.

HS 7/268 89846, Major Pirie's Report: A History of SOE Activities in Greece May 1940–November 1942.

Marshall's Speech File, ML. Appen, 525–528, quoted in Pogue.

NARA Entry 16, Folder 110605–110619, 5 January 1945.

NARA Entry 421, Folder 400,336 (20 March 1947) Sec. 1-A ("Memorandum by the State-War-Navy Coordination Committee to the Joint Chiefs of Staff on Policies for Execution of Assistance Program to Greece," 18 August 1947).

NARA Entry 421, Folder ABC 400, 336 Greece (20 March 1947) Sec. 1-A, Appendix F.

NARA RG 226: Entry 172 Folder 227, 4 December 1944.

NARA RG 226: L49839.

NARA RG 226: L49839.

NARA RG 226:83476.

NARA RG 226: 83476.

NARA RG 226: L49838.

NARA RG 226: XL 2683.

NARA Entry 16, Folder 110924–110936, 8 January 1945.

NARA Entry 210, Folder 1, 31 January 1945.

NARA RG 226: Entry 172, Box 4, Folder 227, 4 December 1944.

NARA RG 226: Entry 172, Folder 227, 4 December 1944.

OKW Diaries, Band II (Kaiegstahgehich des Oberkommando des Wehrmacht, 1940–1945, 4 vols. ed. H. Greiner and Percy E. Schramm, Frankfurt-am-Main, 1961–1966).

UP story in "Note for Record," 11 February 1948, in P & O 000.7 (TS), Sect. I, Case 1, Army Staff Records, NA, quoted in Jones.

Newspaper Articles

Akropolis, 2.11.40.

Avgi, 13.7.60.

Elinikon Ema, 15.10.43.

Elinikon Ema, 6.12.43.

Kommounistiki Epitheoresi, February 1944.

Rizospastis, 15.11.44.

Rizospastis, 1.10.44; 31.10.44.

Rizospastis, 5.12.44.

Rizospastis, 25.10.43.

Rizospastis, 28.10.45.

The Times, 4.12.44, "Crowd Fired on in Athens."

The Times, 7.12.44, "A Tragedy of Errors."

Washington Post, 11.12.44, Drew Pearson, "Daily Washington Merry-Go-Round."

Books and Essays

Acheson, Dean, *Present at the Creation: My Years in the State Department*. New York: Norton, 1969.

Aldrich, Richard J., *The Hidden Hand: Britain, America and Cold War Secret Intelligence*. New York: Overlook Press, 2002.

Alvanos, Stavros, *To Phenomeno Makronisos: Ena Protognoro Egklematiko Peirema*. Athens: Ellinka Grammata, 1998.

Augeropoilos, G., et al. (eds.), *St' Armata St' Armata! Chroniko tis Ethnikis Andistasis 1940–1945*. Athens: Geranikos, 1964.

Avgoustidis, Angelos, "EEAM: The Workers' Resistance." *Journal of the Hellenic Diaspora*, Vol. 11, No. 3 (1984).

Baerentzen, Lars, "The Demonstration in Syntagma Square on Sunday the 3rd of December, 1944." *Scandinavian Studies in Modern Greek*, Vol. 2 (1978).

Baerentzen, Lars, "The Arrival of the Soviet Military Mission in July 1944 and KKE Policy: A Study of Chronology." *Journal of the Hellenic Diaspora*, Vol. 13, Nos. 3 and 4, Fall–Winter 1986.

Bakopoulos, Konstantinos Th., *I Omeria ton Pende Andistratigon: I Zoe ton—Stratopeda Sygendroseos*. Athens: n.p., 1948.

Bartziotas, V., *E. Ethniki Andistasi kai Dekemvris 1944*. Athens: Sygchroni Epochi, 1979.

Bartziotas, V., *O Agonas tou Dimokratikou Stratou Elladas*. Athens: Sygchroni Epochi, 1982.

Bartziotas, V., *Exinda Chronia Kommounistis*. Athens: Sygchroni Epochi, 1986.

Bartziotas, Vassilis, *I Politiki Stelekhon tou KKE sta Teleutea Deka Chronia*, in *Deka Chronia Palis*, edited by Nikos Zachariadis. Athens: Poria, 1978.

Benetatos, D., *To Chroniko tis Sklavias 1941–1944*. Athens: n.p., 1963.

Beswick, Major J. C. H., *Eleventh Battalion*, "Liberation of Greece and Civil War," King's Royal Rifle Corps in Wake, H. and Deeds, W. F., *Swift and Bold: The Story of the King's Royal Rifle Corps in the Second World War, 1939–1945*. Aldershot: Gale and Polden, 1949.

Bouras, Basilis, *I Politiki Epitropi Ethnikis Apeleftherosis PEEA: Eleftheri Ellada 1944*. Athens: Diogenis, 1983.

Byford-Jones, W., *Greek Trilogy: Resistance, Liberation, Revolution*. London: Hutchinson, 1945.

Carouphalis, Dimitrius, ed. "Ta Eglimata ton Eamokommouniston," *E Ellas*, Tuesday 2 January 1945.

Chondrymadis, Iakovos, *E Mavri Skia stin Ellada: Ethnikososialistikes kai Fasistikes Organosis stin Ellada tou Mesopolemou kai tis Germanikis Katochis, 1941–1942.* Athens: Monographia tis Stratiotikis Istorias, 2001.

Christidis, Ch., *Chronia Katochis: Martyries Imerologion, 1941–1944.* Athens: n.p., 1971.

Churchill, W., *Triumph and Tragedy*, Vol. 6. London: Houghton Mifflin, 1953.

Churchill, W. S., *Closing the Ring*, Vol. 5. London: Houghton Mifflin, 1951.

Churchill and Roosevelt: The Complete Correspondence, 3 vols. Ed. W. F. Kimbal. Princeton: Princeton University Press, 1984.

Clive, Nigel, *A Greek Experience 1943–1948.* Salisbury, Wiltshire: Russell, 1985.

Clogg, R., "Pearls from Swine," in *British Policy towards Wartime Resistance in Yugoslavia and Greece*, edited by P. Auty and R. Clogg. London: Macmillan, 1975.

Clogg, R., "The Special Operations Executive in Greece," in *Greece in the 1940s: A Nation in Crisis,* edited by John O. Iatrides. Hanover and London: University Press of New England, 1981.

Close, D. H., "The Police in the Fourth of August Regime." *Journal of the Hellenic Diaspora,* Vol. 13, Nos. 1 and 2 (1986).

Close, David, "The Reconstruction of a Right-Wing State," in *The Greek Civil War, 1943–1950: Studies in Polarization,* edited by David Close. London: Routlege, 1993.

Close, David, *Greece since 1945: Civil War and Reconstruction, 1945–1950.* London: Longman, 2002.

Creveld, M. Van, *Hitler's Strategy 1940–1941: The Balkan Clue.* Cambridge: Cambridge University Press, 1973.

Cruickshank, Charles, *Deception in World War II.* Oxford: Oxford University Press, 1979.

Dafnis, G., *I Ellas Metaxy Dyo Polemon 1923–1940,* 2 vols. Athens: Ikaros, 1974.

Deakin, F. W., *The Brutal Friendship.* London: Weidenfeld and Nicolson, 1962.

Djilas, Milovan, *Conversations with Stalin.* London: Penguin, 1962.

EAM White Book. May 1944–March 1945. New York: n.p., 1944–1945.

Eden, Anthony, *The Reckoning: The Memoirs of Anthony Eden, Earl of Avon.* Boston: Cassel, 1965.

Ehrman, J., *Grand Strategy.* London: HMSO, 1956–1976.

Elephandis, A., *I Epangelia tis Adinatis Epanastasis: K.K.E. kai Astismos ston Mesopolemon.* Athens: Themilio, 1976.

Fleischer, Hagen, "The Anomalies in the Greek Middle East Forces, 1941–1944." *Journal of the Hellenic Diaspora,* Vol. 5, No. 3 (Fall 1978), pp. 5-36.

Fleischer, Hagen, "Contacts between German Occupation Authorities and the Major Greek Resistance Organizations: Sound Tactics or Collaboration," in *Greece in the 1940s: A Nation in Crisis.*

Fleischer, Hagen, *Stemma kai Swastika.* Athens: Papazisis, 1988.

Fleischer, Hagen, and Nikolas Svoronos (eds.), *Praktika tou Diethnous Istorokou Synedriou, I Ellada 1936–44: Diktatoria, Katochi, Andistasi*. Athens: Morphotiko Institouto, 1989.

Frangopoulos, Theophilos, "Betrayals," in *The Silent Border*. Athens: Ekdosistou Philon, 1995.

Gasparinatos, Spyros G., *Apeleutherosi, Dekemvriana, Varkiza*, 2 vols. Athens: I. Sideris, 1998.

Gatopoulos, D., *Istoria tis Katochis*, Vol. A. Athens: Melissa, 1949.

Georgiou, Vasos, *I Zoi Mou*. Athens: n.p., 1992.

Gerolymatos, Andre, "The Role of the Greek Officer Corps in the Resistance." *Journal of the Hellenic Diaspora*, Vol. 11, No. 3 (Fall 1984).

Gerolymatos, Andre, "The Security Battalions and the Civil War." *Journal of the Hellenic Diaspora*, Vol. 12, No. 1 (Spring 1985).

Gerolymatos, Andre, "American Foreign Policy towards Greece and the Problem of Intelligence, 1945–1947." *Journal of Modern Hellenism*, No. 7 (1990).

Gerolymatos, Andre, "Greek Democracy on Trial: From Insurgency to Civil War, 1943–1949," *The Review of International Affairs: Center for Eurasian Studies*, Vol. 2, No. 3 (Spring 2003).

Gerozisis, T., *To Soma ton Axiomatikon kai E Thesi tou stin Sygchroni Elliniki Koinonia, 1821–1975*. Athens: Dodoni, 1996.

Gilbert, M., *The Road to Victory: Winston Churchill 1939–1941*, Vol. 7. Toronto: Stoddard, 1986.

Hadzis, Thanasis, *E Nikiphora Epanastasi pou Chathike: Ethnikoapeleutherotikos Agonas, 1941–1945*. Athens: Dorikos, 1982.

Hammond, N., *Venture into Greece: With the Guerrillas, 1943–1944*. London: William Kimbers, 1983.

Henderson, Mary, *Xenia–A Memoir, Greece 1919–1949*. London: Weidenfield and Nicolson, 1988.

Hinsley, F. H., et al. (eds.), *British Intelligence in the Second World War: Its Influence on Strategy and Operations*, Vol. 1. New York: Cambridge University Press, 1979.

History of the Great Patriotic War, Vol. 1. Moscow: Military Publishing House of the Ministry of Defense of the USSR, 1960–1965.

Hoffmann, Peter, "Roncalli in the Second World War: Peace Initiatives, the Greek Famine and the Persecution of the Jews." *Journal of Ecclesiastical History*, Vol. 40, No. 1 (January 1989).

Hondros, J. L., *Occupation and Resistance: The Greek Agony 1941–44*. New York: Pella, 1983.

Hondros, John L., "Too Weighty a Weapon: Britain and the Greek Security Battalions, 1943–1944." *Journal of the Hellenic Diaspora*, Vol. 15, Nos. 1 and 2 (1988).

Hyde, H. Montgomery, *Stalin, The History of a Dictator*. New York: Farrar, Straus and Giroux, 1971.

Iatrides, John O., *Revolt in Athens: The Greek Communist "Second Round,"* *1944–1945.* Princeton: Princeton University Press, 1972.

Ioannidis, G., *Ellines kai Xenoi Kataskopoi stin Ellada.* Athens: Ekdosis A. Mavridis, 1952.

Ioannidis, G., *Anamniseis: Provlimata tis Politikis tou KKE stin Ethniki Andistasi, 1940–1945.* Athens: Themilio, 1979.

Jane's Fighting Ships of World War II. New York: Military Press, 1989.

Jenkins, Roy, *Churchill.* New York: Farrar, Straus and Giroux, 2001.

Jones, Howard, *"A New Kind of War": America's Global Strategy and the Truman Doctrine in Greece.* Oxford: Oxford University Press, 1989.

Kanellopoulos, P., *Imerologio: 31 March 1942–4 January 1945.* Athens: Kedros, 1977.

Kedros, A., *I Elliniki Andistasi 1940–44,* Vol. A. Athens: Themelio, 1981.

Keegan, John, *The Second World War.* Toronto: Penguin, 1989.

Keeley, Edmund, *The Salonika Bay Murder: Cold War Politics and the Polk Affair.* Princeton: Princeton University Press, 1989.

KKE Episema Keimena 1940–1945, Vol. 5, Athens: Ekdosis tou KKE Esoterikou, 1979.

Klaras, B., *O Adelphos mou o Aris.* Athens: Dorikos, 1985.

Klingaman W. K., *1941: Our Lives in a World on the Edge.* New York: Harper and Row, 1966.

Kofas, Jon V., *Authoritarianism in Greece:The Metaxas Regime.* New York: Columbia University Press, 1983.

Kokkoroyiannis, K., "Dialogos me tin Istoria: Oi Ektelesis tis Ithopoiou Elenis Papadaki." *Labyrinthos,* Vol. 7 (January 2004).

Koliopoulos, J. S., *Greece and the British Connection 1935–1941.* Oxford: Oxford University Press, 1977.

Koliopoulos, J. S., "Esoterikes Exelixeis apo tin Protin Martiou os tin 28 Octovriou 1940," in *Istoria tou Ellinikou Ethnous: Neoteros Ellinismos apo 1913 os 1941.* Athens: Ekdotiki Athenon, 1978.

Koliopoulos, John S., *Plundered Loyalties: World War II and Civil War in Macedonia.* New York: New York University Press, 1999.

Konstas, Panagiotis E., *I Ellas tis Dekaetias 1940–1950.* Athens: n.p., 1955.

Kotsakis, Spyros A., *Eisphora, sto Chroniko tis Katochic kai tic Ethnikis Adistasis.* Athens: Stin Athena, 1986.

Kotsis, Spyro, *Midas 614.* Athens: n.p., 1976.

Kousoulas, D. G., *Revolution and Defeat: The Story of the Greek Communist Party.* London: Oxford University Press, 1965.

Kousoulas, D. G., *KKE: Ta Prota Chronia, 1918–1949.* Athens: Elliniki Euroekdotiki, 1987.

Lanz, General Hubert, "Partisan Warfare in the Balkans," in *Historical Division European Command: Foreign Military Studies Branch,* MS No. P-995a, Koenigstein/Ts 15 September 1950.

Leeper, R., *When Greek Meets Greek*. London: Chatto and Windus, 1950.

Lemkin, Raphael, *Axis Rule in Occupied Greece: Laws of Occupation, Analysis of Government Proposals for Redress*. New York: H. Fertig, 1973.

Leontis, Artemis, *Topographies of Hellenism: Mapping the Homeland*. Ithaca and London: Cornell University Press, 1995.

Levidis, A., *Yia Hare tis Alithias: Intelligence kai Andistasi*. Unpublished manuscript, Athens, 1975.

Lewis, Bernard, *What Went Wrong? Western Impact and Middle Eastern Response*. Oxford: Oxford University Press, 2002.

Linardatos, S., *I 4i Augoustou*. Athens: Ekdosi Dialogos, 1975.

Logothetopoulos, K., *Idou i Alitheia*. Athens: n.p., 1948.

Loulis, J., *The Greek Communist Party, 1940–1944*. London: Croom Helm, 1982.

Louvaris, N., "Golgothas enos Ethnous." *Ethnikos Keryx* (2 April 1950–6 November 1950).

Macmillan, Harold, *The Blast of War, 1939–1945*. London: Macmillan, 1967.

Macmillan, Harold, *War Diaries, The Mediterranean 1943–1945*, London: Macmillan, 1984.

MacVeagh, Lincoln, *Ambassador MacVeagh Reports: Greece, 1933–1947*. Ed. J. O. Iatrides. Princeton: Princeton University Press, 1980.

Makka-Photiadis, Despina, *Reminiscences from December 1944*. Unpublished manuscript, Athens, 1990.

Makris-Staikos, Petros Kitsos Maltezos, *O Agapimenos ton Theon*. Athens: Okeanida, 2000.

Marsan, Polybias, *Eleni Papadaki: Mia Photerini Theatriki Porea me Aprosdokito Telos*. Athens: Kastianiotis, 2001.

Marton, Kati, *The Polk Conspiracy: Murder and Cover-Up in the Case of CBS News Correspondent George Polk*. New York: Random House, 1990.

Matthews, Kenneth, *Memories of a Mountain War: Greece 1944–1949*. London: Longman, 1972.

Maule, H., *Scobie: Hero of Greece, The British Campaign 1944–45*. London: Arthur Barker, 1975.

Mazower, Mark (ed.), *After the War Was Over: Reconstructing the Family, Nation, and State in Greece*. Princeton: Princeton University Press, 2000.

Mazower, Mark, "The Cold War and the Appropriation of Memory: Greece after Liberation," in *The Politics of Retribution in Europe: War and Its Aftermath*, edited by Istvan Deak et al. Princeton: Princeton University Press, 2000.

McCullough, David, *Truman*. New York: Simon and Schuster, 1992.

McNeill, W. H., *The Greek Dilemma: War and Aftermath*. New York: Lippincott, 1947.

Medlicott, W. N., *The Economic Blockade*, 2 vols. London: HMSO, 1978.

Metaxas, Ioannis, *To Prosopiko tou Imerologio,* edited by C. Christidis (Vols. 1–2, 1896–1920), by P. M. Siphnaios (Vol. 3, 1921), by P. Vranas (Vol. 4, 1933–1941). Athens: Ekdoseis Gkobosti, 1951–1964.

Michel, Henri, *The Shadow War: Resistance in Europe 1939–1945.* Trans. Richard Barry. London: Andre Deutsch, 1972.

Myers, E., "The Andarte Delegation to Cairo: August 1943," in *British Policy towards Wartime Resistance in Yugoslavia and Greece.* London: Macmillan, 1975.

Myers, E., *Greek Entanglement.* Gloucester: Hart-Davis, 1985.

O'Ballance, Edgar, *The Greek Civil War.* New York: Praeger, 1966.

O'Brien, Richard, *Recollections.* Unpublished manuscript. London, no date.

Papagos, A., "I Pros Polemou Proparaskevi tou Ellinikou Stratou 1923–1940," in *Archigeion Stratou Diefthnisis Stratou.* Athens: Ekdosis Diefthynseos Istorias Stratou, 1969.

Papastratis, P., "Diplomatika Paraskinia tis Ipografis tis Stratiotikis Symfonias Vretanias—Elladas stis 9 Martiou 1941," *Mnimon,* Vol. 7, 1979).

Papastratis, P., *British Policy towards Greece during the Second World War 1941–1944.* Cambridge: Cambridge University Press, 1984.

Partsialidis, Mitsos, *Dipli Apokatastasi tis Ethnikis Andistasis.* Athens: Themelio, 1978.

Petropoulos, J. A., *Politics and Statecraft in the Kingdom of Greece, 1833–1843.* Princeton: Princeton University Press, 1968.

Petropoulos, J., "Traditional Political Parties of Greece During the Axis Occupation," in *Greece in the 1940's: A Nation in Crisis,* edited by J. O. Iatrides. Princeton: Princeton University Press, 1981.

Phlountzes, A., *Akrovafplia kai Akronafpliotes.* Athens: Themilio, 1979.

Pogue, F. C., *George C. Marshall: Statesman.* New York: Viking, 1987.

Poulos, Constantine, "The Lesson of Greece." *Nation* (March 27, 1948).

Protaios, Stelios, *E Diki ton Ex.* Athens: Chrisima Vivlia, n.d.

Pyromaglou, K., "Ta Tagmata Asphalias." *Istoriki Epitheoresis,* Vol. 6 (October–December 1964).

Pyromaglou, K., *O Georgios Kartalis kai i Epochi tou, 1934–1957:* Vol. A. Athens: n.p., 1965.

Pyromaglou, K., *I Ethniki Andistasis: EAM-ELAS-EDES-EKKA.* Athens: Dodoni, 1975.

Pyromaglou, K. (ed.), *Istorikon Archion Ethnikis Andistasis,* Vol. 2. Athens: n.d.

Rallis, Ioannis, *O Ioannis Rallis Omilei ek tou Tafou.* Athens: n.p., 1947.

Rigopoulos, Rigas, *The Secret War: Greece–Middle East, 1940–1945, The Events Surrounding the Story of Service 5–16–5.* Paducah: Turner, 2003.

Roskill, S. W., *The War at Sea 1939–1945.* London: HMSO, 1954.

Rousos, Petros, *I Megali Pendaetia 1940–1945: I Ethniki Andistasi kai O Rolos tou KKE.* 2 Vols. Athens: Ekdoseis: Sygchroni Epochi, 1978.

Sakellariou, Alexander, *Enas Navarchos Thimatai,* 2 vols. Athens: Dimitrakos, 1971.

Saloutsos, Th., *The Greeks in the United States*. Boston: Cambridge University Press, 1964.

Sarafis, Stafanos, *ELAS, Greek Resistance Army*. London: Merlin Press, 1980.

Saranda Chronia tou KKE 1918–1958. Athens: Sygchroni Epochi, 1958.

Seaton Watson, G. H. N., "Afterword," in *British Policy towards Wartime Resistance in Yugoslavia and Greece*. London: Macmillan, 1975.

Smith, Michael Llewellyn, *Ionian Vision: Greece in Asia Minor 1919–1922*. Michigan: University of Michigan Press, 1973.

Smith, Ole, "The Greek Communist Party, 1945–1949," in *The Greek Civil War, 1943–1950: Studies in Polarization*, edited by D. H. Close. London: Routledge, 1993.

Smith, Ole, "History Made to Fit All Occasions: The KKE View of the December Crisis." *Journal of the Hellenic Diaspora*, Vol. 22, No. 2 (1996).

Spais, Leonids, *Peninda Chronia Stratiotis*. Athens: Melissa, 1970.

Stafford, D., *Britain and European Resistance 1940–1945: A Survey of the Special Operations Executive, with Documents*. London: Macmillan; Oxford: St. Anthony's College, 1980.

Staktopoulos, Grigoris, *Ypothesi Polk: E Prosopiki mou Martiria*. Athens: Ekdosis Gnosi, 1984.

Stavrakis, Peter, *Moscow and Greek Communism, 1944–1949*. Ithaca and London: Cornell University Press, 1989.

Stavrianos, L. S., "Mutiny of the Greek Armed Forces, April 1944." *The American Slavic and East European Review*, Vol. 9 (December 1950).

Stavrianos, L. S., *The Balkans Since 1453*. New York: New York University Press, 1958.

Stavrou, A., *Allied Politics and Military Interventions: The Political Role of the Greek Army*. Athens: Papazissis, 1970.

Stevens, J. M., "Report of Lt.-Col. J. M. Stevens on Present Conditions in Central Greece," in *British Reports on Greece 1943–44*, edited by Lars Baerentzen. Copenhagen: Museum Tusculanum Press, 1982.

Stinas, A., *EAM-ELAS-OPLA*. Athens: Diethnis Vivliothiki, 1984.

Stinas, A., *Anamniseis: Evdominda Chronia Kato apo ti Semaia tis Sosialistikis Epanastasis*. Athens: Dithnis Bibliothiki, 1985.

Sweet-Escott, Bickham, *Greece, A Political and Economic History*. London: Royal Institute of International Affairs, 1954.

Sweet-Escott, Bickham, *Baker Street Irregular*. London: Methuen, 1962.

Sweet-Escott, Bickham, "SOE in the Balkans." *British Policy towards Wartime Resistance in Yugoslavia and Greece*. London: Macmillan, 1975.

Syndomi Istoria tou KKE, Meros A 1918–1949. Athens: Ekdosi ticke tou KKE, 1988.

Tsakalotos, Th., *40 Chronia Stratiotis tis Ellados*, Vol. A. Athens: n.p., 1960.

Tsolakoglou, Georgios, *Apomnemonevmata*. Athens: the *Acropolis* newspaper, 1959.

Tsouderos, Emmanouil, *Ellinikes Anomalies stin Mesi Anatoli*. Athens: n.p., 1945.

Tsouderos, Emmanouil, *Logoi*. Athens: Aetos, 1946.

Tsouderos, Emmanouil, *O Episitismos 1941–1944: Mesi Anatoli*. Athens: Papazisis, 1948.

Tsouderos, Emmanouil, *Diplomatika Paraskinia*. Athens: Aetos, 1950.

Ulunian, Ariom A., "The Soviet Union and the Greek Question," in *The Soviet Union and Europe in the Cold War, 1943–1953*, edited by F. Gori and S. Pons. New York: St. Martin's Press, 1996.

Vafeiadis, M., *Apomnimonevmata*, Vol. 1. Athens: Diphros, 1984.

Vansittart, R., *The Mist Procession*. London: Hutchinson, 1958.

Vatikiotis, P. J., *Popular Autocracy in Greece 1936–41: A Political Biography of General Ioannis Metaxas*. London: Frank Cass, 1998.

Venezis, Elias, *Archiepiskopos Damaskinos*. Athens: Estias, 1981.

Voglis, Plymeris, "Between Negation and Self-Negation: Political Prisoners in Greece," in *After the War Was Over: Reconstructing the Family, Nation, and State in Greece*, edited by Mark Mazower. Princeton: Princeton University Press, 2000.

Vontitsos-Gousias, Giorgis, *Oi Aities Gia tis Ittes ti Diaspasi tou KKE kai tis Ellinikis Aristeras*. Athens: Na Ypiretisoume to Lao, n.d.

Vukmanovic, Svetozar, *How and Why the People's Liberation Struggle of Greece Met with Defeat*. London: Merlin Press, 1950.

Wallace, D. J., "Conditions in Zervas-Held Territory." *British Reports on Greece 1943–44*. Copenhagen: Museum Tusculanum Press, 1982.

Ward, M., *Greek Assignments: 1943 SOE–1948 UNSCOB*. Athens: Private publication, 1990.

Wiskemann, E., *The Rome-Berlin Axis: A History of the Relations between Hitler and Mussolini*. London: Oxford University Press, 1949.

Wittner, Lawrence S., *American Intervention in Greece, 1943–1949*. New York: Columbia University Press, 1982.

Woodhouse, C. M., *The Apple of Discord*. London: Hutchinson, 1948.

Woodhouse, C. M., *The Struggle for Greece 1941–1949*. Chicago: Ivan R. Dee, 1976.

Woodward, Sir L., *British Foreign Policy in the Second World War*, Vol. 1. London: HMSO, 1970.

Zachariadis, Nikos, *Kainourgia Katastasi, Kainouryia Kathikonda*. Nicosia: n.p., 1950.

Zalokostas, Ch., *To Chroniko tis Sklavias*. Athens: Estia, 1949.

Zannas, Alexander, *I Katochi: Anamniseis-Epistoles*. Athens: Estias, 1964.

Zaousis, A. L., *Oi Dio Ochthes: 1939–1945*. Athens: Papazisis, 1987.

Zevgos, Kaiti, *Me ton Yianni Zevgo sto Epanastatiko Kinima*. Athens: Ekdosis Okeanida, 1980.

Zubik, Vladislav, and Constantine Pleshakov, *Inside the Kremlin's War: From Stalin to Khrushchev*. Cambridge: Harvard University Press, 1996.

Interviews and Personal Correspondence

Correspondence with Dione Dodis, 10 November 2003.
Correspondence with Dione Dodis, 13 November 2003.
Interview with Dione Dodis, October 2003.
Interview with Kostas Katsuris, October 2003.
Interview with Leo Katsuris, Vancouver, 8 March 2004.
Interview with Ron McAdam, West Vancouver, January 2004.
Interview with Efthimia Phanou, 15 January 2004.
Interview with George Rallis, Athens, 1989.

INDEX

torture at, 5–6
See also specific prisons
Prometheus, 74–75
Prometheus II, 75, 76–77
Pro-Nazi-pro-Fascist Greek, 55
Protopapadakis, Petros, 1, 3
See also Six (execution)
Psarros, Dimitris, 69, 75
Pyromaglou, Komninos, 73, 75

Rallis, George, 168–169
Rallis, Ioannis
attitude towards resistance, 50
Papadaki and, 168–169
puppet government of, 92–93, 94
Refugees to Greece
following defeat in Turkey, 8–9, 14, 25
with Greek independence, 23
KKE and, 8–9
Regnier, Augustus, 221, 222
Renaissance, 20
Report on SOE Activities in Greece and
Islands of the Aegean Sea, 35
Resistance (occupation)
acknowledgement of contribution,
194, 233
Alexatos (Odysseus), 60–62, 75–76
Athenian underground, 65, 70
Atkinson, 63–66
attitudes towards, 100–101
"class warfare" and, 202
delegation to Cairo, 84–85
demobilization of, 100–101
description, 59–60
domination by communist groups,
40, 43, 63, 70–71
during first year, 59
food shortages/famine and, 41–42,
55–56
in governmental role, 118
Greek armed forces and, 56
Greek officers and, 50–51
Italian counterintelligence, 64–66
justice and, 202
multiple organizations of, 73–76
official denial/negating role of,
193–194, 233, 237
prisoners of war escapes, 59, 63–64
SOE and, 60–62, 66–70

Tsigantes Mission, 67–70
See also civil wars; specific
organizations
Revolutionary Committee
military power and, 9
Pangalos in, 6
Right-left schism. See Left-right schism
Right-wing gangs
after 1949, 233, 237
See also White Terror
Rigopoulos, Rigas, 111–112
Rizospastis (the Radical), 8, 83, 124
Rogakos, Panagiotis, 68–69
Rommel, Erwin, 78
Roosevelt, Franklin
death of, 207
Percentages Agreement, 127
Plastiras-Damaskinos compromise,
86–87
resistance demands and, 84
Rousos, Petros, 71, 121, 124
Royalist-republican schism, 94, 184
Russia
as protecting power, 16
See also Soviet Union
Russian party, 24–25

Sacred Association of Nationalists
Officers (IDEA), 203–204
Sacred Squadron
December Uprising, 144
liberated Greek army and, 119, 120
Sakellariou, Alexander, 39
Santas, Apostolos, 54
Sarafis, Stefanos
Caserta Agreement, 95
December Uprising, 136
ELAS, 7, 95
guerrilla activity, 75
the Six and, 7
Sarigiannis, Ptolemaios, 97
Scobie, Ronald
armistice meetings, 181
Battle of Athens, 109, 113, 136, 141,
142, 144, 145–146, 177, 181
Churchill's directive to, 113, 117
as Greek/British force commander,
120–121
Popov visit, 158